Landscapes and the Law

Landscapes and the Law

Environmental Politics, Regional Histories, and Contests over Nature

Gunnel Cederlöf

OXFORD
UNIVERSITY PRESS

OXFORD
UNIVERSITY PRESS

Oxford University Press is a department of the University of Oxford. It furthers the University's objective of excellence in research, scholarship, and education by publishing worldwide. Oxford is a registered trademark of Oxford University Press in the UK and in certain other countries.

Published in India by
Oxford University Press
2/11 Ground Floor, Ansari Road, Daryaganj, New Delhi 110 002, India

First Edition published by Permanent Black in 2008
Second Edition published by Oxford University Press in 2019

ISBN-13 (print edition): 978-0-19-949974-8
ISBN-10 (print edition): 0-19-949974-8

ISBN-13 (eBook): 978-0-19-909927-6
ISBN-10 (eBook): 0-19-909927-8

Typeset in Adobe Jenson Pro 10.7/13.3
by Tranistics Data Technologies, New Delhi 110 044
Printed in India by Gopsons Papers Ltd., Noida 201 301

For

Leif, Erik, and Gustav

Contents

Illustrations and Maps

Illustrations

Maps*

* Maps by Markku Pyykönen

Glossary

adivasi	original inhabitant/s
amildar	revenue collector
casbha, causba	revenue village
circar, sarkar	government
cutcherry	administration office
diku	non-tribal, outsider
duffadar, kolkar	Indian Army cavalry officer, equal to sergeant
fanam	coin, mostly silver
hookumnamah	instruction
inam, inamdar	grant of land with discount of revenue; inamdar, the grantee of the inam
jagir, jagirdar	grant of land to an army officer; jagirdar, the grantee of the jagir
jajmani	a system of mutual reciprocity and hierarchical dependence between castes (*jati*) in a particular location
janmam, jenmi	birth, hereditary ownership

jenmi, jenmikaran	person holding hereditary rights over land in Malabar
jenm-koodian	person holding a lease on jenmi land
kanam	lease, mortgage, or usufructuary mortgage
kanakaran	holder of a lease or mortgage
kaniachi	land control, right to land
kararnamah	agreement
kumri (warg and sarkar kumri)	shifting cultivation, under landlord or government control
menon	village accountant
mirasi, mirasidar	customary right, particularly to land; customary, privileged landholder, *kaniachidar*
monigar	lowest-level government official, representing a revenue village
mund, mudr	Toda settlement
munsif	subordinate magistrate
nad, nadu	territory, administrative geographical unit
patta	title deed to land on condition of rent payment
pattadar	landholder, holder of a *patta*
peishkar, peshkar	administrative head of a revenue office
ryot	cultivator
saraf ('shroff')	money-changer
sheristadar	head clerk, accountant
shola	high-altitude stunted evergreen forest, from Tamil: *solai*, thicket, grove, forest
tahsildar	low-ranking administrative executive officer in the revenue department of a district
taluk	administrative subdivision of a district
tharavadu	household, landed matrilineal household in Malabar
zamindar	landlord, holder of an estate

Preface to Second Edition

As is the nature of research, we set out guidelines and, once the work gathers speed, it takes off in unexpected ways, moved by evidence and conversation. The study that resulted in *Landscapes and the Law* began in this manner, with clear directions and with a goal on the horizon. As part of every-day research, new results triggered new questions, and the assumed goals were refined. A decade has now passed since the publication of the first edition. As with other texts, once your thoughts are put into print, the text takes on a life of its own in the eyes of the reader. Conversations begin already at the threshold when creative and critical reading open up new possibilities to better understand and develop ideas.

Some responses arrived a bit unsuspected, as on several occasions when I found the book on the shelves of anthropology, not history. Not that I minded. And, true, the study has been much influenced by anthropological works. Part of the history that is discussed, in fact, is about how ethnology and the origins to anthropological scholarship influenced the formation of nineteenth-century law. Discussions with my colleagues in anthropology were important for me in order to understand how something as deeply rooted in historical research as land law and revenue history had depended on the searching eyes of ethnographers and ethnologists. But I doubt that such considerations made a librarian put this publication under the section of anthropology. Rather, it must have been the first edition's cover photo of Mrs Narsam, dressed for a bow and arrow ceremony in her *putkuli* shawl that caused the classification. A lady looking 'tribal' most likely referred the book to the sphere of culture rather than of history.

Mrs Narsam herself has lived through the consequences of such racialized perceptions, where just the glance on a person labelled her not only as belonging to a 'tribe' but also assumed her life to be somehow timeless or not quite part of the history of India. Countless tourists have taken her picture to keep as a memory of their experience of ancient culture and authentic nature when they have visited the Ooty botanical garden in the Nilgiri Hills. The nature surrounding her home and settlement has been the object of onlookers' projections across two centuries. From the first arrival of Europeans onwards, romantic and aesthetic values have placed her community on par with animals, grazed hillocks, and groves as if they were of the same matter and quality. Sometimes such views have benefitted the community but mostly they have been to their disadvantage. Simultaneously and in contrast to romanticist ideas, the Nilgiri natures have also been defined in line with utilitarian thought. To privilege usage for the sake of the public as defined by a government has dominated over knowing land from the meanings ascribed to it by people living there. Market-oriented assessments of land have mostly valued nature as a material resource. This has worked to detach people from the land. Yet it was not a simple trajectory of events that resulted in this dislocation of rights from land. The half century encompassing the early formation of legal rights in land in the Nilgiri Hills turned out to be much more complicated.

When I made the first sketches of my project, I naively thought that I would find a clear case of overpowering conquest. I was pretty sure I would discover a native population facing the force of colonial subjugation, represented by armed bureaucrats of the British East India Company. Without much deliberation, they would have mowed down any opposition. Guns, revenues, and resource exploitation would have combined to rob defenceless local people of their livelihoods and their land.

Arriving in the Nilgiris at 2,000 metres above sea level from the agrarian highlands of the Coimbatore district in Tamil Nadu where I worked in the 1990s, I soon realized that I had moved away from the historian's craft to the academic realms of the anthropologist. A fairly short geographical distance had taken me far from the assumed caste-structured and economically hierarchical society of old state formations—an old fiefdom of historians. I was now in an area described as tribal and, therefore, as anthropological territory.

My expectation of finding sharp, binary conflicts between colonial power and colonized subjects was founded in dominant discourses among historians at the time. It also corresponded to everyday realities that were reflected in my political involvements, from those I gained from schoolmates arriving as refugees from Latin American dictatorships to those in the anti-apartheid movement and in the critical debates on the demands for structural adjustment programmes for vulnerable African economies. These political experiences matched theoretical debates on dependency theory, subaltern studies, and history from below, schools of thought which contributed a necessary and critical rereading of the colonial pasts. Seen from outside European and Western perspectives and experiences, the histories of Asia, Africa, and Latin America changed the entire equation for research into the history of the last 200–300 years. I was inspired by the brilliant works of Ramachandra Guha, Ranajit Guha, and James C. Scott, and was convinced I would find yet another case of expediently violent formation of British rule.[1]

Occasionally it happened that the baby was thrown out with the bathwater. Those who emphasized the complexities of Indian society and its integration with colonial rule were at times ridiculed for being soft on Empire. Certain ideologically founded narratives of domination and subordination tended to ignore native agency and, therefore, by default, make Indians, not least those at the lower end of socio-economic scales, appear passive and incapable. In their criticism of nationalist historiography,

[1] Ramachandra Guha, *The Unquiet Woods: Ecological Change and Peasant Resistance in the Himalaya* (New Delhi: Oxford University Press, 1989); Ranajit Guha, *Elementary Aspects of Peasant Insurgency in Colonial India* (New Delhi: Oxford, 1983); James C. Scott, *Weapons of the Weak. Everyday Forms of Peasant Resistance* (New Haven: Yale University Press, 1985).

scholars in the early subaltern studies collective described an autonomous domain of subaltern consciousness, where there was agency but little room for divergence. Reflecting on a disappearing 'subaltern' in subaltern studies, in 2001 Sumit Sarkar argued that a colonial cultural domain that is stripped of complexities and variations 'faces an indigenous domain eroded of internal tensions and conflicts ... the colonized subject is taken to have been literally constituted by colonialism alone'. Seen in a longer perspective, the debates of the 1990s around the positions of historians within subaltern studies helped me to find more nuanced views on the mechanisms of the formation and consolidation of colonial rule and the relationship between the colonial and the colonized subject.[2]

In the Nilgiris, there were also complicated pasts, preceding a European presence, in which conflicts were played out. Dominant social groups, different communities, and royalty fought over space, revenues, social control, and loyalties. Apparently, here the formation of British rule had not come into place by brute force alone, but by mediation, negotiation, multiple transactions, and, at times, the most unexpected alliances. The consolidation of colonial government had come about slowly, as a powerful and densely woven texture. Its force did not seem to hinge on the presence of an unstoppable and powerful colossus. There was an everyday underbelly to its formation, which was challenging to understand. If I was to comprehend the ways in which the Nilgiris came under British rule, I needed to explore these everyday mechanisms of its formation.

I was occasionally reminded that this was *south* India. South India was often said to be different; but different from what? What was the norm against which the south was measured?

[2] Gyan Prakash, 'Writing Post-Orientalist Histories of the Third World. Perspectives from Indian Historiography', *Comparative Studies in Society and History* 32, no. 2 (1990); 'Can the "Subaltern" Ride? A Reply to O'Hanlon and Washbrook', *Comparative Studies in Society and History* 34, no. 1 (1992); Rosalind O'Hanlon and David Washbrook, 'After Orientalism. Culture, Criticism, and Politics in the Third World', , *Comparative Studies in Society and History* 34, no. 1 (1992); Sumit Sarkar, 'The Decline of the Subaltern in *Subaltern Studies*', in *Reading Subaltern Studies. Critical History, Contested Meaning, and the Globalisation of South Asia,* ed. David Ludden (New Delhi: Permanent Black, 2001), 408; Gyan Prakash, 'Postcolonial Criticism and Indian Historiography', *Social Text*, no. 31/32 (1992).

The question brought me to Bengal and the expanding Bengal Presidency. The region was far away from the southern hill ranges of the Western Ghats. But at the beginning of the nineteenth century, the issues at stake turned these two presidencies into quarrelling neighbours. As David Washbrook and others have often pointed out, the Madras administration habitually ended up on a collision course with its Bengal counterpart.[3] If we are to understand the history of one, we also need to understand the other. These new enquiries gave rise to the study *Founding an Empire on India's North-Eastern Frontiers, 1790–1840*.[4]

To me, the two studies are intimately related. The social, legal, and environmental history of the Nilgiris was my reference point when I ventured into the pasts of what are today North-East India, Burma, and Bangladesh. But I realize that the relationship between the two studies may not be as obvious to others as it is to me. The two regions are seldom seen in the same framework, except when discussed in the most general sense of British imperial conquest or in vague notions of a 'colonial discourse'. Readers who are interested in either north or south India may not necessarily search for literature outside their preferred regional limits.

The differences between the two presidencies seem obvious. The regions are geographically far apart. Climate, topography, ecology, polity, culture, socio-economic and political contexts, and historical trajectories all differ. Comparing the limited space of the Nilgiri Hills and the large expanse of the old North-Eastern Frontier that extended from the Brahmaputra towards Burma is no easy undertaking. The divergence of scale is dramatic.

Yet these geographically distant regions shared a common political feature—the influence of the British East India Company, which expanded its operations extensively across the Indian subcontinent from the late eighteenth to the mid-nineteenth century. In the south, troops under British and Hyderabadi banners fought those led by French and

3 David A. Washbrook, 'South India 1770–1840. The Colonial Transition', *Modern Asian Studies* 38, no. 3 (2004): 487–89.

4 Gunnel Cederlöf, *Founding an Empire on India's North-Eastern Frontiers, 1790–1840. Climate, Commerce, Polity* (New Delhi: Oxford University Press, 2014).

Mysore officers. We know these battles as the four Anglo-Mysore wars, from 1767 to 1799. They paved the way for British sovereign rule in the south. The Nilgiri Hills were part of the gain.

Parallel to these events, in Bengal (at the north-eastern extreme of the British territories) the officers who combined commercial and administrative trades in the EIC strove to determine what territories came with the Mughal *diwani* grant of 1765. EIC troops, cartographers, bureaucrats, and surveyors battled with physical realities to demarcate the limits of territories that they aimed to bring under sovereign control. War with Burma in 1824–6 became a major push for British control of the North-Eastern Frontier. There were kingdoms and small polities here too that became part of the EIC's gain. In both the south and the north-east, imperial logics can be seen in everyday chores and, conversely, the diversity of micro-histories can help us explore the macro-historical logic.

The growing British Empire was a market of opportunity for seasoned merchants and socially mobile young fortune-seeking men from across Europe. Many failed, but some prospered, and some of that group became both wealthy and powerful. We can see this in the south, for example, in the case of John Sullivan, the collector of Coimbatore district of which the Nilgiris were a part, who secured absolute property in land corresponding in extent to a large estate. Or in that of Robert Lindsay, the collector of Sylhet district, who became one of the wealthiest men of his time from trading in limestone and in the cowry currency. This was also a time when the Company was seriously questioned for overstepping the limits of a mercantile corporation. It was eventually crippled by the amended Charter Act of 1833.

The tug of war between, on the one hand, the corporation and its merchants and, on the other, the monarchy and the British parliament characterized many conflicts within the bureaucracy. Observing their struggle helps us to explain priorities and decisions in the two presidencies, including at the level of daily routine. Cooperation between the bureaucracies of the corporation and the British state was not without friction, nor did the interests of individual merchants always fall in line with those of the Company. As bureaucracies function by regulations, the law was a major arena for such disputes. Law was applied wherever soldiers and administrators marched. And there was hardly a case brought before a judge in which the quality and the interpretation of acts and regulations went unquestioned. Every law has a prehistory. There is a reason why it is regarded as necessary at a particular point in time. More often than not, it is established to mediate in disputes. Once it is passed, a post-event history begins, when the correct interpretation of the law is debated, in both the courtroom and the public square. As a rule, EIC officers used legal arguments to prove the legitimacy of conquest. Legal procedure had to be followed, even in the smallest matters.

The early phase of the formation of British rule in the south Indian mountain ranges is also a display of some of environmental history's key questions. We could say it was a peaceful colonial conquest. No guns were fired. Yet by the force of bureaucracy and courts, people's rights in nature were dramatically remade across time. In the Nilgiris, the grazing of land diminished, shifting cultivation became increasingly permanent, and plantations began to turn hillsides into monoculture units. It was all argued to be 'in accordance with law', and laws last long. Once in place, they are not easily done away with. This makes law appear neutral to the shifts of time. Yet, at every turn of events, codes and regulations were reinterpreted and adjusted to the specific situation in which they were to be applied. In the Nilgiris, a social system of reciprocity and hierarchy was first replaced by claims to absolute property and ancient aboriginal right, soon to be overruled by the weaker 'occupational' right, usufruct and 'compensation for loss of privilege'—all arguments claimed to be solidly legal while simultaneously based on race theory. Across no more than a generation, the legal framework that regulated people's access to nature, their control over grazing grounds, forests and groves, had changed in the law code while its implementation took longer. Such legal elaboration adds a dimension to what is meant by 'conquest'.

These disputes are now almost 200 years old, but some of the arguments resound in the recent decades' battles for rights in Indian forest and hill tracts, and in the conflicts and claims for indigenous people's rights. Such long-term legacies make it particularly important to understand the details of conflicts when the foundational laws of legal rights in nature and, specifically, land were laid down. In the Nilgiris, nature was made the location for projections and ascriptions of people's identities, histories, and rights to access and control the land. The privilege of interpreting the meaning of the legal principles for the rights that were vested in the land was soon removed from the communities in the hills to the officers who came to investigate their claims. It may seem as if people's voices disappeared from the documents. But for us who read the officers' reports and letters, to a large extent, the explanations and counter-arguments facing them still remain in their notes. People objected in many different ways. Their voices are seldom found in the summary high-level reports which are easily accessible, but in the day to day communications on the ground. Therefore, as a cure to the malady of allowing vested interest to determine historical narratives stands the patient work in archives and the critical reading of texts that allow for a multitude of often contradictory voices to speak.

The Nilgiri conflicts were not unique. There was a global shift for reformulating and regulating human–nature relations. As in the Nilgiri Hills, the negotiated process of making law worked to dislocate particular rights from nature. The European officers in the Nilgiris, driven by particularistic interests and with the force of government, thus enforced a slow violence by means of law. They targeted rights in nature to wrench land out of people's hands. Partly as a consequence of such processual changes, legal frameworks shaped a polity, in south as well as in north-east India. We could say that the everyday practices and administrative procedures that were subsequently turned into regulations and formalized in legal jurisdiction provided the form and glue of polity. There were particular reasons for why these legal foundations came into being, and why they took the form they did. But in the rear-view mirror, those reasons may seem narrow and even insignificant. The lawmakers may never have had such conclusive consequences in mind as the shaping of a polity. Yet if we follow the trail of such regulations across decades, we may see how what was once a practical solution to an immediate problem became a cornerstone of the larger structure of Empire. Through the microcosm of the Nilgiri Hills we may better understand the global transformations that shaped the moulds of laws for rights in nature.

Gunnel Cederlöf
Lundbacken, January 2019

References

Cederlöf, Gunnel. *Bonds Lost. Subordination, Conflict, and Mobilisation in Rural South India, C. 1900–1970*. New Delhi: Manohar Publications, 1997.

______. *Founding an Empire on India's North-Eastern Frontiers, 1790–1840. Climate, Commerce, Polity*. New Delhi: Oxford University Press, 2014.

Guha, Ramachandra. *The Unquiet Woods. Ecological Change and Peasant Resistance in the Himalaya*. New Delhi: Oxford University Press, 1989.

Guha, Ranajit. *Elementary Aspects of Peasant Insurgency in Colonial India*. New Delhi: Oxford, 1983.

O'Hanlon, Rosalind, and David Washbrook. 'After Orientalism. Culture, Criticism, and Politics in the Third World'. *Comparative Studies in Society and History* 34, no. 1 (1992): 141–67.

Prakash, Gyan. 'Can the "Subaltern" Ride? A Reply to O'Hanlon and Washbrook'. *Comparative Studies in Society and History* 34, no. 1 (1992): 168–84.

______. 'Postcolonial Criticism and Indian Historiography'. *Social Text*, no. 31/32 (1992): 8–19.

______. 'Writing Post-Orientalist Histories of the Third World. Perspectives from Indian Historiography'. *Comparative Studies in Society and History* 32, no. 2 (1990): 383–408.

Sarkar, Sumit. 'The Decline of the Subaltern in *Subaltern Studies*'. In *Reading Subaltern Studies. Critical History, Contested Meaning, and the Globalisation of South Asia*, edited by David Ludden, 400–29. New Delhi: Permanent Black, 2001.

Scott, James C. *Weapons of the Weak. Everyday Forms of Peasant Resistance*. New Haven: Yale University Press, 1985.

Washbrook, David A. 'South India 1770–1840. The Colonial Transition'. *Modern Asian Studies* 38, no. 3 (2004): 479–516.

Preface to First Edition

Books written over longish periods of time tend to take an unexpected course, sometimes achieving analytic depth as time passes. What began nearly ten years ago as a set of fairly straightforward questions about conflicts over land and natural resources in the Nilgiri Hills of South India, in a project titled 'Claims and Rights', soon asked other questions. An initial assumption which mainly derived from the results of earlier studies—for my part presented in the volume *Bonds Lost. Subordination, Conflict and Mobilisation in Rural South India c. 1900–1970* (New Delhi: 1997)—namely, that people at the losing end of society were not merely passive, helpless victims of some social juggernaut but possessed agency enough to influence their immediate situations—helped to break down the stereotyped dichotomies of dominant and subordinate, ruler and ruled.

In most detailed historical accounts, the complexities of everyday life surface. Many of the questions emerging in the present study have also arisen from the array of arguments and rhetoric that were voiced in escalating land disputes within the Nilgiris. In the early nineteenth century, when the British East India Company was conquering new territory, a wide variety of interests materialized and made claims on nature.

However, when particular rights were claimed, it was not just a matter of 'money talking'; historical narratives, competing legal principles, evolutionary theory, political visions, ethnology, and race were also invoked as legitimate grounds for claims on nature. A variety of contradictory claims on and appropriations of land and natural resources thus competed for legal justification. Accordingly, the process of making law came into focus as much as the actual implementation of law.

In my search for a broader environmental history of law that simultaneously encompasses the social, economic, political, and ideological aspects of legal conflicts over nature, I have benefited immensely from numerous discussions with scholars in different fields. For most of the time, Beppe Karlsson has remained my closest colleague and discussion partner. Our joint project and his research in north-east India have been constant sources of inspiration. As we moved office within Uppsala University together with our project—from the Seminar for Development Studies (earlier hosted by the Department of Government and subsequently by the Collegium for Development Studies) via years of fellowships at research institutes in Sweden and abroad, spending the last five years back in Uppsala in the Department of Cultural Anthropology and Ethnology—my thinking has been much influenced and enriched by different approaches to these questions in the various disciplines concerned. Throughout these years I have been in close contact with fellow researchers in the Department of History at Uppsala University, and it seems only appropriate that I concluded this historical study as a research fellow in that department.

As a fellow of the Swedish Collegium for Advanced Study (SCAS) I had the privilege of developing the initial outlines of this work in the most inspiring research environment. I am grateful for the formal and informal conversations I was able to have with the other fellows in the spring of 2000, and would particularly like to thank Björn Wittrock, Barbro Klein, Göran Therborn, and Heléne Andersson, who formed the heart of SCAS. During a one-year fellowship at Oxford University, affiliated with Queen Elizabeth House, I benefited from discussions in the context of the many and diverse seminars, lectures, and social gatherings associated with that university. David Washbrook, Barbara Harriss-White, Judith Heyer, and Karen Middleton, in their different ways, formed my own and my family's closest network of colleagues and friends. The warmth of their friendship remains an inextricable part of my life and work. During my many visits to the British Library, Hanna Hodacs and Mary Hilson generously opened their home to this vagabond from Oxford.

Alongside this work, my research collaboration also developed on the theme of nation, nationalisms, and appropriations of nature for the sake of identity, interests, and rights. In this parallel project over a four-year period with K. Sivaramakrishnan, which resulted in *Ecological Nationalisms. Nature, Livelihoods, and Identities in South Asia* (Delhi 2005 and Seattle 2006), I benefited immensely from our discussions, Shivi's many thoughtful comments, and his friendship.

During my periods of fieldwork in the Nilgiri Hills I had the privilege of collaborating with C.R. Sathyanarayanan, who at the time was working for the Anthropological Survey of India in Mysore. His long experience of anthropological and ethnographic research in the region made him a knowledgeable co-traveller and colleague. I would also like to express my gratitude for the hospitality and generous sharing of their life experience by people in the Toda settlements of Kandelmund, Manjakalmund, Marlimund, Kengodumund, Malcodmund, Minicmund, Karikadumund, Ankurthkulimund, Nedimund, and Tapkodumund. Ms Vasamalli, Mr Pothili, Mr Peter Raj, and Mr Rajan patiently guided us to many new contacts. Dr Ayyavoo kindly informed us about the work of the Sheep Breeding Research Station at Sandynallah.

For discussions, comments, and all manner of assistance because of which this book has improved through its various drafts to its final shape, I am grateful to Maria Ågren, David Arnold, Arun Bandopadhyay, Neeladri Bhattacharya, Stuart Blackburn, Judith Brown, B.B. Chaudhury, Dipesh Chakrabarty, Max Edling, Sverker Finnström, Claude Garcia, John Hall, Paul Hockings, Martha McLaren, Jeanette Neeson, Ulrika Persson-Fischier, Ric Sims, Tanka Subba, Rolf Torstendahl, and David Washbrook. I am also grateful to Deborah Sutton for our many fruitful discussions, which resulted in a joint article wherein we were able to combine our fields of competence in Nilgiri nineteenth century history. Mahesh Rangarajan, K. Sivaramakrishnan, and Heather Goodall have taken the trouble to read and comment on the whole manuscript or major portions of it. Their detailed comments and our subsequent discussions have guided me immensely in clarifying my major arguments and making this volume more cohesive.

I have benefited from comments on texts presented at seminars at the Department of History and the Department of Cultural Anthropology and Ethnology, Uppsala University; at St Antony's College and Queen Elizabeth House, Oxford University; and at the Madras Institute of Development Studies. Important insights were gained from presentations at conferences organized by Jawaharlal Nehru University in Delhi in 2002, by the University of Calcutta's Department of History in 2003 and 2005, and by the Centre for World Environmental History at Sussex University in 2005, as well as at two larger meetings: the South Asia Conference at the University of Wisconsin in Madison in 2001, and the 17th European Conference on Modern South Asian Studies in Heidelberg in 2002. Three articles were published on the basis of the papers presented at these seminars and meetings, and the arguments pursued in them have formed the backbone of three of the chapters exhaustively rewritten in this volume. These articles are 'The Agency of the Colonial Subject. Claims and Rights in Forestlands in Early Nineteenth-Century Nilgiris,' *Studies in History* 2 (2005), also published as a longer version in *People of the Jangal. Reformulating Identities and Adaptations in Crisis,* edited by Marine Carrin and Harald Tambs-Lyche (Delhi: Manohar, 2008); 'Narratives of Rights. Codifying People and Land in Early Nineteenth-Century Nilgiris,' *Environment and History* 8 (2002); and 'The Toda Tiger. Debates on Custom, Utility and Rights in Nature, South India 1820–1843,' in *Ecological Nationalisms. Nature, Livelihoods and Identities in South Asia,* edited by Gunnel Cederlöf and K. Sivaramakrishnan (Delhi: Permanent Black, 2005, and Seattle: University of Washington Press, 2006).

I am grateful to the staff at the British Library and the India Office Records; the Bodleian Library and the Indian Institute at Oxford University; the University of Birmingham Library, Special Collections; the Tamil Nadu Archives; and the Nilgiri Library in Ootacamund. I have also benefited from my visits to the well-equipped library of the Department of Social Analysis at the Tamil Nadu Theological Seminary, Madurai, and from discussions with scholars connected with the department. I would like to thank Markku Pyykönen for producing the excellent maps in this volume and Martin Naylor for his careful editing of the language in a way that often forced me to rethink and clarify both wordings and arguments in the text. I am grateful to my editor Rukun Advani for his support and generous guidance through the process of publication.

None of this would have been possible without financial support. I am deeply grateful for the research grants that have been made available by the Bank of Sweden Tercentenary Foundation, the Research Council for Developing Countries at SIDA (the Swedish International Development Co-operation Agency), the Swedish Council for Planning and Coordination of Research (FRN), and the Swedish Council for Research in the Humanities and Social Sciences (HSFR).

During these years, as always, I have shared this part of my life, too, with those closest to me: my husband Leif and our sons Erik and Gustav. On our joint travels and in our shared concern for the issues at stake, I have always found encouragement and rest in their love and support.

GUNNEL CEDERLÖF
Lundbacken, July 2007

1 *Histories of Rights in Nature*

An Introduction

Oshthaars remains a scar, a festering wound in the memory of old Toda men in Kandelmund. Whenever the fate of Oshthaars is told, voices grow harsh, eyes seek your attention.

In the soil beneath St Stephen's Church, right in the middle of Ootacamund town, the Toda divinity still dwells. The Christian church, built within a decade of the first European settlements in the Nilgiri Hills of South India, is said to have supplanted the Toda temple of Oshthaars, which sanctified the earth. The men tell me I need to understand the gravity of the injustice, the extent of the violation, the unspeakable act of eradication of Toda pasts embodied by this Christian 'temple' that has overlooked Ootacamund ever since 1830. The younger generations in the *mund* are aware of the loss, the old have given it a name: Oshthaars. The very first generation of British officials in the Nilgiris had to learn that Toda divinities not only reside on the land of their temples, but that the temples and all that is connected with them—lands, buffaloes, pens, sheds, water—*are* divine.[1] Occasionally, when passing the gates of the churchyard, Nanicane, the senior most man of Kandelmund, stops, faces the church, and salutes his gods. For him, the Toda divinity still lives beneath the Christian church and burial ground.[2]

Violating places of religious worship was strictly against recommendations issued by the British East India Company (EIC) to its officers in India. Such acts ought therefore to have left some imprint in colonial files. However, a thorough search of colonial documents fails to uncover anything on the settlement or mund of Oshthaars,[3] which would have been very small, not big enough to encompass the handful of houses in a settled mund. There would only have been the barrel-shaped temple and the modest dwelling place of the priest. Still, its religious significance for the Toda ought to have merited the careful attention of administrators. Yet, neither in correspondence, minutes, or reports, nor in petitions, depositions, and private collections is there any trace of either settled or temple munds inside or near the site of the church. In his matter-of-fact way an imperial historiographer of the early twentieth century, Frederick Price, asserted that the government assigned a property named Woodville, belonging to the EIC and occupied by a Captain Clubbey, for the building of the church. Miscalculations that led to a substantial overrun of the budget for its construction were debated in correspondence. Likewise, its inauguration ceremonies were described in the most high-flown terms despite the fact that the building then lacked many fixtures. In a lithograph of 1834 accompanying Price's text, the land surrounding the building is empty and a Toda family—father, mother, and child—are pointing towards the church as if admiring the edifice.[4] But Oshthaars is nowhere to be seen.

Men and women of the Toda munds, which today are engulfed by Ootacamund town, often recollect their lost lands by naming buildings subsequently erected on the sites—the Ootacamund Club, the governor's bungalow, the Botanical Garden and, not least, St Stephen's Church. Large areas were sold for a pittance, and people deceived by government officials. It is with bitterness and resignation that the Toda of Kandelmund and Manjakalmund speak of their past.

The legacy of Oshthaars remains strong among the people of Kandelmund, though the details of the tale change from time to time.

Ill 1 St Stephen's Church Ootacamund, 1834. In Robert Baikie (1834), *Observations on the Neilgherries, including an account of their topography, climate, soil & productions, and of the effects of the climate on the European constitution.*
(Reproduced courtesy British Library.)

No specific descriptions of the old Oshthaars temple site exist, nor names of the priests who once served there. A narrative, or a story, with a beginning, a middle, and an end that can describe the fate of the mund doesn't seem to exist. The only thing that people say for certain is that it once existed. When the Europeans entered the land, the place and its sacred buffaloes became polluted and the Toda moved out. As a violent rupture in the Toda past, the meaning of Oshthaars seems to be that it is now lost. Relating this grim fate and calling upon the divinity in its old dwelling place are constant re-enactments of a lived experience of loss.[5] Nanicane explains that Oshthaars was 'the place where our deities assembled, danced and sang'—*Oshth* meaning coming together to enjoy, *aars* meaning deities.[6] Today, Kandelmund carries a heritage of alienation.

But it is not that once-and-for-all loss of land to colonial conquerors 180-odd years ago that causes resentment. It is the subsequent and continuing experience of losing control over and access to land as government officials bend and reinterpret the texts of regulations and land settlements. Within such a heritage, past and present collapse. The narrative of Oshthaars demonstrates the selectiveness and inventiveness of memory—its emancipating qualities, its capacity to bridge mental and physical landscapes, and its indifference to time. The memory of Oshthaars continues to cause pain, just like the phantom pains of a lost life-world. Searching out a detailed classical ethnography of Oshthaars is therefore not important, any more than establishing the actual sequence of events that led to its destruction; it is the quality of the event that matters.[7]

But the Toda in Kandelmund realize that there must be old documents tucked away in government files which can prove people's legitimate rights in specific lands. These are the same documents that Forest Department officials keep referring to, but are so reluctant to disclose. Rather than sharing copies of such documents, low-level officials who visit the mund prefer to relate the meaning of the texts. At present, varying and contradictory copies of government documents are kept in Kandelmund, some typed, others handwritten, some signed, others looking more like scribbled notes. The perception among the Toda is that there are other, older documents on the shelves of government departments, and in them lies the hope that

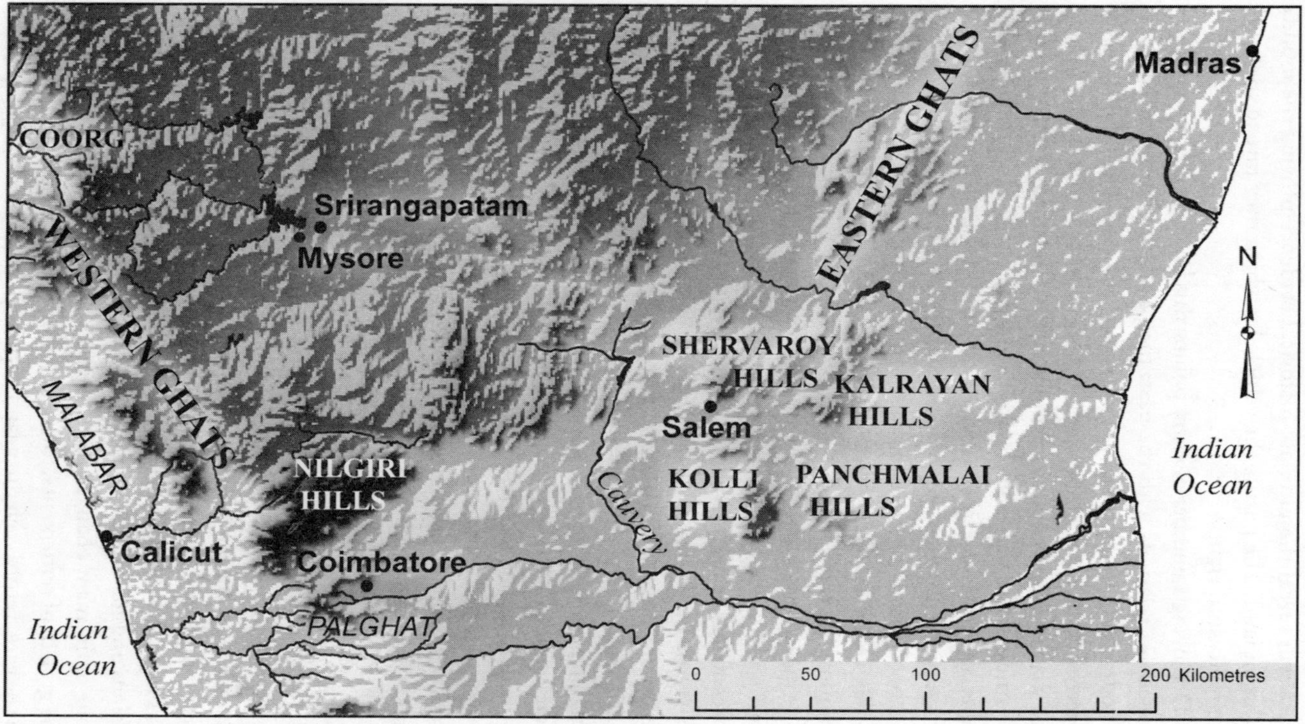

Map 1 Central South India

these will reveal the ultimate historical evidence proving the mund's rights in land. The past is the vehicle by which they intend to secure their ancestral rights.

Deploying a number of entry points, this book centres on questions of people's relations with the past: the past as a point of orientation, a node of common relations, an archive of knowledge for targeted searches, a narrative to be continuously reshaped or reproduced, and a powerful resource for ascertaining rights. The book is thus a historical study of the processes by which rights in nature, reformulated by colonial officers in the narrower sense of land settlement and rights of usage, were redefined and codified in law. The empirical focus of the book is on the transformation of the Nilgiri Hills between the 1790s and the 1840s, when the region came under British colonial administration.

It may seem anachronistic to refer to present situations in the region within such a historical study, but the intention is not to make inferences about the past from observations of the present. Nonetheless, field visits have been crucial to my understanding of the past, even though the period under study is no longer part of lived experience or living memory. At the outset, my field visits were made primarily for the sake of finding documentation of the early nineteenth century. Copies of documents were originally made for the district, presidency, and London files, but individual documents tended to go missing in various places. As my work progressed, it became important to enquire about place names and names of individuals, and ask questions that required an insight into linguistic issues because several languages were used in the Nilgiris: English among the Europeans, Tamil among the native EIC servants, Toda (a language without a script), Malayalam in Wynad, and a form of Kannada among the Badaga community, 'their language being very imperfectly understood by the Cutcherry servants.'[8] More profoundly, it became clear the landscape was the battleground in the conflicts of the early nineteenth century. Contesting rights in particular plots of land was more than a battle over soil; it was simultaneously a contestation of visions and life-worlds which shaped the landscape. Needless to say, in spite of the many changes over 180 years on account of afforestation and the growth of settlements, towns and modern infrastructure, the reports in the early records refer to a landscape of peaks, rivers, temples, munds,

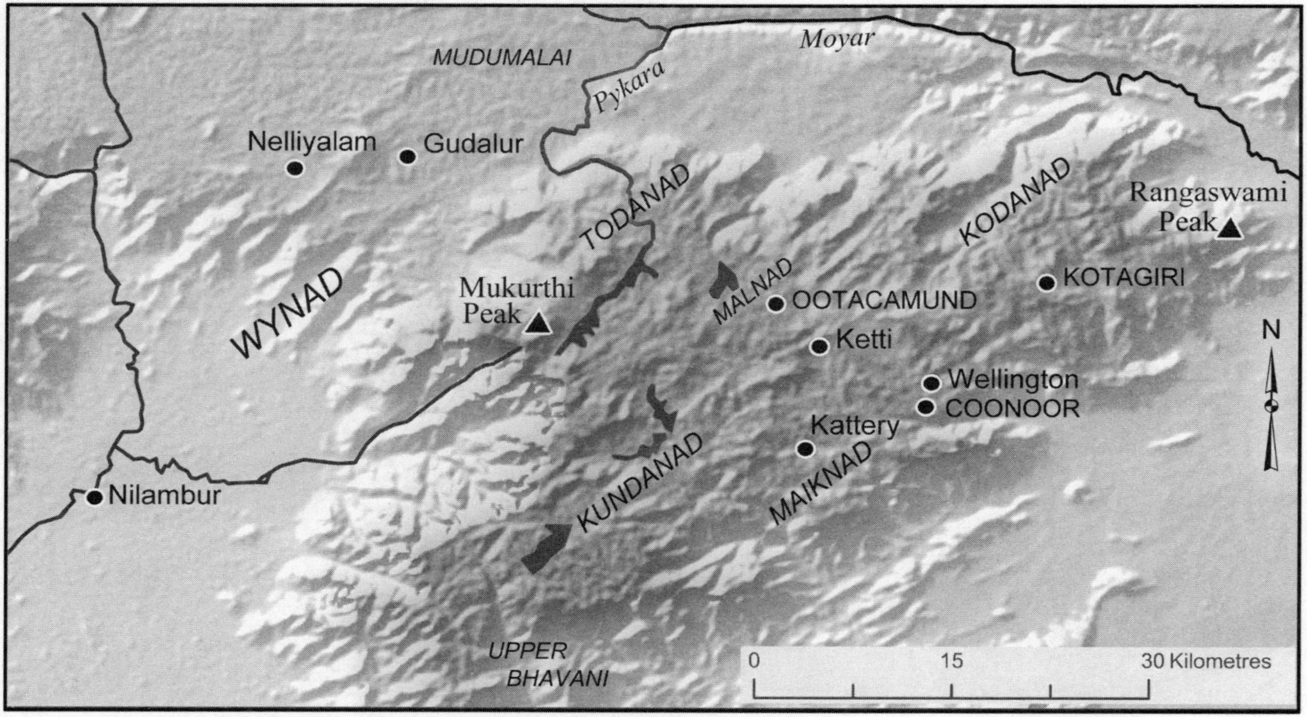

Map 2 The Nilgiri Hills, eastern Wynad and north-western Coimbatore District

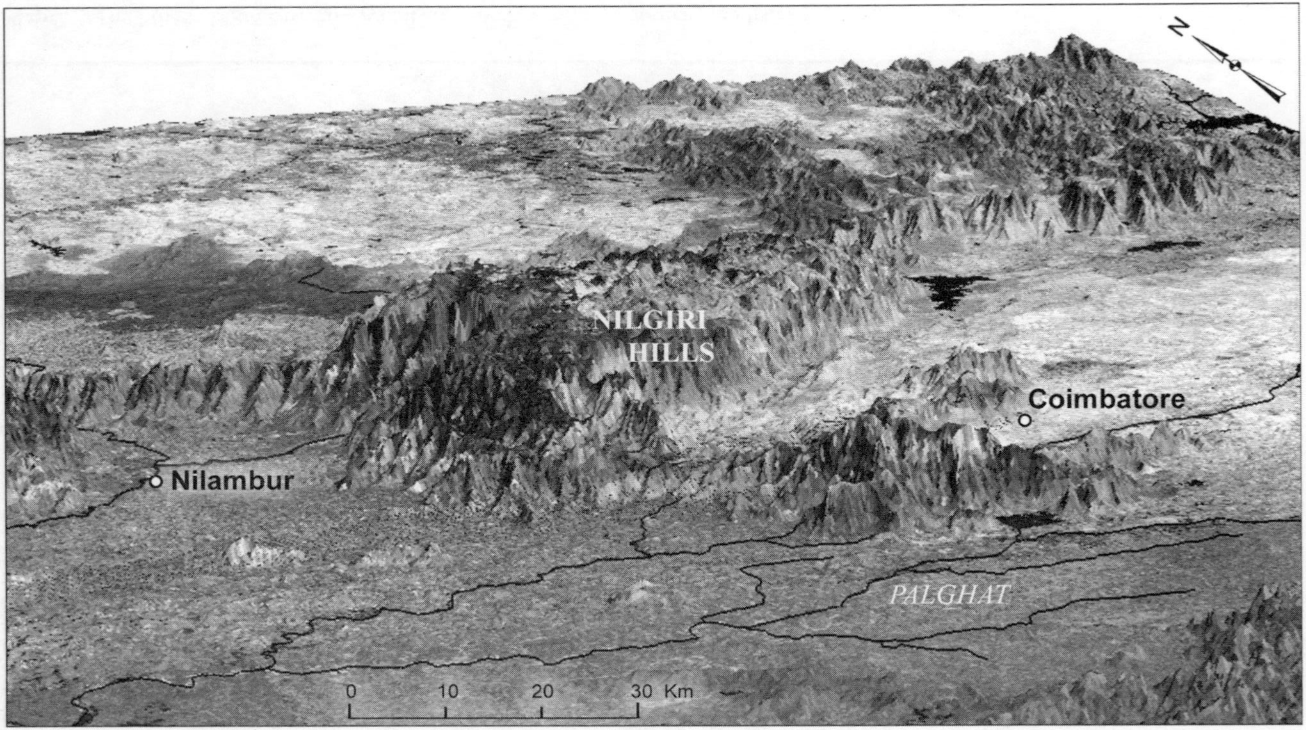

Map 3 The Nilgiri Hills seen from south-west

and physical distances in which a historian who has not walked some of these distances moves half blind.

The past was always present in my communication with people during field visits, and I realized that after each such visit (in 2001, 2002, 2003, and 2005), however brief in time, I began to ask new questions of the written documents of the 1820s, 1830s, and 1840s. These questions remain in the text, while only small portions of the field notes introduce each chapter. These field visits were made with C.R. Sathyanarayanan, who has worked as an anthropologist for the Anthropological Survey of India at its Southern Regional Centre in Mysore for the last sixteen years, conducting anthropological and ethnographic studies in the Nilgiris; my work benefited greatly from Sathyanarayanan's thorough enquiries on his other visits to the Nilgiris during the period 2001–5.

The trust which people placed in the written document was striking. In marked contrast to the academic debates about the extent to which such colonial archives are compromised by their imperial and Orientalist biases, and that remnants of Indian pasts should rather be traced via memory and myth,[9] the Toda living in Ootacamund, like many other people claiming rights in hills and forest lands when disputing the Indian government, ask for century-old colonial documents. These documents are then considered for their legal and objective value, almost irrespective of the context in which they were produced. Retrieving the documents means setting the record straight. Rather straightforwardly for the historical facts that they are thought to contain, these documents are thought to serve as a corrective to the historiography in which people have been marginalized as victims of the onslaught of state power.

Yet incorporated with this situation is a complex and contradictory relationship to the past and to history. People appear to relate to the past both for its existential and evidential value, and the histories produced become histories that carry meaning. On the one hand, narrations of the past that can be heard in Kandelmund convey the fragrance and the inner sense of people's long experience of being marginalized, betrayed, and separated from a past in which they were actors and not only acted upon. The act of narrating is deeply existential in its aspiration to ascertain spatially and temporally rooted identities. To borrow from the anthropologist Michael Jackson's elaboration of the narrative imperative in situations of deep crisis, storytelling is a human strategy for 'sustaining a sense of agency in the face of disempowering circumstances.'[10] On the other hand, people who strive to regain control over their lives and livelihoods look to the state for the information it controls about their pasts. The state archives, which were organized by colonial authorities according to the needs of the colonial state, then become the doorways to the documentation that will reveal violations against the people, prove the validity of their claims, and correct historiographies that have been imposed on their pasts. To gain control of a history based on evidence, the Toda in Kandelmund also claim written historical documentation. Consequently, the dividing line between searching the past for its existential and evidential value is not absolute; the two are not opposite ends of the scale with which to measure history. As the situation in Kandelmund shows, they can be mutually constitutive. Where there exists a notion that facts, perhaps even truth, can be established through written documents, evidential value becomes as real as immediately experienced existential value.

Stuart Blackburn speaks of the desire, through narrative, to establish one's identity by arriving at a correct version of past events in one's life. Although his study focuses on Tamil folk tales and legends, it contains useful parallels with the way in which the Toda of the Nilgiris struggle to grasp their past. Blackburn observes how, in the tale, the life of a hero is made a vehicle to reveal 'what really happened'; the experience of an individual is the central plot of the narrative. As with oral histories, folk tales provide no date for either content or composition. They present themselves as timeless and therefore of general value. As they claim to speak the truth, they carry collective moral weight. When the narrative is uncovered, the plot is the timekeeper that organizes otherwise random experiences. Applying Blackburn's observations to our terrain, we can substitute the individual human being with the individual node of Toda life—the sacred mund: Oshthaars.[11]

The search for history is an enterprise that people in Kandelmund share with numerous others—tribals, indigenous people, dalits—all over the subcontinent. As has often been observed, people at the margins of state concerns are usually less well represented in historical works and archives than are elites, governments, and colonial rulers. Sometimes this has mistakenly led scholars to assume that their 'voices' are absent from the colonial archives, or that they exist only in 'mirror images' of the colonial mind and can best be recovered by means of reversal. It would in fact be truer to say that, for too long, people writing history have been reluctant to trace the resonances of such subaltern voices in the archives.

Two Debates: History *vs* Memory, and History within Modernity

The critical role of the past in arguments over rights in nature runs as an undercurrent through this book, which addresses both the perceived and the experienced pasts of colonizer and colonized. It therefore moves both at an ideological level of interests and worldviews, and at the level of experienced events, trespassing the boundaries of various academic debates. These debates are those in which scholars have sought to come to terms with, on the one hand, the assumed silences and lack of documentation of subaltern social groups, and on the other, the dominant role of the West or Europe in the reconstruction of non-European pasts. Partly to address the silences, and partly as contribution to an epistemological critique of the scholarly discipline of history and scientific methods that have broadly developed from the European Enlightenment, academic debates have taken a new turn in the last couple of decades. These debates are profoundly methodological in nature. For a study such as this, which is located within the tide of scholarly discussion arising from the contradictory flows of Enlightenment thought, and which targets the trajectories of contested natures—wherein reconstruction of the past remained vital to all the parties involved—these debates are of special importance.

As will become evident in the following chapters, a key characteristic of the legal settlement of rights throughout the long process of immigration, encroachment, resistance, negotiation, settlement, and subsequent renegotiation was that the issue of rights was continuously seen through the prisms of past and history. Simultaneously, the project of defining rights became closely entangled with European scholarship as the empirical sciences also increasingly became a resource for the legitimization of colonial expansion. For the purposes of this study, we may divide present-day debates into two, both of which focus on the place of history as a discipline and a relationship to the past, and, simultaneously, on the place of Europe as colonizer, claiming mastery of scholarly knowledge. The first contrasts history with memory, at times projecting it as a matter of scientific history *versus* native subaltern memory, while also attempting to bridge the gap. The second focuses on the impact of evolutionary science on the production of history as an imperial project and as an aspect of modernity.

Scientific History *vs* Subaltern Memory?

In response to the difficulties involved in tracing the histories of subaltern people, methods qualitatively different from those based on the search of written material have been suggested, and the significance of myth and memory for historical reconstructions has been emphasized. Methods dealing with memory and time have been debated. Günther Schlee captures the relationship between history and memory in his metaphor of a plant, where both stem and root grow out of the seed, i.e. out of the present, one downwards and one upwards, the one dependent on the other. The image of continuously developing roots usefully visualizes how memory selectively captures images of the past from within the experiences and conditions of the present. From this perspective, there is no true or false memory, there is only lived experience connecting the present to a remembered past, with its representation organized in line with the needs of the individual present.[12]

Long-standing debates on history and memory have raised critical questions about the preference given to written documents as historical evidence. It has been argued that history is an art of memory which is revealed, expressed, or moulded in different forms. The dividing lines between fact, memory, and myth have been blurred, linear perceptions of time have been questioned, and historical reconstructions of the past examined as epistemological modes, language, and rhetoric. A decisive step in displacing the written document from the historian's craft, or, for that matter, removal of the entire discipline of history from acceptably representing popular memories of myth and divinity was taken by Ashis Nandy in his well-known article on the dominance and crisis of the modern historical mode: '[t]raditional India not only lacks the Enlightenment's concept of history; it is doubtful that it finds objective, hard history a reliable, ethical, or reasonable way of constructing the past.' Nandy's alternative is a search for myths and legends in which oral traditions preserve histories of a different nature. Such a history is one of diversity, located in the worldview of 'victims' who have been deprived of a past. For Nandy, memory tends to stand opposed to history and is not an integral part of its constitution.[13]

In a discerning critique of such claims, developed in a literary study of late medieval to early modern South Indian texts, Velcheru Narayana Rao, David Shulman, and Sanjay Subrahmanyam show how history in South India has been written in many genres that are related to changes in a community's preferred mode of literary production. They argue that this significant body of literature, written in the vernacular, *is* history. The preferred genre of history which dominated nineteenth-century Western Europe developed as something that was relatively fixed and stable and which, according to some Western historians, embodied truth; however, this does not refute the production of history in India prior to colonial rule. The methodological argument of this work makes universal claims of applicability; this is not an India-only form of history; the authors state that such history requires a combination of the skills of the social and literary historian.[14]

Attempting to reconstruct the past of people native to the Dang forests of western India, Ajay Skaria searches along lines similar to Nandy for alternatives to what he sees as ill-suited methods developed in Europe. He blames the marriage of history and 'western modernity' for blinding the discipline to the only 'original' sources of the past, i.e. memory and speech. Eventually, according to Skaria, history 'displaces its moment of origin, memory'. In this view the place of memory in the search for knowledge of the past becomes identified with a critique of science as it developed in Europe, in forms that are claimed to have rendered it incapable of establishing reliable knowledge in non-European contexts. Simultaneously, memory is identified with people suppressed by colonial power. Establishing memory thus becomes one of many alternative methods of unearthing histories of the subaltern. Skaria weaves his study of Dang society into the two webs of *mogali* and *mandini*, the two spheres (Skaria calls them 'epochs', but without chronological determinants) defined by people in the Dangs as those of freedom and of subordination to colonial rule. However, in his attempt to capture Dangi pasts Skaria almost takes the Dangs out of history, or represents them as being just as timeless as they were represented in the narratives of his informants.

In a sharp critique of this position Sumit Guha adopts a more distant stance to popular narratives and observes that Skaria's aim of portraying the complex and multilayered life of the Dangi communities leads him to stereotype their 'other', the plains. Guha also suggests that Skaria simultaneously downplays internal differences within Dangi communities as well as the impact of other important social groups on Dangi society. Arguing with reference to a study by Ghanshyam Shah for the need to historicize the core term of Skaria's work, Guha claims that Skaria ignores the fact that the present notion of 'Dangi' itself has a short history, being recently reconstituted and spanning barely three decades.[15]

Nandy's and Skaria's studies are two examples of works in which debates about, on the one hand, the nature of modern science and the place of memory in history and historiography and, on the other, the consequences of dominant historiographies for marginal and subaltern people—i.e. silencing and making invisible their pasts—have become intertwined. Both debates are no doubt concerned with methods of establishing knowledge, either in non-European contexts or for subordinate groups. But in spite of their obvious connecting themes, the two debates are not identical, and the critique of dominant historiography should not be mistaken for siding with the form of discourse analysis which dismisses a 'European-based, post-Enlightenment discipline of history' as incapable of representing non-European or Indian pasts.[16]

From another perspective, Partha Chatterjee introduces 'the Popular' as an analytic domain in its own right. By suggesting the notion of the Popular, he does not mean this domain can replace academic history with a new or more 'original' philosophy of history. He intends the Popular to be incorporated into the discipline of history as a necessary readjustment, allowing space thereby for popular practices of memory. In his Introduction to *History and the Present* he opposes memory to history on account of the way in which history—the academic discipline and the history-writing that stems from it—tends to invalidate memory as evidence, 'a self-constructed cage of scientific history', while viewing memory as the most immediate expression of the popular domain. Other earlier attempts at methodological refinement, based on a systematic inclusion of memory as a source for the past, may not agree with a description which so sharply contrasts history and memory. Many important historical studies, relying heavily on memory, have been provided by works in the fields of cultural history, history of mentalities, historical anthropology, or, more specifically, trauma and post-conflict studies.[17] However, Chatterjee places his contribution in 'a moment of critique, of self-reflection of disciplinary practises', searching in this particular moment for more truthful and ethical historiographical methods. His methodological suggestions, vested in the Popular, result from experiences drawn from history-from-below movements and Subaltern Studies. Yet in the various essays in *History and the Present* it appears that the importance of introducing the notion of a Popular domain is not to bring memory into historical analyses—this was done long ago—but to more carefully elaborate memory in relation to the present, through its meanings, negotiations, representations, and historicizations, and thus to circumvent elitist history from making universal claims to represent the past.[18]

A common strand within studies that deplore the lack of written sources on subaltern pasts is the notion that memory is more than a source of knowledge—it is a source specific to subordinate and marginalized historical experience. Modernity and the modern state place certain restrictions on the production of history by means of techniques or of interests and purposes that work to exclude memory. Memory is eventually invalidated and choked in the webs of modern institutions and the modern mind. However, the arguments in this viewpoint tend to go a step further, claiming in addition that not any or all memory is silenced, but specifically subaltern memory. We are thus left with the idea that memory plays a different or no role at all among elites and in dominant institutions—clearly, this is a problematic notion.

In *Memory of the Modern* Matt Matsuda argues the case for a memory which positions the present in relation to the past in a way that is distinctive for modernity. For him, modernity stands out as one of history's grand epochs.[19] Matsuda contrasts 'archaic memory' with 'modern memory'; the archaic is primordial, organic memory working subconsciously in human behaviour, while the modern has reshaped ancient habits into new cultural forms. He locates the transformation of perceptions of historical knowledge within the development of modernity. Here, modernity is not defined as distinctively European or structured by a dominant European paradigm that worked to dominate other parts of the world through colonial expansion. It is treated as a general transformation, which Matsuda studies through a case from late-nineteenth-century France. The notion of linear and accelerating time and the increasing technological capacity to preserve disappearing pasts by means of systematic record-keeping, archives, and modern media lead, in effect, according to Matsuda, to a narrowing down of knowledge about the past as a consequence of decisions about what elements to trust within contested images of former times. Thus, 'modern memory' is questioned rather for what it withholds than for what it reveals, and history within the modern world also becomes an art of oblivion.[20]

When James Scott argues that '[c]ertain forms of knowledge and control require a narrowing of vision', conceptually his argument reflects ideas similar to Matsuda's, though they are introduced in a different field of research. Taking scientific forestry in the late nineteenth century as a significant example, Scott observes how the authoritarian high-modern state dramatically limits access to information and produces the most extreme form of selective knowledge and recordkeeping. Here, selectivity is not, as in Matsuda's argument, merely the result of form—i.e. knowledge and memory that do not fit the forms designed to preserve them will disappear into the margins of dominant historical memory. In the high-modern state, Scott says, information is selected for the purpose of reorganizing society according to the interests of the state. More than being only a consequence of technological capacity, knowledge is a tool of power. One of the most obvious examples is the colonial state, specifically its revenue surveys and archives.[21]

For my work, however, Scott's argument is somewhat premature. I would even ask whether such a state ever appeared in its totality on the Indian subcontinent. As indicated also in Scott's subtitle, the grand schemes failed more often than not, both because of a lack of capacity in the face of opposition, and for lack of will—due to complex realities and conflicts internal to the EIC. As a state of a modern character grew in India, it encompassed both homogeneity and diversity. At the broader level, observed by C.A. Bayly, there was during the nineteenth century a growing global contemporaneity and uniformity of ideas, economic life, statecraft, and religion, at the level of both institutions and embodied practice. Yet such homogenizing trends were interspersed with internal complexity and local diversity, uniformity and diversity together forming the core character of this modernity.[22] In early-nine-teenth-century India there was, instead of an all-encompassing state, the bureaucracy of an increasingly institutionalized trading company, mixed up in war. In the process, the recording of information was the backbone of administration. Selectivity operated at all levels, from the native subordinate company servant gathering day-to-day information and reporting to his immediate superior, to the records of the Board of Control. But this selectivity was based on different principles, interests, and concerns. No monolithic colonial voice is heard in the archival files; there is a polyphony. Taking the Nilgiri Hills as an example, only from the 1840s onwards—when open conflicts over land had largely become a matter for the bureaucracy—was there any sign of the Madras government attempting to act as a strong state with extensive means of control, using historical selection and neglect to justify land settlements. The early EIC bureaucracy was certainly authoritarian, but its powers to implement such policies were limited. The narrow vision of the state, in Scott's terms, may be traced to decision-making in the higher echelons, but it was not a primary characteristic of the everyday colonial encounter.

Memory also penetrated recording—a fact that is often neglected. Reports, correspondence, and other communications which have ended up in the files were based on a mix of memory, empirical observation, and assumptions about historical, social, and biological evolution which organized the narratives of informants and authors of particular reports. When we read these files it is difficult, even unproductive, to assume a clear opposition between local (native, subaltern) memory and universalizing, official historiography. For the purposes of searching for subaltern or popular pasts in modern archives, it may be more useful—after distinguishing homogenizing trends in colonial administration and 'modern' science from the simultaneous presence of a variety of voices, including those of 'marginal' regions and people—to observe how both *together* constitute modern memory and knowledge.

Colonial surveys also laid the foundation for decisions on the rights in land and natural resources to be granted to people in the Nilgiris from the mid-nineteenth century onwards. Reflecting a desire to record the fact that the legal settlement of land had been carried out in an orderly and civilized manner, the revenue files overflow with correspondence, reports, and minutes documenting thorough investigations carried out by rule-abiding officials. However, socio-political and economic changes, together with changing interests within the state, meant that regulations and laws were never immutable. People in the Nilgiris and, in particular, the Toda have faced constant reinterpretations by government officials of the historical documents, from the first invention of the rules down to the present. As is argued throughout this book, the past was almost always considered a legitimate point of reference for making claims to rights in nature. History was taken as a pretext for extensive claims to land, as well as used to provide justification when encroachments were turned into legal settlements. The past was, simultaneously, the immemorial ancestry to which people native to the Nilgiris referred when they claimed authority over or customary access to land. Throughout the nineteenth century, the past was identified through a variety of means, articulated in different arenas, and neglected or disavowed for the purpose of claiming specific rights in nature. The colonial administration searched for, but rarely found, documentation on property in the Nilgiris and, as a result of its efforts, documentation was produced. Paradoxically, today these are the very documents which individuals among the Toda hope to use as historical evidence to prove their rights against the government as well as against financially powerful entrepreneurs who claim and sometimes encroach on their lands.[23]

Among people in Kandelmund there is a sense of frustration in their being sure that events which they have now forgotten, and agreements that are now being violated, are documented and yet unavailable to them, in government departments. It is as if they distrust their own memory; or, rather, they do not seem to assign it any weight. When they relate the trajectory of their community under colonial rule, it is the voices of Western anthropologists who have done fieldwork in the Nilgiris that emerge, rather than 'original'—sometimes called 'authentic'—Toda memory. Shared memories, like that of Oshthaars, tend to take longer to emerge. Although such memories are deeply rooted in the narratives told in the mund, it seems that they do not account for the 'history of the Toda'. Occasionally, the narrative of 'Toda history' relies heavily on imperial manuals and gazetteers, which were produced to provide a source of knowledge for colonial officers and to make administration more efficient.[24] Such publications were thus public, government-sanctioned historiographies. Given their wide distribution, they influenced public memory—a memory that helps to structure and order the ideological context in which decisions regarding citizens and subjects are made. We may think of the term in contrast to collective or shared memory, since a historiography that was once sanctioned by government is hardly ever shared by all subjects as experience. Over time, however, owing to the reach and constant reiteration of official publications of the kind described, the history which a public memory conveys tends to contribute to the reconstruction of a remembered past that is beyond the living memory of people. In the Nilgiris, it appears as if the expert voice has managed to silence the many voices, the collective memories. As a reflection of their alienation from state authorities, people repeatedly remark: 'Our history is even hidden away in the big libraries in London, so you have to tell us about our past.'[25]

Most Todas living in the munds of Ootacamund, when seeking to explain the present state of their lives, will point to the role of John Sullivan, the first district collector in the Nilgiris when the region was made part of Coimbatore district. At the time of his collectorship in the Nilgiris he was in constant dispute with his superiors and, today, is acknowledged as a champion of Toda rights. 'The discoverer of Ooty and the father of modern Nilgiris', the title ran in pamphlets produced by the Save Nilgiris Campaign, his memory honoured by a full-page article, 'One Man's Ooty' in *The Hindu* in 2005, commemorating the 150th anniversary of his death. *The Hindu*, one of India's leading newspapers, proclaimed Ootacamund, or Ooty for short, as the invention of this British officer, and the oak that he planted was described as an appropriate metaphor for Ootacamund—'gnarled, knobbed and twisted'.[26]

Stories about Sullivan have been told so many times among the Toda that the same formulations constantly recur, and the details have withered away. Just as the notion of a singular 'Toda past' essentializes clans and families among the Toda and munds near and far from Ootacamund as part of a uniform experience of subjugation, so Sullivan has attained a converse mythical status in the stories. Younger generations give little ironic smiles on hearing the stories but, even so, they go on narrating them. The best-known tale about John Sullivan is how he got hold of a very large piece of land when he arrived as one of the first 'white men' in the region. Sullivan, 'who always cared for the Toda', turned to the Toda of Kandelmund and Manjakalmund and asked for an area of land no larger than the size of a sheepskin. They agreed to the bargain when Sullivan paid with a gold coin. But when he measured the land after concluding the agreement, he cut the sheepskin into a thin strip which he stretched over the ground, enabling him to claim an enormous piece of land.

To an outsider the tale immediately raises many questions. Is it not somewhat reminiscent of the ancient Roman poet Virgil's story of how Queen Dido acquired Carthage? When did sheep begin grazing the grassy hills of the Nilgiris? The tale portrays Sullivan as a villain; how can it have become such a famous story among the Toda if he is their hero? Is this not, rather, a mocking story told among British settlers who were highly critical of Sullivan's quick move in the 1820s to secure for himself a government grant of almost 2,000 acres: a colonial tale of the Toda champion cheating poor tribals? The story, in fact, belongs to a well-known folk tale theme and to a category known as the 'Deceptive Bargain'. There are versions of it in Finnish, Estonian, Icelandic, Catalan, Czech, Russian, Serbo-Croat, and American English, though similar stories in India tend to have a different plot. But whether or not the Sullivan story is of European origin and has been adopted by people native to the Nilgiris from European settlers, such tales are not in general intended for factual scrutiny. They have an important but different significance: they appear, rather, to make the present situation comprehensible. Things did not happen by chance; there were greater circumstances within which the Toda's fate can find a meaning.[27]

The Toda's search for evidence to verify their past in written documentation may therefore seem at first to contradict the prominence given to modern myths as told in the munds and in the modern media. And, given the processes of bias and selection that are present in any compilation of archives, the former colonial, and now state, archives may not yield the information they seek. But the problem they face when they approach the state is less one of selective record-keeping than of not having had interpretive precedence in that record. The collections in the colonial archives are certainly selective in the broadest sense of the term, since the information was compiled for the sake of securing colonial rule. But the magnitude of these archives, the wealth and variety of the information they contain, and the many liberal critics of the colonial enterprise both within and outside the colonial pay-rolls who are well represented in the files, all point rather to a problem of selection in the investigator's encounter with the archives—both among latter-day government officials interpreting laws and regulations, and among academic scholars producing historical texts.

Until quite recently, historical studies of the nineteenth-century Nilgiri Hills—including those which claimed to represent tribal history—were based almost exclusively on summary government reports from throughout the nineteenth century and imperial gazetteers from 1880 and 1908.[28] This led some authors to conclude that the documentation was scanty and that imperial biases tended to resonate in the texts. But compared with the day-to-day reflections on events in correspondence, or the different interests represented in petitions and depositions, such reports mostly had the policy purpose of demonstrating the superiority of certain colonial or imperial policies. That there are bound to be imperial biases in imperial gazetteers should not surprise anyone; the many contradictory voices—the surviving evidence of the various observers, recorders and narrators, speaking from within their own worlds and worldviews—are more likely to be found in other kinds of documentation. Giving up on the task of finding written documentation of tribal or dalit pasts, or dismissing such documents by labelling them as colonially biased will eventually lead to tribal and dalit experiences being deemed unverifiable modern myths, and as no more or less valid than elitist and other such histories.

Apart from the difference in detail and the heterogeneity of voices represented on the one hand in reports compiled at presidency administrative offices, and on the other the day-to-day accounts of low-level officials, petitioners, and interviewees in depositions and private letter writers, there is the difference in temporality. Temporality is not to be taken here as a synonym for history; it will not answer questions about 'what happened in the past'. Just as locality may be understood both as a particular place and as the way in which that place is perceived from a particular position within or outside it, temporality may usefully be understood as how individuals or a collective perceive their location in time, i.e. how she, he, or they relate to time and locate themselves in temporal terms. Ancestry, heritage, memory, visions, experience, trauma, public historiographies, narrative trajectories (for example, those of a nation state, or people, or a family), and so on, all speak of different temporalities. These will mediate human activity, such as when people seek to root place-based identity in narrated pasts, or when people construct national commonalities in the particular trajectories of a community. Thus, St Stephen's Church simultaneously represents continuity and rupture. Placed at the physical and social centre of the newly settled territories in the Nilgiri Hills, it was evidence of a continuously evolving British society and nation. The elaborate narrative of its establishment in Price's imperial historiography of 1908 should be viewed in its broader framework: a history of the foundation of a town in the rapidly growing British empire.[29] The church represented the Protestant faith and was a necessary building block of English, or perhaps we should say British, nationality and sovereignty. In contrast, to the Toda of Kandelmund the very same building represents a landmark of historical change affecting their relationship to ancestral lands. For them the land is the timekeeper, holding within it ancestral pasts. Such different perceptions of the past are seldom coherent, although identities may seek to bridge incoherences so as to maintain a sense of order or control in a situation of inconsistent life experience. In particular, in situations of conflict, adherence to varying temporalities may become incommunicable and form part of narratives that legitimize violence.

Evolutionary Histories and Many Europes

We may now return to the debate centring on the relationship between history, historiography, and historicism under the impact of nineteenth-century imperialism and modernity. The evolutionary narrative dominating European historiographies of non-European societies, which has been thoroughly debated in studies of Orientalist discourse, also had a decisive influence on nineteenth-century events in the Nilgiris. It was not a singular narrative, but one of the many facets by which people were both essentialized into timelessness and yet placed within a scheme of evolution and change. It may appear paradoxical that, at the time of the consolidation of the British empire and European global pre-eminence, European historians were increasingly preoccupied with writing the history of nations and nation states. Continuing the theme of temporality, we may observe how, in the formation of nation states, the nation tends to be ascribed a temporal logic of its own; a people with a mission determined by evolution, a scattered 'volk' with a common ancient culture and language, or a people of many religions and languages sharing a historical continental past. In their elaborations of the state and statecraft, British historians tended to separate the history of the British Isles from imperial history, and liberal historians such as John Robert Seeley depicted the history of the colonies as emancipated and integral parts of the history of Greater Britain. Thus, the transformation of Europe into competing nationstate projects seems to contrast with the synoptic view of empire. These European imperial projects had varying success, projecting Europe either through the experience of unending imperial conquest or as the empire that never came to be. Yet it was within the discursive realm of nations that history worked to legitimize colonial sovereignty. The imperial grand narratives, well represented in gazetteers and other official publications, were firmly founded on theories of race, civilization, and evolution. As will become evident in the following chapters, in the process of codifying people's rights to access and use nature into written law, people were identified in relation to particular landscapes and their rights were determined by their perceived historical relationship to the land. Orientalist discourses such as classical Orientalism played an important role in this process. Yet in order for us to understand the means by which land relations were transformed in the Nilgiri Hills, we need to avoid simplistic ideas of the 'Orientalist' view held by colonizers.[30]

Interestingly, one of the major nineteenth-century debates has recently reappeared in a new form on the historian's agenda. Some historians active in parallel debates are those seeking genuinely Indian histories, undistorted by European notions of history. One of the core concepts under attack has been historicism, with its roots in nineteenth-century European scholarship. In tandem with the process of professionalization among historians in the nineteenth century, there was an ambition to construct linear narratives of human social forms that could connect individual events into meaningful wholes, while at the same time proposing methodologies that would safeguard the autonomy of past ages from normative reading through the political lenses of the present, i.e. the development of *Historismus*.[31]

Historicism, as it is more commonly known in Anglo-American debate, has recently gained renewed attention in discussions within the philosophy of history. Among German historians, critical discussions about stereotyped definitions and usages of *Historismus*—'this chameleon of a word'—have led to revisions of the concept. Irmline Veit-Brause identifies two broad sets of arguments in the debates. One distinguishes *Historismus* as a scientific, methodological approach to the past which constitutes a phase in the historiography of human sciences and history. It is a 'major epoch', according to Friedrich Jaeger and Jörn Rüsen, and as such is prominently represented in nineteenth-century imperial historiography, but one that now belongs to the past. The other position does not primarily look for methodological developments within the academic discipline of history, but discerns therein a fundamental philosophical problem of modernity. This is the modern historical sense, which has developed out of the European Enlightenment, as a notion of progress and evolution. Obviously, this critique does not take account of differences within the broad and, at times, contradictory ideological trends of the Enlightenment, but has instead chosen to emphasize the Enlightenment legacy in the singular; as well as the notion, or shall we say the grand narrative, of Europe. Given the emphasis this viewpoint gives to plurality, diversity, and heterogeneity within non-European traditions, its homogenization of the Enlightenment is, to say the least, ironic. To that extent, also, it tends to be a view more from the outside than from the inside.[32]

The latter position connects closely with academic works that aim to formulate a theoretical critique and establish an analytical discourse which does not reproduce Orientalist epistemologies in the broad sense, as in *Writing Post-Orientalist Histories of the Third World* by Gyan Prakash, or in a narrower sense target historicism as a modern phenomenon, as in *Provincializing Europe* by Dipesh Chakrabarty. Some would argue that the criticism of *Historismus* as a linear historical development of progress, in which specific social formations are assigned a unique value, is a bit belated. Theoretical paradigms such as social-structural history have long since dethroned *Historismus* from its position of influence on historical writing. However, Chakrabarty does not see *Historismus* as an evolutionary idea contained within a certain phase of academic historical thinking. He argues in line with the second position in Veit-Brause's characterization: that it permeates every aspect of European modernity. According to Chakrabarty, the history produced within a master narrative of historicist thought, which he refers to as a 'modern, European idea of history', serves to organize histories for every other part of the world and characterizes much written history today; he thus locates the disciplinary discourse of history in post-Enlightenment Europe. Simultaneously, he defines 'Europe' as a hyper-real concept encompassing an imagined Europe of reified categories, structured in terms of domination and subordination and of a development ideal that results in fulfilment for Europe, while for non-Western regions it results in a 'lack'. The imagined 'Europe' thus becomes an ideal impossible to fulfil for all non-'Europes' or non-Western regions of the world.

Chakrabarty's argument reflects Homi Bhabha's discussion of colonial 'mimicry' and the 'slippage' it produces. According to Bhabha, mimicry is the imitation of the colonial ideal, which is a discourse that is structured around ambivalence, producing a desire for reform and simultaneously a slippage, a lack, and a difference of non-achievement.[33] Closely mirroring Bhabha's argument, Chakrabarty writes of historicism as a strategy, a political project integral to the idea of modernity, thereby making the concept less abstract and more political than is assumed in Veit-Brause's typology. Chakrabarty writes: 'Historicism enabled European domination of the world in the nineteenth century. … Historicism is what made modernity or capitalism look not simply global but rather as something that became global *over time*, by originating in one place (Europe) and then spreading outside it.' However, while Bhabha's argument is clearly located in post-Enlightenment English colonialism, Chakrabarty claims Europe is the site for the projection of such stereotyped ideals. Profoundly, though, this Europe is a British colonial or an Anglo-American 'Europe', thus lacking the diversity to which an inclusion of other simultaneous stereotyped ideals prevailing in Europe would have contributed. 'Europe' thereby remains a concept that reads 'empire'.[34]

Ideas of this kind remain abstractions on a scale so grand that they can hardly be verified or falsified via empirical studies. Empirically rich work, such as *Green Imperialism* by Richard Grove, or studies centring on ideologies within the British empire like Thomas Metcalf's *Ideologies of the Raj*, point to deep ambivalence and contradictory notions within the imperial vision, in spite of the indubitable general trends. Perhaps the 'Europe' envisioned by Chakrabarty may not even be intended by him to be drawn into such an exercise. Consequently, the dramatically conflicting notions and visions of the ideal societies that European settlers—officers, ethnographers, and entrepreneurs alike—hoped would materialize in the Nilgiris of the early nineteenth century can only with difficulty find an explanation in terms of Chakrabarty's singular, reified 'Europe' that had penetrated discourses to the extent that it had become equal to the air people breathed. References were in fact more often made to Scotland, England, and Austria than to Europe, indicating the more common stereotyped identifications with specific nations, rather than with Europe. In contrast, references to 'Europe' often meant 'the Continent' and the arch-enemy, France.

Certainly in the terrain I look at, projections of Scottish highland qualities, the simple peasant, and the entrepreneurial industrialist onto Indian societies were modelled on abstract ideas of particular European regional landscapes and their inherent capacities while the idea of Europe was intersected by racial categories. Europe with its industrial towns, polluting both nature and the minds and bodies of people, was often in fact described as the very negation of the healthy and strong life found in the South Indian hills. As in Arcadia, people here were understood to be rooted in this landscape, to originate and belong to this place. Therefore, the place itself and the people living there, promised development, and ideas of romanticism and progress went hand in hand. In short, within the early-nineteenth-century colonial encounter with the South Indian hills, the singular and reified idea of Europe and its adherents is remote from our terrain; rather, we must speak of many Europes.

In parallel with the epistemological debates of the nineteenth century, there was no less vigorous a discussion about the empirical methods that could be used to critically assess the validity of sources of knowledge of the past. Objective knowledge was often seen as an unachievable, yet necessary, ideal. Johann Gustav Droysen concluded in 1868 that the past could only be reached indirectly: 'we cannot bring forth the past "objectively" but can produce only an idea, a picture, and a reflection from the "sources".'[35] While taking account of the very limited histories that could be produced if source criticism was the only method by which to obtain knowledge about the past, we would do well to remember that, when positivist methodologies and rules for the use of sources were further developed at the turn of the twentieth century, they were seen as ways of critically scrutinizing nationalist historiography, and as a counterforce to the incorporation of historians into nationalist political projects. A methodology of critical treatment of sources represented, in that sense, an endeavour to protect the integrity of scholarly work from the influence of political and ideological meta-narratives of state power. This was much like the aims both of present-day historians who seek to guard academic history from being co-opted by the political projects of religious groups, and of the historians, discussed above, who suggest a theoretical alternative towards a genuinely non-European, non-Western historical epistemology.

Contested Space in a Delimited Region

The historical events, trajectories, and contexts which this book aims to uncover centre on a region that has been thoroughly marked out and delimited in numerous histories over almost two centuries. While the main characters and perspectives have changed in accordance with the aims and interests of each study, the region has remained intact. As an ecological enclave, a tribal realm, or a political boundary zone the Nilgiri Hills have remained an unquestioned region in their own right, with a unique history. Even in recent works that seek to demonstrate the influence of precolonial states on the Nilgiris, the boundaries of this particular region remain undisturbed. Much important scholarly work has come out of research in the Nilgiris, in particular anthropological, linguistic, and ecological studies.[36] The point here is not to question the value of these contributions, but to observe that unquestioned and generally accepted boundaries, including those of linguistic and administrative units, tend to produce blind spots.

Most of the studies undertaken have been concentrated in the centremost part of the Nilgiri Hills, the upper plateau approximately 2,000–2,600 metres above sea level. This part of the region was dominated by montane grasslands, with low-stature shola forests in valleys, and along slopes above 1,800 metres. The present study, however, encompasses a larger region, from the low-lying Nilambur plains in the west, at 80 metres above sea level below the steep western scarp, across evergreen forests meeting the plateau, to the eastern slopes that gradually merge with scrub forests towards the Coimbatore plateau and, further north, along the Moyar river. From the northern slopes rising from the Mysore plains and the dry and moist deciduous forests, like that of Mudumalai, the region under study also includes the continued hill ranges of the Upper Bhavani towards Palghat in the south. The topographical complexity and spread of the region, including its vast variety of vegetation zones, has had a major impact on conditions for human life and livelihoods. The importance of internal, locally specific conditions, and of migrations into and within the region at large, may usefully be seen in the light of climatic and ecological conditions. The wide range of rainfall zones, from 500 to 7,000 mm per year, and the regionally varying length of the dry season, from only about a month in the west to six months in the eastern plateau, serve to show the broader Nilgiri region as not a singular entity or a sealed-off enclave.[37]

In several studies it has been taken as self-evident that the central hilly plateau at 2,000 metres, which could be reached only by climbing hill slopes, formed a naturally given space that completely determined human life and social organization. However, we need to see how this space, including its climate and ecology, was experienced, understood, and lived in, in ways that dissolved the exactness of such fixed boundaries. As discussed in Chapter 2, temporal notions were read into past histories of the region and of the people living there. Even if a linear evolutionary trajectory was assumed, each racially defined community was ascribed different temporal relations to the region which identified them with histories and past events far beyond the Nilgiris. Ethnographic reports described in detail the relationships between endogamous communities—the tribes—in the hills and emphasized interdependence and hierarchy in terms of economic, social, and ritual exchange. Yet, in spite of representations of a closed system of Toda pastoralists, Badaga shifting cultivators, and Kota artisans and musicians maintaining looser relations with other 'tribes'—such as Kurumba and Irula shifting cultivators, hunters, and gatherers—two of the communities were singled out as having a specific relationship to the past and the future.[38] The Toda were depicted by early European visitors as a people of ancient history, herders in the Rousseauan sense, and assumed most likely to have a European ancestry—they had been moving slowly through time in primitive livelihoods. In contrast the Badaga, being cultivators of the soil, were ascribed a history of skill and progress, marked by dramatic events of flight from northern warfare, and a bright future of entrepreneurship. For the Badaga, time was assumed to move rapidly, while for the Toda it stood still.

The landscape was also immediately ascribed meaning by identifying it with non-Indian sceneries, such as the European Alps and the Scottish highlands. To the Europeans these were landscapes of healing and health, assumed to promote the best human qualities. Yet the area was also described as a transformative landscape. British officers identified suitable hillsides and valleys for the cultivation of European crops and the rearing of European cattle, and roads opened the hills up to exploitation. Widely published lithographs showed European visitors, early tourists, strolling through the landscape to explore its beauty and observe primitive herders. In the far distance, orderly rows of houses in the European settlement of Ootacamund can be seen. However, soon various representations of the landscape came into conflict and discourses changed. In 1829, the oft-quoted ethnographer Reverend James Hough described the encouraging and frank deportment of the Toda as he saw winds catch their hair: this made him think of mountain deer running free and wild over the fields. He said they were well proportioned and muscular, playful and easily amused. Freedom and liberty were the words that came to his mind as he compared them with English peasants, far removed from submissive Hindus.[39] This wilderness, in his account, promised a healthy life filled with opportunities. Less than two decades later, in 1846, another observer writing for a Calcutta newspaper was equally struck by the wildness of nature when he observed the Toda. However, in his report there is no trace of Hough's encouraging absence of Hindoo servility:

> I learn that when stung with hunger they spring upon food with the eagerness of the tiger, when their appetite is sated, they doze away their hours in idleness or sleep, then they are an easy prey to the temptation

> of each wild and passionate impulse, and reckless in their manner of gratifying it. Their passions, wild and turbulent, have been prematurely kindled—their inborn sense of shame prematurely withered—they are imbruted—they are men without a God—they grope their way through a dark world, and know not of hereafter.[40]

Lacking a sense of shame or of God, and unable to control their passions, the Toda were now portrayed as reckless tigers. The wilderness needed to be tamed or, at least, controlled. Compared to the earlier account, in which the simple English peasant was recognizable, the later one depicts an animal-like human with no familiar features. Common to both is a sense of distance, with the authors placing themselves as observers, spectators, away from the landscape, while nature itself engulfs the Toda in the form of the mountain deer or the tiger. This distance is well described by Keith Thomas as resulting from changing views of man's place in the natural world. When English theologians in the late seventeenth century turned from stressing the decay of the natural world, caused by the Fall from Paradise, to an increasing emphasis on the perfection of Creation—in which there was no disharmony between man's needs and subordinate creation—they observed a hierarchical order. In the late eighteenth century this hierarchy found more elaborate distinctions. Man was proven superior to the beasts by his capacity for speech, reason, intellect, and moral responsibility, along with his possession of a religious instinct and an immortal soul. Early modern England felt 'anxiety, latent or explicit, about any form of behaviour which threatened to transgress the fragile boundaries between man and the animal creation'. But men, too, could be 'like beasts'. American Indians could be described as 'herds of deer in a forest' or 'just one degree … remov'd from a monkey'. The Irish lived 'like beasts', women lacked souls, and the poor were 'but brutes in their understanding'. Like the Toda in the South Indian hills, these were people lacking morality, human sensibility, and history.[41]

Early-nineteenth-century descriptions from the Nilgiris show, in an interesting way, how romanticist notions of nature and people collided with utilitarian ideas about the use of nature and the appropriate place of people in the process of progress. It was not unusual for individual Europeans to hold romantic ideas about herders, even as they advocated a rational use of the land through settled cultivation. In the process of defining space and ordering it into larger schemes, the concern over its use became central. At first, the Madras government was unconvinced it had any use at all, considering its location and lack of valuable forest. Early European visitors, who included the district collector Sullivan, argued the need for a resort and sanatorium. But as it became evident that the soil produced good crops, the hill landscape was defined as a proper place for cultivation, thus bringing the Nilgiri landscape within the scope of the general principles of revenue and the notions of settled agriculture that were then the hallmarks of civilization.

Agriculture was a source of revenue and required legal codification. In the process of establishing legal rights in land, the EIC administration revealed internal divisions and conflicts in terms of generations, ideologies, economic and political interests, and visions for the transformation of the region. Such processes have been widely researched in agrarian history. But in contrast with studies that talk in terms either of a gradual inclusion of newly conquered territories into the legacies of British law, of a parallel working of different British and Indian legal systems, or of an adaptation of the former to the latter, legal settlements of rights in land and resources in the Nilgiris clearly demonstrate how conflicts within the EIC combined with pressure from people in the Nilgiris to shape the legal codes that emerged. In the course of the disputes, arguments among British administrators often referred in the first instance to what was considered appropriate for the Nilgiris as a specific region. However, as is discussed in depth in Chapter 3, on almost every occasion it is quite clear that the arguments also reflected positions held in the British parliament, most prominently during the heated debates on enclosure, on the rights of British subjects under common law, and on the principles of government and sovereign rule. The Nilgiris thus became a legally contested space with repercussions, on matters of principle, for similar disputes in other continents.

As has been acknowledged in many earlier studies, ordering knowledge about Indian territories included ordering people within those territories. Such categories were gendered and also followed the lines of race and caste.[42] The gradual transformation of philosophies into natural and social sciences came to have a huge impact on the methods and schemes used to structure the information that had been empirically gathered through surveys. People in the Nilgiris immediately attracted the ethnographer's interest, the Toda more than others, and mythologies spun around their ancestries and habits travelled fast. Anthropologists later paid much attention to the socio-economic order prevalent in the Nilgiris, in which different communities related to each other in a mutual exchange of produce and services, executed within a hierarchical order.[43] But as early as the 1820s, and in the following decades, ethnographers struggled to discern the nucleus of this order and, from a conviction of the uniqueness of the Nilgiris as a region, the system was from the first outlined as a closed one. Chapter 4 brings out how the notion of this racially divided space was subsequently incorporated into the elaboration of legal rights, not to be replicated in legal codes but to be reinterpreted in terms of the specific rights acknowledged for each racially defined community. The arguments followed the logic of utilitarian thought and focused on the specific land-use needs of each 'hill tribe', whether herding cattle or cultivating the soil. Liberal political thought and race theory combined in this way to create law, which then became particularist rather than universal.

European settlement in the Nilgiris expanded gradually and, from the vantage point of people living in the hills, may have been seen as immigration rather than conquest. However, the British themselves reported it in terms of an expansion of territory and the establishment of British administration and rule. In spite of an increasing number of buildings, plots taken up for cultivation, and revenue assessments (if erratic), it took a decade for anyone to react against British intrusion into the central part of the Nilgiri plateau. This was also the region in which the Toda retained unquestioned authority over the land, and it was only after being called upon to sign a document renouncing their control of parts of the land that the Toda in this particular region realized that a change had already taken place which they had not previously perceived. The administrative move to legalize occupation of the land through documented ownership in the late 1820s triggered years of conflict, involving a broad range of actors. Notwithstanding the very limited size of the Toda population—an estimate in 1832 put it at 600 individuals,[44] the highest figure recorded during the early decades of the British presence—it was not until 1843 that the first regulations on land rights in the Nilgiri Hills could be passed. The time span itself reveals the complexity of the conflicts.

As indicated earlier, confrontations in these South Indian hill tracts differ from those in the general narratives of dichotomous conflicts between on the one hand the colonial state, and on the other the indigenous population—the superior and the subaltern, Europe and its Other. The use of armed force in combination with decisive revenue assessments would most likely have made short work of any native resistance in the Nilgiris. But there were significant differences between the situation here and the way in which open confrontation took place in East and North India, as described in several historical studies.[45] As Chapter 5 will show, analysing the situation in terms of two opposing entities of colonial force and native resistance will not encompass the conflicts as these evolved out of different claims to the same lands. There were divisions within the EIC administration as well as within the indigenous population. These divisions appeared both between communities and within them, and with other actors—such as with the strong lords of the neighbouring Wynad region. The latter made use of the conflicts by siding with the Toda to get at the British, their former enemy. Information about divisions within the communities of the Nilgiris is not easily available. Colonial ethnographies describe them as closed ethnic entities, defined according to racial categories, and the administration found no reason to question such schemes. It is in the reports from periods of conflict, when the Toda of the central Nilgiris seem to have acted somewhat erratically, changing position from time to time, that divisions can be seen. During conflicts, hierarchies of authority and decisions based on clan affiliations come to the fore. Thus, what at first sight looks like indecisive tribals was most probably the result of tensions within Toda society.

There are often good reasons to compare the process of territorial conquest in India with that on other continents. But when making such comparisons we need to acknowledge their limited applicability, owing to fundamental historical differences between the continents and regions. Analyses of expanding European rule on the Indian subcontinent need to take account of the fact that the Europeans were not newcomers, but had trading relationships with native merchants and states going back more than 300 years. Territorial conquest generally built on pre-existing contacts and alliances, which had implications for colonial administration. For example, respect for 'native law' was given particular emphasis in South India and, consequently, when an argument for the right to take over empty land, *terra nullius*, was voiced in the Indian context it had different implications compared with when it was voiced in North America and Australia. Furthermore, as this study will show, people in forest and hill regions, too, were accustomed to a situation of multiple authority and hierarchical societies in precolonial times. Therefore they were not completely at a loss when confronted by administrators of the EIC. They acted within a space in which local politics could be played out.

The conflicts that reached a peak in the 1830s came to have a crucial impact on the codification of law, and the discourse of rights in which disputes took place was by no means a singularly transmitted European doctrine. Consequently, the Nilgiris as a space in which rights were asserted cannot be understood in terms of a neat dichotomy between two clearly defined parties, either in the materialist sense—as has been chosen by Ramachandra Guha and Ranajit Guha in their studies of resource conflicts during the expansion of capitalism and colonial rule—or in a deconstructivist sense, as in Skaria's study of the Dang forests of western India. Following the polarized structure of early Subaltern Studies analysis, Ranajit Guha speaks of 'counterinsurgency', Ramachandra Guha of 'rebellion as confrontation', and Skaria of 'counteraesthetics'. In spite of later studies of cross-fertilizations between colonizer and colonized, most studies of South Indian forest tracts remain within the 1980s framework. In order to understand conflicts over rights in the Nilgiris, this analytical divide needs to be problematized further. There is reason to emphasize not merely polarities but also the specific relations created in the meeting—or collision—between conflicting parties.[46]

The less clear-cut situations following in the wake of British conquest in forest and hill tracts have more recently been discussed by K. Sivaramakrishnan. He discerns 'zones of anomaly' in the geographical spaces within which the colonial government tried to establish legal regulations for land settlements, but where their application was thwarted.[47] When British colonizers sought to make people in the Jungle Mahals of Bengal yield to colonial power, for example, they did not rely on troops and revenue collectors alone. The zamindars, controlling the intermediary zone between forest tribes and regional states interacted with the jungle chiefs in what Sivaramakrishnan has termed a 'trade and raid economy, with [a] complicated delineation of jurisdictions'. Achieving political control in these areas involved the deployment of an economy in which the landscape was divided into settled cultivation, wasteland, and forest, i.e. an economy alien to the fluctuating uses of cultivation and forest in a situation of shifting cultivation. The revenue system and physical control of land and population thus combined in what could be called 'ecological warfare ... on the landscape', in which settled cultivation was a key tool.[48] Landscape clearing was also a military strategy in its own right, aimed at preventing rebel forces from taking cover in forests along the roads. As several studies have shown, forests could both offer people shelter during armed movements and provide safe havens for those evading taxes or military service. In colonial narratives the jungle was regarded as an uncivil refuge for bandits and criminal tribes.[49]

Furthermore, regions that were considered to be of low economic value, potentially rebellious, remote, and densely forested—such as Bastar in central India in the early part of the nineteenth century—were more often put under indirect rule and subjected to the payment of tribute or revenue. The system was both cheaper and more convenient since it involved fewer resident British administrators, and any rebellion could be blamed on the king who had failed to meet the needs of the people. But even such apparently limited penetration into local polities never stopped British interests from making claims on natural resources. From the very outset, in Bastar and Chhattisgarh, the British claimed independent rights in forest and mineral assets.[50]

Applying the term 'zones of anomaly' more broadly, it may be suggested that these were geographical spaces where the colonial administration's attempts to incorporate a territory into its legal codification and framework were contested and fought by people living in the territory. Norms, epistemologies, and perceptions of nature and of rights to access and use its resources, clashed. Such zones emerged 'at different stages in colonial statemaking', according to Sivaramakrishnan, and were particularly troublesome for an expanding modern state seeking singularity, rationalization, and centralization. They thus became an extended 'frontier', differing from the sharp line drawn between two opposing and essentially different worlds in that it allowed for interaction, exchange of information, a measure of interdependence, and uncertainty about the acting subjects' influence on the course of events. This brings into focus the importance of place, and is distant from the notion of a 'frontier' behind which an intact European/colonial polity and society had taken control.[51]

Sivaramakrishnan's analytic frame can usefully be refined using Mary Louise Pratt's concept of a 'contact zone' to encompass, in addition, processes in which interaction between colonizer and colonized showed how internal conflicts as well as interests and identifications transgressed and blurred the major divide. Introducing the concept in this context is also intended to facilitate an analysis of codification in which European and indigenous Indian legal norms, notions, and perceptions needed to communicate and, therefore, often mutually invented the necessary terminology and its interpretations. As the present book focuses on the wrestling and negotiation that took place between different legal interests in a situation where conflicts ran deep but did not erupt as physical violence, understanding the social and relational articulation of conflicts requires analytical tools that go beyond mere descriptions of an unclear situation. The notion of a contact zone was introduced in Pratt's work on travel writing to denote a space of co-presence, interaction, and interlocked understandings and practices resulting from colonial encounters and representations of the 'domestic subject'. This is therefore not a geographical but a social space, and in that sense it is not the space in which they actually meet, but the space that is created by their meeting. This meeting may be highly asymmetrical in terms of domination and subordination, yet the subjects are constituted in and by relating to each other. The contact zone is thus a space for relational processes of mutual formation and, consequently, encompasses the socially complex situation in which rights were negotiated in the Nilgiri Hills.

Thinking in terms of transculturation—as a phenomenon concerned with how subordinate groups select and invent from material transmitted by a dominant culture (in the shape of norms, language, institutions, hierarchies, etc.)—may also serve as a way of reflecting on the complexities of popular strategies to oppose and distort government initiatives to impose sovereign rule.[52] Chapter 5 also seeks to explore the consequences of conflicts within the colonial administration over the scope which people had to negotiate, distort, and delay the introduction of colonial sovereign rule. As I will show, such conflicts opened up a space for the assertion of rights, a space that was utilized for local politics. In the process, resistance moved into the sphere of dominant power. My intention is therefore to ground Pratt's concept in an analysis that takes account of the importance of territory and space.

As discussed later, these conflicts were expressed at crucial points in the abstract and normative language of courtrooms, before officials who were vested with the powers of a judge. Here, different claims were made to specific entities of land with criss-crossing boundaries. These lands were claimed for their perceived economic, social, religious or other value, and the arguments noted in the many depositions reflected ideas of nature that were worlds apart and yet which tried to communicate. Pratt's concept captures the complexity of conflicts displayed in such social spaces. But, more than that, the conflicts were acted out on the land itself, in operations and actions that depended on territorial and ecological knowledge, as well as on the measure of force supporting them. Disputes took place in physical locations, for example in places vested with symbolic authority such as the *cutcherry* (the British administration office) or Toda temple sites and their sacred grounds. The land—with its hill slopes, fields, rocks, streams, and roads—was inspected on site, by means of surveys. Officials undertaking these went in search of demarcation stones and well-versed informants among either members of a Toda settlement, who claimed the land as their grazing ground, or individual Badaga shifting cultivators, who claimed it on the basis of their cultivation. Such surveys were performed to 'rectify miscomprehensions about land tenure', i.e. to prepare the ground for new administrative principles.

For a long period of time, however, legal principles that were asserted for the entire hill region remained largely a matter of paperwork, only mattering in spaces where outsiders actually built houses or ploughed the land. As Vinita Damodaran observes with regard to British encroachment into Chotanagpur, no document in a distant government office could immediately transform people's complex relationship to the land. Referring to Peter Gow's study of western Amazonia, she notes that land was a lived space, in which people's experiences were closely bound to the landscape. In addition, we need to consider that, depending on the extent of penetration into physical and social natures, people's experiences of and relationships to a particular landscape changed. In the longer term, this becomes even more important, for example, in situations like those described by Mahesh Rangarajan for the Gir forests of Junagadh in today's Gujarat. Here, resident and transient people were present at all times amidst the fluctuating appropriation and use of forest tracts by succeeding states, from Mughal times through British indirect rule to the present. Over these 400 years, nature was in constant flux and subject to multiple claims, the land being used as pastoral ground or a marcher region contested by rulers of princely states; as a timber reserve; a hunting ground; a protected forest; a sanctuary; and now eco-development and Hindutva nationalism.[53]

The legal process itself partly explains the one-sided historical accounts in which, in particular the Toda community, but also the Badaga, received such immense attention—disproportionate attention, one might say, from an ethnographic point of view. The Irula, Kota, Kurumba, and other communities in the hills were dealt with in a more offhand manner. From the standpoint of land rights, authority, and sovereign colonial rule, however, all but the Toda and the Badaga were considered insignificant, since they were not in a position to claim rights to land. Apart from their presence in purely ethnographic accounts, they appear almost exclusively as woodcutters and bearers in colonial files.

In contrast to regions such as Uttarakhand, Bastar, and Bengal, military force was never used for the purpose of conquering the Nilgiri Hills. Army troops were only deployed in the Nilgiris for recreation or training purposes, not to force people to leave their lands or to accept British rule. Here, the brutality of conquest lay in the way in which law was deployed as the instrument of conquest. Within the Company administration, disputes over institutions and institutional measures were themselves arenas in which conflicts over authority, resources, and legal principles were played out. For almost fifteen years the principles used to settle land rights divided the district and presidency administrations; the one seeking private property and some liberty for private enterprise, the other claiming sovereign rule. Pastoralists and shifting cultivators, caught in the crossfire of Europeans making contradictory claims on lands over which the Toda claimed authority, then moved to employ local politics.

Claiming and Negotiating Rights

As a consequence of what has been argued above, South India may stand out as different, as exceptional, in an all-India account of the expansion of colonial rule into Indian forest and hill tracts. Needless to say, though, such a statement rests on assumptions regarding the regions and situations singled out as the norm and against which all others stand out as the exceptions. We may also ask whether the more violent encounters have been assumed to be the common historical trajectory of colonial conquest simply because of the more voluminous traces they tend to leave in colonial files. This apart, there may still be regional differences of another kind.

On exploring the legal settlement of rights in South Indian hill regions, we discern the early structure of the colonial state as it began to form in the Madras Presidency. The findings of this book may appear to stand in stark contrast to historical works that portray early-nineteenth-century colonial rule in terms of a military fiscal state. The centralized and authoritarian character of EIC rule through its corporate and militarized organization does not easily fit the Nilgiri situation, with this area's unclear and improvised administration in constant collision with higher authority. David Washbrook, who emphasizes the corporate structure of early colonial rule and its willingness to adopt the imagined despotism of the Orient, says the Company ran 'a world-wide business empire and, at least theoretically (and whatever its men-on-the-spot might actually have done), ran it under extremely centrist forms of authority'.[54] I try to look very closely at the words in brackets, for what the 'men-on-the-spot' actually did came to have a profound influence on people's lives. The wrestling of contradictory interests, crosscutting alliances, and negotiations meant that the centrist ambitions of government and boards remained no more than theory until policies had been heavily moulded through lengthy processes of negotiation on the spot. Without offering an alternative interpretation or critique of the notion of an authoritarian state, I seek to contribute a more balanced picture of how the early colonial state functioned, and how the institutional framework began to penetrate issues such as conflict management at the local and regional level. In the Nilgiri Hills the strength of a military fiscal state was unnecessary—military force was not required, the revenue was insignificant. After the 'pacification' of Wynad and the death of the last rebellious raja in 1805, only a limited and very passive military presence remained in the region. The situation reveals, rather, how state-like institutions were used by individuals and groups with colliding interests, thus constantly redefining the authority and expediency of such institutions.

Central authorities, like the Madras government, worked to systematize governance. But they did not do so primarily in order to streamline administration, or for the sake of allowing policies to be copied in every region. A high degree of political pragmatism prevailed. Consequently, officers invoking legal principles could still arrive at legal settlements that appeared to contradict the logic of such principles, and the law was used in almost an instrumental way to achieve certain aims. In the courtrooms, as in many other arenas of dispute, adherence to higher principles was a core discourse of debate, but the practical application of those principles preceding the actual settlement could take account of a range of local conditions which, in fact, ran contrary to the principles being professed. This situation underlines the need to let historical research move far beyond the summary revenue reports and final wordings of regulations, given the fairely dominant place which general policies and principles tend to have in such documents.

Another aspect of the endeavour to systematize governance emerges clearly in the Nilgiris when the Madras government acted forcefully to establish administrative hierarchies within the EIC. In the process of consolidating colonial rule, it took firm action against individual officers who had taken personal advantage of their position within the administration. Such criticism not only affected the district collector, who was vested with far-reaching authority regarding land, revenue, and judicial matters; the many private Indian and European entrepreneurs who immigrated in the hope of being landowners were also affected when the government attempted a clean sweep in order to put all land under government sovereignty.

This situation further illustrates the analytic problems that arise from positing a strict dichotomy of state *versus* people. Such a dichotomy obscures understanding of the crosscutting alliances that formed during conflicts over authority with regard to land. Yet it is not inappropriate to use the word 'resistance' as a powerful term in the analysis of confrontations between colonial power and indigenous populations in forest and hill regions. The term does capture the response of people subjected to external threat, conquest, or authoritarian and bureaucratic state force, without presupposing by that term the singular identity of such people.

As Scott has shown, a refusal to accept dominant power need not be violent in order to remain an effective, popular struggle. Low-key noncompliance in everyday life may achieve a powerful distortion of government agendas among people who lack the capacity to risk open confrontation. Going absent is another effective means of avoiding an encroaching state. Revenue assessments and demands for forced labour became impotent when people simply absconded into the forests. The strategy of evasion among the Baiga and Gond in the Central Provinces has been explained by Rangarajan in terms of flight, a common pattern of resistance. Both strategies were used among the Toda in their conflicts with the government.[55]

In exploring the situation in the South Indian hills I have chosen to discuss resistance also in terms of negotiation, i.e. as a strategy of acknowledging, influencing, and making use of the other party's domain of authority—a strategy of keeping confrontation to a minimum and making gains without open conflict. In a variety of such ways, a new space for the assertion of rights was defined, a space in which both parties sought to use the other's terminology to their own advantage. This is the social space with connotations similar to Pratt's 'contact zone': a space created by the interaction between parties and, in the Nilgiri case, by conflict. Negotiation as a strategy of confrontation resembles the form of interaction existing between ruler and subject, which acknowledges a certain interdependence and in which both possess economic, political, and symbolic resources that may influence the course of events. This strategy has mostly been interpreted as accounting for British relations with Indian elites, however, it is also useful to elaborate in these same terms the relations between a ruler and subjects belonging to a much lower strata.

The taking of a deposition may serve as an example. During the conflicts of the 1830s in the Nilgiris, depositions were taken on a number of occasions. In order to fix certain land rights in written documents, the papers had to be signed, and this could not be done at gunpoint. Since the British administration was divided on the issue of native rights, the principles of legal process were carefully adhered to. The purpose of calling people for questioning was primarily to get the vital signatures. The term 'deposition' may give the impression that the 'deponent' was the only party to initiate the proceedings. But in fact, apart from being an important way of getting information, these depositions were mainly a means by which the colonial administration arranged for certain documents to be signed. In this sense, Sverker Finnström's slightly sarcastic term 'imperial dialogue' is appropriate, since there was rarely a genuine dialogue, or reciprocity, between colonizer and colonized. There was rather a one-sided appropriation of meaning, formulated by colonial agents. Yet deliberate and complete disregard for native conceptions would not have produced the signatures or the peaceful submission of subjects under colonial rule. In this sense, the depositions reflect the need for understanding why the opponent argued according to a certain logic, and what the specific rights he referred to actually implied.

Depositions were at times signed by up to twenty-six individuals, indicating both their personal names and the names of their respective munds. The statements recorded were mostly characterized by the respondent's or deponent's elaborate explanations of particular phenomena, well known to him (there were no women among the interviewees). These are among the types of documents in which we may discern subordinate voices, even when the various filters of translation, interpretation, and selection by colonial authorities through which the statements passed are taken into account. The existing balance of power in the region did not demand such an elaborate course of action; it was the legal procedure itself and the fact that the British administration incorporated conflicting interests that made negotiations necessary. As indicated earlier, in the context of legal disputes the arguments voiced in conflicts over land and resources encompassed different and contradictory legal principles. Some emphasized the importance of securing trust in the EIC among Indian subjects, others referred to principles of equity—the fair and reasonable application of law. Arbitration and negotiation were thus given a part to play, not only in the settlement of land disputes but also in the codification of land rights. This state of affairs further explains that power relations need not be equal for a situation to remain 'negotiable', and for us to analyse the situation in terms of negotiation. The power relations were, of course, deeply unequal. Yet the situation had nonetheless opened up a space within which cattle herders and shifting cultivators, too, had an impact on the codification of law.[56]

The main body of research on subaltern assertion in forest tracts, which has now been debated for about a quarter of a century, has tended to emphasize confrontation, and therefore conflicts are analysed with terms such as 'uprising', 'insurgency', 'rebellion', and 'revolt'. Similarly, the observation of a specific kind of conflict between ruler and subject in precolonial and colonial states was long an important feature of the historical narrative. Ramachandra Guha's sharp distinction between different forms of confrontation among peasant communities within earlier kingdoms, and with the colonial state in Tehri Garhwal and Kumaun in the western Himalayas, is quite representative of the line of argument in such work. The term 'rebellion as custom' is used here to describe rebellion under pre-industrial and pre-capitalist monarchies. This form of resistance, Guha claims, drew its legitimacy from custom and did not seek to overthrow the social order since, within such societies, authority rested on 'an idiom of reciprocity' that could sustain peasant subsistence. In contrast, 'rebellion as confrontation' refers to rebellion against an alien, centralized, and bureaucratic state built on uniform administrative structures and claiming forest resources for an economy with its centre far outside the region. Here, according to Guha, the level of violence and intensity of conflict depended on the strategic importance of the region and its accessibility to colonial administrators and troops.[57] In principle, the argument is a reflection of Michael Adas's description of precolonial societies in Burma and Java, where peasants were easily drawn into elite feuds and, to avoid these, resorted to strategies of avoidance that found legitimacy within the social order. At the time of Dutch colonial conquest, the situation changed. However, Adas prefers to emphasize the importance of the organization of the state, rather than single out alien colonial forces as such, to explain the change. When precolonial states gradually centralized into bureaucracies, peasants' defence mechanisms began to erode. In the process, conflicts with the ruling power grew more violent.[58]

A study of early modern ruler–subject conflicts in west and central Indian forest tracts, similar to Adas's work in its sensitivity to detail, is by Sumit Guha. Proceeding from a sharp critique of Gadgil's romanticization of precolonial tribal societies, Guha points to intensive interaction between hill and plains societies and the mobile character and changing resource-use patterns of many communities in the forests. Resistance strategies, such as flight and migration, and forest clearance as a state strategy to control rebellion, were common in early modern India, according to Guha.

Similarly, drawing on empirical evidence, Chetan Singh questions Ramachandra Guha's 'simplistic' description of social organization in precolonial Himalayan regions. In contrast with ideas of a movement from collective to individual use of forests, and a destruction of village communities in the transition to colonial rule, Singh points to the role of the raja as the owner of forest and waste in Himachal. In the villages, pressing decisions were made by consensus among the peasants, yet a clear-cut village community may never have existed. Uncultivated waste was often controlled by grantees of land or the raja, not by a village community sharing property in common. We would also do well to remember the broader research context immediately preceding the debates of the 1980s about tribal confrontations with colonial power, in which K.S. Singh observed the considerable regional and historical differences between tribal communities and societies. Mughal rulers actively opened up forests to cultivation, trade, and roads for transport by offering various incentives to peasant castes and others. Singh specifically pointed out that communities, later identified as tribes, such as the Bhil, Mina, Koli, and Gond, were not leading a secluded life in the forests and hills but were recognized as dominant communities by the Mughal empire. More importantly, he noted the rise of states either from within these societies or as a result of the policies of Rajputs and other castes who established their power in Orissa, Central India, Gujarat, and Rajasthan. Though made in the 1970s, Singh's observations still serve to complicate the situation into which colonial forces advanced and within which conflicts escalated.[59]

Likewise, the sharp distinction made in Ramachandra Guha's study does not work well in an analysis of a hill region in the early nineteenth century, such as the Nilgiris and upper Wynad. A more gradual change, simultaneously involving various rulers with claims on the region, better depicts the transformation. At the time of the European intrusion the region had been incorporated to varying degrees into state polities and revenue assessments and was claimed almost simultaneously by strong lords among the royal houses of Malabar, the Mysore State, and the government of the EIC.

In a more recent article, Guha (together with Gadgil) shows a slight shift in his earlier emphasis on the question of resistance, clearly influenced by the theories of Scott and Adas. Having maintained that peasants tended to discard 'weapons of everyday resistance' for more open and confrontational forms of protest, Gadgil and Guha now argue along similar lines to Scott and Adas, claiming that resource users in the forests of the western Himalayas mobilized a variety of strategies against colonial state intervention. These were 'avoidance strategies' such as theft, foot-dragging, the retraction of testimony in court, and other measures to undermine the colonial state's efforts to impose forest laws on the region. Interestingly, in contrast to Adas's observation that such strategies tended to disappear under more centralized states, Gadgil and Guha now argue that these 'hidden' forms of resistance were an equally effective strategy in thwarting colonial forest administration.[60] David Hardiman casts doubt on the success of such protests in his introductory comment on their argument, and claims that the documentation in the article itself proves the opposite, i.e. that open revolt won fuller concessions from the British authorities. The weapons of the weak were obviously rather weak. But just as important as exploring the effects of such forms of resistance is understanding the ways in which people read the situation and chose to respond to it, and how they perceived their power resources. In Gadgil and Guha's work we find the Forest Department introduced one prohibition after another to limit peasant access to forest resources, and peasants either bargained with the authorities or broke the law. The study thus reveals just how weak policy implementation and colonial administration were, despite the fact that, over time, peasants were subjugated to colonial power and drawn into the dominant system of agrarian production.[61]

The description of polarized conflicts between the colonial state and tribal communities has been further modified in recent research relating to the term *diku*, the non-tribal outsider. Tribal communities responded not only to European intrusion, but to any encroachment on their lands. Damodaran speaks of a 'period of rebellion' to describe the constant unrest that erupted into open rebellion in Chotanagpur during the major part of the nineteenth century. The notion of the diku included local zamindars and traders, as well as Europeans. Likewise, the complex conflict that Hardiman explores in *The Coming of the Devi*, which originated among communities in the Dang forests of western India in the early twentieth century, reveals a nexus of exploitative moneylenders and liquor dealers penetrating adivasi society at large in south Gujarat and the neighbouring regions. The dominant binary opposition between tribe/indigenous people and state is thus in fact coming apart in complex ways.[62]

In the act of confrontation, many authors have observed a process of renegotiating collective identities as an indigenist reaction or response to the external aggression of colonial or independent states. Arguments have, step by step, moved away from Ranajit Guha's assertion that 'a sense of identity was *imposed*' on peasants and tribals; that the peasant's 'identity amounted to the sum of his subalternity', a negation of the properties and attributes of his superior.[63] Dwelling on tribal assertion in the Kol 'disturbances' in Chotanagpur in 1832, Guha wrote in 1983:

> The tribe ... was not merely the initiator of the rebellion but was its site as well. Its consciousness of itself as a body of insurgents was thus indistinguishable from its recognition of its ethnic self. 'The tribe remained the boundary for man, in relation to himself as well as to outsiders': this observation made by Engels about the Iroquois was true of the Indian adivasis, too, not merely when they lived in peace with themselves and the Raj, but even more so when they took up arms both as a positive and a negative affirmation of their ethnicity.[64]

Already, in his 1987 study, Hardiman found that the term adivasi was derived from a historical experience of subjugation under colonial rule: such an experience of resistance generated an awareness of adivasis being in complete opposition to outsiders. The community itself was therefore a form of consciousness rather than a fixed social body.[65]

In her study of Chotanagpur, Damodaran places even greater emphasis on the agency of indigenous communities. Here, groups such as the Munda, Ho, and Oraon saw growing Indian and British colonial encroachment on their lands. Although precolonial natures were far from pristine, and were largely managed human landscapes, the unprecedented transformation of nature took off from the mid nineteenth century onwards, spurred by the demand for timber for railway sleepers. Damodaran argues that colonial territorial expansion and cultural incursion into Chotanagpur marginalized people, who responded with protests and uprisings. As early as 1816 unrest arose in Tamar, and in 1832 the Munda rebellion erupted. Consequently, in the process of exclusion, an awareness of cultural difference in opposition to 'outsiders'—Indians and Europeans—gave rise to an identity as indigenous nations, or adivasi, firmly rooted in the territory and landscape of Chotanagpur. Damodaran observes how such identities were furthered by missionary and colonial representations which essentialized tribes into ethnic or racial entities, and how the formation of a common tribal identity was shaped in the confrontation between indigenous identity and colonial ethnology, which she sees as mutually constitutive. Her study thus contrasts with Hardiman's work on tribal conflicts in the Dang forests, in which Hardiman also brings out internal divisions among tribal communities despite their identification as adivasi. In that region, in other words, the intra-community identity, formed in opposition to colonial and non-tribal Indian aggression, was internally structured along community and class lines.[66]

In contrast to the Chotanagpur situation, the corresponding pan-Toda and pan-tribal identities never appeared in confrontations over land in the Nilgiris less than a decade earlier. In order for us to understand native responses to colonial encroachment on land in the hills and colonial interference with the social, ritual, and political order, we need to acknowledge the gradual and overlapping changes in authority in the region. In high-level colonial reports, it may appear as if the British administration 'took over' control from earlier authorities and created institutions where these were seen to be lacking. However, authority was never lacking in the Nilgiris. Different forms of authority were at work, simultaneously competing for their realms of influence. Resistance took many forms, and among the more prominent were those articulated within the frames of colonial institutions. However, such negotiations did not conform to preset, fixed agendas, but became part of setting the agendas. While the Toda and Badaga were *identified* by colonial rulers as certain fixed communities, their *identities* were not 'imposed', nor are there any indications of broad native alliances that resulted in a common oppressed identity. Rather, within processes that resulted in subjugating people in the Nilgiris to colonial rule, we may discern splits between communities and clans. At the same time, people made use of fractions and divisions that existed within the EIC. This situation calls for a redefinition of our understanding of resistance to colonial expansion in forest and hill tracts.

* * *

In an attempt to grasp the complexity of the situation under study, I examine the conflicts over rights in Nilgiri nature from a number of different angles. In Chapter 2 perceptions of the Nilgiris and the visions projected onto the landscape and people by the early European visitors and settlers are discussed, together with a reconstruction of regional history in the broad sense. Chapter 3 elaborates the general legal debates and different positions through which property and land rights were argued over in the Nilgiris. Chapter 4 brings out how the empirical sciences, particularly ethnology, merged with historically specific interests in the hills, and how various settler and government claims, through ethnological treatment of people, justified the acquisition of land. Chapter 5 looks in detail at the conflicts between two Toda munds and the Madras government. These conflicts deepened in the late 1830s and lasted until the early 1840s, and were to form the basis for the first regulation of land grants and Toda rights in the Nilgiri Hills. The chapter focuses in particular on how the EIC administration tried to institute a form of rule by record-of-rights, while negotiating forcefully, though not always successfully, in pursuit of their intention of establishing sovereign rule.[67]

Bringing these insights together into what may tentatively be termed an environmental history of law, the final chapter thematically explores a number of core issues deriving from the study as a whole. These are the importance of acknowledging the competing interests of individual absolute property and government sovereignty; the necessity of focusing on the process of making law, in contrast to treating law as a given; the specific characteristics of resistance in a situation of multiple authority and internal divisions; and, lastly, the problem of defining regions in regional history. As this book shows, the Nilgiris, though only a small region in the hills, reveals the large issues that were at stake.

Notes

1. Walker, 1986, *The Toda of South India. A New Look*, 120–1.
2. The documentation of Toda munds referred to in this chapter is from my field notes in November 2001, December 2002, September 2003, and February 2005. Field notes of C.R. Sathyanarayanan also from January 2004 and September 2005.
3. A mund is a settlement among the Toda community, consisting of the closest kin, i.e. brothers and their wife/wives and children, unmarried siblings and parents. A mund was therefore a small settlement. A seasonal mund was the settlement to which the family migrated on a seasonal basis with their buffaloes. A temple mund was a mund with no dwelling houses, only a temple and the priest(s) serving it.
4. See illustration no. 1. Price, 2000 (1908), *Ootacamund, a History*, 69. BUL, Special Collections, Church Missionary Society, 3, Proposals. For the institution of a grammar school on the Nilgherries, 8 April 1830, para 4. Clubbey is misspelled 'Clubley' in Grigg.
5. Of the many anthropological works exploring the profound changes in nature—environment, landscape, ecology—that dramatically alter people's life conditions, Gold and Gujar's study of Rajasthan is exceptionally sensitive to the experience of loss due to deforestation, new technology, and production systems that include imported knowledge and affect the sense of meaning, identity, and community life. All are intrusions that are experienced as non-reversible. Gold and Gujar, 2002, *In the Time of Trees and Sorrows. Nature, Power, and Memory in Rajasthan*, ch. 10, specifically 281–3.
6. Aars also means 'royal'. The translation here follows Nanicane's own explanation.
7. The inspiration for these ideas came from lectures by Michael Jackson in Uppsala, January—February 2003. See also Jackson, 2004, *Existential Anthropology. Events, Exigencies, and Effects*, 11–13, 143–8.
8. Cutcherry, administrative office. OIOC, MBRP, 20 August 1835: 9241, to the Secretary to the Board of Revenue, from I. Haig Esq. at Ootacamund.
9. Nandy, 1995, 'History's Forgotten Doubles'; Skaria, 1999, *Hybrid Histories. Forests, Frontiers, and Wildness in Western India*.

10. Jackson, 2002, *The Politics of Storytelling. Violence, Transgression, and Intersubjectivity*, 14–15.
11. Blackburn, 2004, 'Life Histories as Narrative Strategy. Prophecy, Song, and Truth-Telling in Tamil Tales and Legends', 204–5, 217, 222.
12. Schlee, 2002, 'Introduction. Approaches to "Identity" and "Hatred". Some Somali and Other Perspectives', 9.
13. Nandy, 1995, 'History's Forgotten Doubles', 63.
14. Narayana Rao, D. Shulman and S. Subrahmanyam, 2001, *Textures of Time. Writing History in South India, 1600–1800*, 3–5, 19–23.
15. Skaria, 1999, *Hybrid Histories. Forests, Frontiers, and Wildness in Western India*, 6–11, 15–16; Guha, 2000, 'Review. *Hybrid Histories. Forests, Frontiers and Wildness in Western India* by Ajay Skaria'; Chatterjee and Ghosh, 2002, *History and the Present*, Introduction.
16. Prakash, 1990, 'Writing Post-Orientalist Histories of the Third World. Perspectives from Indian Historiography'; Nandy, 1995, 'History's Forgotten Doubles'; Chakrabarty, 2000, *Provincializing Europe. Postcolonial Thought and Historical Difference*.
17. For some recent contributions in the different fields, see Pohlandt-McCormick, 2000, '"I Saw a Nightmare ...". Violence and the Construction of Memory (Soweto, 16 June 1976)', 23–44, on violence, the silencing of memories and the individual's will to engage with and contest collective memory and official history. Eyal, 2004, 'Identity and Trauma', 5–36 discusses the problem of individual and collective memory from the perspective of a historically specific will to remember and declaring it defective measured against an ascribed function and purpose. See also *History and Memory*, Fall 2005, which has a thematic focus on Germany in the twentieth century from the perspective of the Holocaust, the Third Reich, and the unification of Germany.
18. Chatterjee and Ghosh, 2002, *History and the Present*, 15–23.
19. Björn Wittrock distinguishes usefully between the commonly used temporal and substantive conceptions of Modernity, i.e. either as an epoch in world history, or as distinct phenomena and processes in a given society at a given time. In a critical account, Wittrock argues for multiple modernities that were formed by heterogeneous processes and in which transformations in different parts of the world were interconnected. Wittrock, 2000, 'Modernity. One, None, or Many? European Origins and Modernity as a Global Condition', 31–5.
20. Matsuda, 1996, *The Memory of the Modern*. See also Patrick H. Hutton's discussion of Matsuda's work in Hutton, 1997, 'Mnemonic Schemes in the New History of Memory'.

21. Scott, 1998, *Seeing Like a State. How Certain Schemes to Improve the Human Condition Have Failed*, 11, 87–9.
22. Bayly, 2004, *The Birth of the Modern World, 1780–1914. Global Connections and Comparisons*, Introduction.
23. For further discussion, see Cederlöf and Sutton, 2005, 'The Aboriginal Toda. On Indigeneity, Exclusivism and Privileged Access to Land in the Nilgiri Hills, South India.'
24. For a clear example, see Walker, 1986, *The Toda of South India. A New Look*, ch. 8. See also Cederlöf, 2002, 'Narratives of Rights. Codifying People and Land in Early Nineteenth-Century Nilgiris,' 344–52.
25. Fieldnotes, December 2002.
26. Pamphlet, 'Remembering John Sullivan Father of Modern Nilgiris,' Save the Nilgiris Campaign, 16 January 2005; *The Hindu Magazine*, 16 January 2005: 1. I am grateful to Erik Cederlöf for bringing this article to my notice.
27. The Deceptive Bargain is also known as 'Aarne-Thompson 2400 The Ground is Measured with a Horse's (or ox's) Skin.' I am grateful to Stuart Blackburn for pointing this out and showing that similar stories in India of deceptive land sales, in which the buyer gets as much land as a horse can travel in one day, have parallels in the Mahabharata.
28. For further discussion, see Cederlöf, 2002, 'Narratives of Rights. Codifying People and Land in Early Nineteenth-Century Nilgiris,' 344–52.
29. Price, 2000 (1908), *Ootacamund, a History*, 69–92.
30. John Robert Seeley (1834–1895). Louis, 1999, 'Introduction,' 3–10; Wittrock, 2003, 'History of Social Science. Understanding Modernity and Rethinking Social Studies of Science,' 80–1, 86–8.
31. Tosh, 1999, *The Pursuit of History*, 4–9; Torstendahl, 2003, 'Fact, Truth, and Text. The Quest for a Firm Basis for Historical Knowledge around 1900,' 307–14.
32. Jaeger and Rüsen, 1992, *Geschichte des Historismus. Eine Einführung*; Veit-Brause, 1996, 'Historicism Revisited,' 103. Arguments in accordance with the latter position can be found in Wittkau, 1994, *Historismus. Zur Geschichte des Begriffs und des Problems*.
33. Prakash, 1990, 'Writing Post-Orientalist Histories of the Third World. Perspectives from Indian Historiography'; Bhabha, 1994, *The Location of Culture*, 122–3; Chakrabarty, 1994, 'Postcoloniality and the Artifice of History. Who Speaks for "Indian" Pasts?'; Ibid., 2000, *Provincializing Europe. Postcolonial Thought and Historical Difference*.
34. Ibid., 7.

35. Torstendahl, 2003, 'Fact, Truth, and Text. The Quest for a Firm Basis for Historical Knowledge around 1900', 307–14 quoting Johann Gustav Droysen, 1868, *Grundriss der Historik.*
36. For an excellent overview of the rich literature on the Nilgiris, see Hockings, 1978, *A Bibliography for the Nilgiri Hills of Southern India.*
37. Daniels, 1996, 'The Nilgiri Biosphere Reserve. Review of Conservation Status with Recommendations for a Holistic Approach to Management India'. I am grateful to Claude Garcia for helping me find this publication.
38. See specifically the works by Hough, 1829, *Letters on the Climate, Inhabitants, Productions, &C., &C., of the Neilgherries, or, Blue Mountains of Coimbatoor, South India* and Harkness, 1832, *A Description of a Singular Aboriginal Race Inhabiting the Summit of the Neilgherry Hills or the Blue Mountains of Coimbatoor, in the Southern Peninsula of India.*
39. Reverend James Hough was a chaplain on the Madras establishment. Hough, 1829, *Letters on the Climate, Inhabitants, Productions, &C., &C., of the Neilgherries, or, Blue Mountains of Coimbatoor, South India*, 64–5.
40. *Calcutta Oriental Christian Spectator*, 29 September 1846, 'From our correspondents, Ootacamund'.
41. Thomas, 1983, *Man and the Natural World. A History of the Modern Sensibility*, 20, 32–3, 38, 42.
42. One of the most perceptive studies of the phenomenon of caste in Indian society remains Bayly, 1999, *Caste, Society and Politics in India from the Eighteenth Century to the Modern Age.* Nancy Lee Peluso and Peter Vandergeest's idea of a racialization of the landscape in the course of colonial conquest has also inspired studies of tribal history. Peluso and Vandergeest, 2001, 'Genealogies of the Political Forest and Customary Rights in Indonesia, Malaysia, and Thailand'.
43. Rivers, 1906, *The Todas*, ch. 27; Hockings, 1980, *Ancient Hindu Refugees. Badaga Social History 1550–1975*, chs 4, 5; Walker, 1986, *The Toda of South India. A New Look*, ch. 1.3.
44. OIOC, BC, 16 February (no. 3), 1836, Mr Sullivan's Minute, para 12.
45. See, for example, Guha, 1989, *The Unquiet Woods. Ecological Change and Peasant Resistance in the Himalaya*; Sivaramakrishnan, 1999, *Modern Forests. Statemaking and Environmental Change in Colonial Eastern India*; Mey, 2005, 'Shifting Cultivation, Images, and Development in the Chittagong Hill Tracts of Bangladesh'.
46. Guha, 1983, *Elementary Aspects of Peasant Insurgency in Colonial India*; Guha, 1989, *The Unquiet Woods. Ecological Change and Peasant Resistance in the Himalaya*; Skaria, 1999, *Hybrid Histories. Forests, Frontiers, and*

Wildness in Western India. See Singh, 1998, *Natural Premises. Ecology and Peasant Life in the Western Himalaya, 1800–1950*, for a study offering a more complex argument about conflictual relations in disputes over nature.

47. Sivaramakrishnan, 1999, *Modern Forests. Statemaking and Environmental Change in Colonial Eastern India*.
48. Ibid., 45–8.
49. Rangarajan, 1996, *Fencing the Forest. Conservation and Ecological Change in India's Central Provinces, 1860–1914*, 96–104; Sivaramakrishnan, 1999, *Modern Forests. Statemaking and Environmental Change in Colonial Eastern India*, 56. In important ways, recent works have drawn attention to interrelated developments in European and South Asian regions of the British empire. Specifically, structural similarities between Ireland, Scotland, and India under the aggressive impact of British industrialization and territorial incorporation have been emphasized. See, for example, Bayly, 2000, 'Ireland, India and the Empire. 1780–1914', 377–97.
50. Sundar, 1997, *Subalterns and Sovereigns. An Anthropological History of Bastar, 1854–1996*, 90–2, 103.
51. Sivaramakrishnan, 1999, *Modern Forests. Statemaking and Environmental Change in Colonial Eastern India*, 19, 30, 33, 65.
52. Pratt, 1992, *Imperial Eyes. Travel Writing and Transculturation*, 6–7. Pratt's concept has also been usefully elaborated in social history in Frenz, 2003, *From Contact to Conquest. Transition to British Rule in Malabar, 1790–1805*, 47–9.
53. Gow, 1995, 'Land, People, and Paper in Western Amazonia'; Rangarajan, 2001, 'From Princely Symbol to Conservation Icon. A Political History of the Lion in India', 405–11, 419–30; Damodaran, 2005, 'Indigenous Forests. Rights, Discourses, and Resistance in Chotanagpur, 1860–2002', 127. See also Ingold, 2000, *The Perception of the Environment. Essays on Livelihood, Dwelling and Skill*, for his discussion of 'dwelling'.
54. Peers, 1995, *Between Mars and Mammon. Colonial Armies and the Garrison State in India, 1819–1835*; Washbrook, 1999, 'India, 1818–1860. The Two Faces of Colonialism'; Ibid., 2004, 'South India 1770–1840. The Colonial Transition', 513–14.
55. Rangarajan, 1996, *Fencing the Forest. Conservation and Ecological Change in India's Central Provinces, 1860–1914*, 118–26; Scott, 1998, *Seeing Like a State. How Certain Schemes to Improve the Human Condition Have Failed*.
56. Finnström, 2003, *Living with Bad Surroundings. War and Existential Uncertainty in Acholiland, Northern Uganda*, 51–2.
57. Guha, 1989, *The Unquiet Woods. Ecological Change and Peasant Resistance in the Himalaya*, chs 4, 5.

58. Adas, 1981, 'From Avoidance to Confrontation. Peasant Protest in Precolonial and Colonial Southeast Asia', 218–27, 240–1.
59. Singh, 1977, 'Presidential Address', 380–1; Singh, 1998, *Natural Premises. Ecology and Peasant Life in the Western Himalaya, 1800–1950*, 92–3, 146, 208–9; Guha, 1999, *Environment and Ethnicity in India, 1200–1991*, 42–6, 49–52.
60. Guha and Gadgil's study focuses on Jaunsar Bawar and Tehri Garhwal. Gadgil and Guha, 1992, 'State Forestry and Social Conflict in British India', 125–31, referring to Adas, 1981, 'From Avoidance to Confrontation. Peasant Protest in Precolonial and Colonial Southeast Asia', and Scott, 1998, *Seeing Like a State. How Certain Schemes to Improve the Human Condition Have Failed.*
61. Gadgil and Guha, 1992, 'State Forestry and Social Conflict in British India', 280–6; Hardiman, 1992, *Peasant Resistance in India, 1858–1914*, 50.
62. Hardiman, 1987, *The Coming of the Devi. Adivasi Assertion in Western India*; Damodaran, 2005, 'Indigenous Forests. Rights, Discourses, and Resistance in Chotanagpur, 1860–2002'. For a similar line of reasoning, see Hardiman, 1987, *The Coming of the Devi. Adivasi Assertion in Western India.*
63. Italics mine. Guha, 1983, *Elementary Aspects of Peasant Insurgency in Colonial India*, 18.
64. Ibid., 286, referring to Friedrich Engels, 1968, *The Origin of the Family, Private Property, and the State, in the Light of the Researches of Lewis H. Morgan*, 529.
65. Hardiman, 1987, *The Coming of the Devi. Adivasi Assertion in Western India*, 11–12, 15–16; Ibid., 1992, *Peasant Resistance in India, 1858–1914*, 9.
66. Damodaran, 2005, 'Indigenous Forests. Rights, Discourses, and Resistance in Chotanagpur, 1860–2002', 118–19, 125, 128, 141–3; Hardiman, 2006, *Histories for the Subordinated*, 9, 13, 20–2, ch. 9. For a critical account of the use of 'adivasi' to emphasize tribal unity and essentialize indigenous communities' relations to nature in Jharkhand, formerly part of Chotanagpur, see Shah, 2006, 'Elephants, Indigenous Communities and the Environment. The Politics of Claims in India's Jharkhand', 4–8.
67. Ch. 3 builds on Cederlöf, 2005, 'The Toda Tiger. Debates on Custom, Utility and Rights in Nature, South India 1820–1843'. Ch. 4 is an extended version of Cederlöf, 2002, 'Narratives of Rights. Codifying People and Land in Early Nineteenth-Century Nilgiris'. An early version of ch. 5 was published in Cederlöf, 2005, 'The Agency of the Colonial Subject. Claims and Rights in Forestlands in Early Nineteenth-Century Nilgiris' and Cederlöf, 2007, 'The Agency of the Colonial Subject. Claims and Rights in Forestlands in Early Nineteenth-Century Nilgiris'.

2 *A Narrative on the Toda and Its Problems*

Ask in a Toda mund about the history of the Toda, and you will mostly end up down a blind alley. Often, a senior man will respond, explaining that before the outsiders arrived all hill people lived in harmony, sharing resources according to the specific skills of each community under the lordship of the Toda. When the British began to settle the region they encroached on Toda land and robbed the Toda of their grazing grounds. Only one man, the district collector John Sullivan, stood by them to protect their rights from the worst atrocities of colonial conquest. The sheepskin tale will most likely be cited, as will the claim that Sullivan paid with a coin for his lands.

In most munds the tale of Sullivan's coin is generally told to prove his honesty; Sullivan actually paid for the lands he took charge of, which is more than most Europeans did. However, in Kandelmund this tale has a special resonance. Once, when Nanicane was relating the story, the old man suddenly went off to his house to fetch the old gold coin. The tale was more than just a tale, and Nanicane intended to prove to me that

Ill. 2 Nanicane showing silver coins depicting Queen Victoria and Indira Gandhi
(Photo by the author.)

Sullivan had in fact paid and that his coin was now with Nanicane, in his house. It had been passed on to him from his father Tilipah as a treasure of Kandelmund, and now he wanted me to see it. But as it turned out the coin was not to be found. Instead he returned with two other coins that were carefully preserved as a heritage of the past among this Toda clan. Both coins looked old and important. One bore the portrait of Queen Victoria in relief, the other of Indira Gandhi—in my eyes, two powerful rulers who made far-reaching claims to state authority and intervention.

Taking a closer look I could see that the Victorian coin had been minted to commemorate the Neelgherry Exhibition in Poona in 1875. This was one of several exhibitions at which Toda, dressed in *putkuli* shawls, together with their ornaments and ceremonial tools, were displayed as exotica. In the 1880s a group of Toda was even contracted for a circus, to be shown as 'ethnological rarities' in Europe, Australia, and North America, this group coming to be known as the 'Travelled Toda'. But nothing of these events now remained in Nanicane's narrative. The two coins had ended up as part of the tale of how the Toda lost their lands.[1]

Idealizing Historical Landscapes

Once you come to think about it, the thought does not leave you: the British officers who had such a decisive influence on the administration of South India were very young. Sullivan was only 13 when he was appointed a civil servant with the EIC. At 16 he was posted as a writer in Madras, and at the age of 29 he was made permanent collector of Coimbatore District, after holding similar positions elsewhere in the presidency. He was obviously one of a career-minded group of British officers with good connections. When he enclosed 500 *bullas*, or 1,910 acres, in Ootacamund three years after his first visit, he was 34 and had already built a house in Kotagiri. In size his landholding resembled the estates of northern England and Scotland in which many EIC merchants invested their profits. One of Sullivan's patrons was Thomas Munro, who was appointed governor of the Madras Presidency in 1819. In their voluminous correspondence the two exchanged opinions on a revenue system without middlemen and on the need to invest far-reaching powers in district collectors. Not surprisingly, they complained vehemently about the new generation of EIC servants arriving from England who were 'utterly ignorant' and lacked practical knowledge of the modes of management that existed before their arrival.[2]

When the first Europeans made their way through the Nilgiri landscape, they found it both untouched and different from all they had seen in India, and yet strangely familiar. This was the landscape they had been searching for: it resembled Switzerland and Scotland, wild and romantic. Reports, correspondence, and articles are full of vivid descriptions of nature. Here, apples, potatoes, and cabbages would grow just as they would on British soil.[3] Such reports reveal landscapes carried over long distances, not only as fond memories of places to which the travellers wished to return in their old age, but also as landscapes that could be transformed into practical possibilities for the people of the Nilgiris. Romantic notions thus blended with projects for a modern society. As argued in Chapter 1, the two were not exclusive sets of ideas but mutually constitutive, sometimes represented in one and the same sentence in letters sent from the Nilgiri Hills. In these, both highland Europe and the Indian hills were idealized, and with them their flora, fauna, and people.

These were also landscapes onto which a romantic cultural heritage could be projected. In many cases, such projections represented a socially embedded Scottishness that drew inspiration from poets and novelists such as Sir Walter Scott. Margot Finn calls the social and extended kin networks of Scottish patronage among Anglo-Indians from the late seventeenth to the early nineteenth century 'strategic Scottishness'. In her study of the gift economy, which laid the foundations for political and social ambitions among Anglo-Indians, she observes the importance of Romantic literature as an ideal object of circulation in British India. The importance of such networks for a successful career in the EIC also explains why teen-aged individuals arriving in India, who had hardly seen the British Isles, much less the Scottish highlands, still wrote long letters about majestic hills that reminded them of similar landscapes 'back home'. Nostalgia and identity politics blended with escapism and romanticism.[4]

This chapter seeks to reveal the often contradictory representations of landscapes and people that characterized the first decades of British reports from the Nilgiris, and which subsequently had a lasting influence on historical and anthropological writings about these hills. In important ways, profoundly romanticist notions of wild nature and primitive people merged with ideas of progress and evolutionary development. I first discuss how these seemingly incoherent ideas mutually reinforced specific transformative visions aimed at improving both the landscape and its inhabitants. Two ethnographic works of the 1820s and 1830s, by Henry Harkness and James Hough, stand out among the many early reports from the region. They were often cited and came to have powerful implications for the legal rights given to people in the hills at the time. Even in twentieth-century studies, these have continued to be quoted as sources of factual information, which would seem to be problematic, given that their observations were made for specific purposes at a particular point in time and need to be read in that light.

Secondly, as has been increasingly and critically observed, portrayal of the Nilgiri Hills as a unique region, defined and bounded by topography and a specific social organization, has obscured a more complex and integrated analysis of these hill tracts in the larger regional history of South India. An attempt is therefore made here to broaden the analytic perspective of territory in order to reopen many taken-for-granted assumptions about regional history. Such an attempt also requires a temporal perspective that bridges the precolonial—colonial divide, and refrains from taking as its point of departure the appearance of the British in the Nilgiris. The dominant basis for periodization in historical works is thereby questioned. Demarcations of time and space in historical analyses tend to reflect the assumptions structuring the work in question, and ultimately, even if unintentionally, assumptions about an isolated Nilgiri uniqueness and a British defining moment in Nilgiri history are an important undercurrent in dominant narratives of colonial historiography which need to be problematized.

Thirdly, the vision of transforming and improving hill society and utilizing its resources also extended to 'improving' its population. Of the communities living in the Nilgiris at the time of colonial intervention, two were particularly favoured by the British: the Toda and the Badaga. The former were immediately associated with romanticist ideas about herders and, as noted in Chapter 1, stereotyped according to gendered values of the natural human being. Written representations as well as images—such as lithographs and drawings—were gendered and depicted a wild but controlled people within a similarly wild but controlled landscape. In contrast the Badaga were ascribed ideas of progress that specifically emphasized the possibility of converting them from 'hill cultivators' into entrepreneurs of a modern, settled agriculture. Through a critical reading of colonial visions for the transformation of the Nilgiris we can thus distinguish the nature of British interest in these hill tracts. As will become evident from the subsequent chapters, there was no singular vision, there were many—just as there were many contradictory interests.

Tim Ingold speaks usefully of a 'dwelling perspective' in which landscapes are the enduring records of the lives and works of past generations who dwelt in them—a 'chronicle of life and dwelling'. The Nilgiris were also in this sense 'pregnant with the past' of the people who had dwelt there; they formed a sense of belonging through human labour and active interaction over many generations, long before Europeans began to settle there. It requires long experience and prolonged presence to read a landscape from within such a dwelling perspective. The Europeans thus perceived past histories as they ventured into the Nilgiris. Yet the chronicles of which Ingold speaks do not appear to have been transparent to them. Both Europeans and immigrant Indians had lived experiences of embodied landscapes that shaped, in different ways, their relationships to the Nilgiris. But these were landscapes from the Indian plains and north-western Europe. To such people, the Nilgiris were 'pregnant' with other pasts. 'Locality is both embodied and narrated and is ... highly mobile: places travel with the people through whom they are constituted,' observes Hugh Raffles. The term he prefers, 'locality', is not equal to location but denotes 'a set of relations ... in which places are discursively and imaginatively materialized and enacted through the practices of variously positioned people and political economies'. By this conceptualization Raffles emphasizes the transformative qualities of place, and the need for constant reaffirmation of place-identities. Places, in other words, were not static and immobile, however 'ancient' and unchangeable they may have appeared to immigrant Europeans. In this sense, localities are created not only in the stories people repeatedly tell, but also in narrated *aspirations* which 'reinforce a personal connection to critical moments of group action involving the landscape'.[5]

Colonial power, in its first encounter with the Nilgiris, did not arrive as a singular entity governed by ideas of rationality and utility, violently enforcing ruthless exploitation over the place. The early reports, rather, breathe of possibilities that existed to transform the place, to bring it more in line with the wild landscapes and farmed valleys in which the immigrant spectators had earlier dwelt. There was also an urgency in the reports, and Sullivan in particular bombarded the presidency administration with letters and applications relating to roads, farmlands, and the opening up of local markets. He appears to have felt that time was short and not to be wasted. His perspective of time—or rather, his relationship to it—certainly did not correspond to that of the people he described. To paraphrase Ingold, their different retentions of the past and 'protentions' of the future influenced, in very different ways, decisions in the present. The people who received most attention were the herders, whom Sullivan saw as simply passing away their days, drowsing in the meadows and idly chasing buffaloes. Although Europeans like him merged their perception of this landscape and 'its' people with that of the British wilderness, they remained spectators. At the same time, the cultivation of both wild nature and people seemed to offer the prospect of a profitable enterprise.

In the 1820s, reports and articles from the Nilgiris compete to paint their descriptions in the brightest colours:

> The increased purity, coolness, and elasticity of the air; the extensive prospect of table land ... covered with a beautiful verdure, adorned with cottages, woods, and the windings of a majestic lake, and bounded by the horizon, with here and there a distant peak to break its uniformity, altogether produce a sensation not to be described, and to be conceived only by those who have been favoured with such a transition from India's scorching plain.[6]

This description by James Hough represents the idea of an ordered, well-structured wilderness. His image resembles a landscape painting in which the scenery has been carefully selected. The view across the tableland is magnificent and the air is pure, cool and elastic. The landscape is 'adorned' with cottages, woods, and a 'majestic' lake; and all is made complete and comprehensible by its boundary, the horizon. This landscape 'produce[s] a sensation': the exhausted, overburdened British officer can withdraw into it from the harsh realities of India. The antithesis of this Nilgiri Eden is the merciless heat of India's scorching plains. The author observes cottages, the dwellings of the English countryside, but leaves out the huts of Indian pastoralists and shifting cultivators.

The ideals behind such Indian landscapes, in their perfect proportions and simplicity, broadly reflect similar ideals of the English aristocratic refuge that was sought in Palladian architecture and style. Such ideals had enjoyed a brief revival on the estates of rural England in the late eighteenth century. Seen from this perspective, Hough's Nilgiri landscape reminds us of the Arcadia which Simon Schama describes in *Landscape and Memory* (1995), a romantic pastoral idyll. Schama links its creation to changes in access to the forest of Fontainebleau in the mid 1850s. Such forests were transformed in the minds of the urban French bourgeoisie when they arrived as visitors and were exposed to carefully designed experiences of wilderness by Claude François Denecourt's promenades. The walks he created were intended to give the hiker a blend of wooded landscapes, rocks, meadows, and brooks occasionally interrupted by 'notable sights', giving the illusion of wilderness without exposing the hiker to any real danger. Schama notes that, for urban 'arch-Romantics', Denecourt had returned the forest from the imperial state to 'the people'—not to woodcutters, charcoal burners, and pig grazers, but to the people of the Romantic Arcadia, the gypsies and herdsmen.[7]

To inspire the reader to make the journey to the Nilgiris, another traveller and author of an early travel guide to the hills, Lieutenant H. Jervis, included copies of letters from people such as the Bishop of Calcutta, praising the possibilities of turning the hills into cultivated lands. In contrast with Denecourt's walks, which were designed to give the visitor to the forest a taste—albeit harmless—of wilderness, Jervis presented the familiar. Unlike the French urban bourgeoisie, longing to escape Paris, British officers in India were homesick for, or perhaps, nurtured a longing for, 'home' as depicted in Scott's Romantic novels. However, both Denecourt's and Jervis's landscapes were escapist projects. Jervis's description of the view that met the visitor arriving in the valley near Ootacamund seems intended to reassure the reader that the journey was worth the effort: 'In the valley of Katey may be seen the beginning of English husbandry, under the care and well-known skill of Major Crewe; Southdown sheep grazing, English cattle in perfect health, and crops of potatoes that would be prized even in the "Land of Murphies".'[8]

The contrast between ideas of romanticism and improvement as well as their mutual reinforcement is well depicted in David Arnold's work on landscape and science in India. Observing that romanticism was only partly about idealization of the past and wild nature, he concludes: 'through association with the doctrines and imagery of capitalism and Christianity, it also helped forge a program for change, emphasizing the need to transform the ruined and debased Indian landscape to create a peaceful and prosperous civilization modelled after an "improved" and industrious Britain.'[9] The climate in the hills was particularly praised for its miraculous effects on the human body, and the region soon became an important object of study for medical topography. This emerging scientific field combined the study of climate, season, and geographical location as a basis for determining the distribution of disease. The warm climate of 'tropical' India was defined as unsuited to European settlement, and the climate itself was considered a source of disease. In the 'temperate' hills, however, Europeans would recover.[10] Members of the medical corps accordingly produced numerous articles on the benefits of Nilgiri location and climate in *The Asiatic Journal and Monthly Register for British India and Its Dependencies*.[11] Just before his first trek to the hills, Sullivan made a journey to Mauritius—like many other officers, he too needed to get away from the Indian plains to restore his health. Now he made the climate a core reason for the EIC to exploit the natural assets of the Nilgiris, which, he argued, was best positioned for a sanatorium. The army being interested in finding a place for recreation, saving both time and money—the alternatives were the Cape and Mauritius—Assistant Surgeon John Jones, Lieutenant Evans Macpherson, Sullivan, and other such officers supplied the military boards with temperature records and notes on the climate to convince them of the Nilgiris' advantages.[12]

A causal relationship between health and environmental factors is an old theme, and in this the ancient schools also influenced the medical corps of the EIC. Hippocrates noted climate's contribution to medicine and, in *Politics*, Aristotle observed its influence on polity. Ibn Khaldun elaborated the impact of climate on human virtues and civilization, and the relationship between the human body and the environment was a theme of Ayurvedic medicine. This relationship was soon made part of the emerging modern sciences of Europe. Topography was particularly closely observed, as were soil conditions, humidity, and the occurrence of wet ground. A hot climate was believed to be debilitating for body and mind, and Europeans who resided for long periods in the 'scorching plains' also ran the risk of suffering a gradual decline in health.[13]

These texts were published at a time of intense debate about the effects of climate and landscape on the human body. There was an urgent need to find ways of dealing with the tropical diseases that tended to heavily reduce EIC troops in the ongoing wars. The problems of insufficient supplies and deteriorating conditions having been noted, theories of race and class also shaped the prevailing understanding of individual tolerance of different climates and susceptibility to tropical disease. On the one hand, a particular race was expected to withstand a particular climate and topography; on the other, the tropics with their hot climate caused ailments ranging from lethargy to epidemic disease.[14]

As Thomas Metcalf and others have pointed out, the Indian subject of British rule was identified through both racial and gendered norms that defined and ordered the hierarchy between ruler and ruled. At the most general level, it may be argued that British and Indian men and women were fitted for distinct roles within the ideology of the Raj. Male virtues of control, self-discipline, and strength were accordingly British, while Indian masculinity was assumed to be degraded, effeminate, and weak—just as Hindu religion was associated with vicious and licentious female deities. At best, Indian masculinity was a caricature of the British man: this was also well known as the description of the English-educated Bengali. The Hindu woman was understood to be degraded by her sexuality and vulnerable to Brahmin influence, and destined only to be sacrificed to the Indian man—a servility that ranged from household slavery to widow burning. Simultaneously, aspects of class affiliation, region of natal origin, education, and similarly influential factors cut across and restructured such simplistic social divides.[15]

In stark contrast, reports on Toda men and women in the Nilgiris diverge markedly from the wider racial and gendered ideas about the Indian subject. The notion of the effeminate Indian man and the servile Indian woman serve in fact as counter-images of the Toda man and woman. The reputation of muscular Toda men, who could wrestle a full-grown male buffalo to the ground, spread quickly. They were portrayed as gigantic: 'from six feet six to six feet eight', according to one visitor who lamented he never had time to see them.[16] Early ethnographies compete in their descriptions of the male Toda—this playful child of nature who could be consumed by 'immoderate laughter' and who refused to be tied by duties of labour or time. His favourite diversion was to prove his strength by besting his 'immense' buffaloes. Hough describes how three or four youths selected the largest of the herd, ran him down, and, seizing him by the hind legs, threw him to the ground, 'which they do with perfect ease and singular dexterity'. Such descriptions of Toda men often ventured into the poetic, as in Hough's animated description: 'It is beautiful to observe the agility with which they bound over the hills, shaking their black locks in the wind, and as conscious of liberty as the mountain deer, or any trueborn Briton. They are remarkably frank in their deportment; and their entire freedom from Hindoo servility is very engaging to the Englishman, and cannot fail to remind him of the "bold peasantry" of a still dearer land.'[17] The author admits the nuisance caused when Toda left trees unfelled for weeks because 'the wild spirit of freedom charms them away'. Yet, he adds, 'who that has been accustomed to observe with pain the servility of Hindoos, would wish or consent to destroy in the Thodawurs this independence of character?'[18]

This account is quite representative of early encounters between Europeans and Toda. The latter had an appealing innocence that both explained and excused their wild nature. Toda men were male, muscular, tall, and free, in contrast with effeminate and submissive male Hindus on the hot plains. The 'cool', 'salubrious', and 'healthy' climate of the hills had been beneficial for the Toda, who were assumed to be the original settlers of this high elevation. They thus possessed all the positive characteristics attributed to the healthy, rustic male. Yet the reports take care to convey that Toda men were not adult or civilized in their behaviour. They were not the equals of the bold peasantry of Britain, only nearly so. In their childish innocence, Toda men posed no threat to the British. They were in need of guidance.

Toda women received even more particular attention. Most observers reveal mixed feelings of attraction and horror at what they perceive to be unusual behaviour for a woman on the Indian subcontinent. The British were mostly mystified by the role of these women in family and society, attracted by their looks and behaviour, captivated by their supposedly accessible sexuality, and horrified by polyandry and practices of female infanticide. The major difference between Indian women in general and Toda women in particular was ascribed to their behaviour. Here, too, we may discern qualities associated with Britain, or rather, with the Scottish highlands. Harkness wrote that the women were: 'perfectly free from the ungracious and menial-like timidity of the generality of the sex of the low country; and enter into conversation with a stranger, with a confidence and self possession becoming in the eyes of Europeans, and strongly characteristic of a system of manners and customs, widely different from those of their neighbours.'[19] In a later account, J. Shortt wrote that, unlike most of the 'Indian races', Toda women were not regarded as mere household slaves. He observed skills among them that were generally associated with those of women in Victorian England. 'They are treated by their husbands with marked respect and attention ... they are left at home to perform what European wives consider their legitimate share of duty' and 'employ their leisure hours in embroidery work, which they execute in a clever off-hand manner; others amuse themselves in singing, of which all appear very fond.'[20]

At a time when mortality rates among European troops were high, and when Lord William Bentinck referred to the 'want of physical strength and of moral energy in the sepoy [soldier]', the strong, tall, and athletic Toda of the Nilgiris were seen as ultimate proof of the unique and healthy climate of the hills. Consequently, when Sullivan appealed for the establishment of a sanatorium for officers, it was not just a call prompted by financial considerations, but one that also resonated with the scientific debates of the time.[21] Marmaduke Thompson, an enthusiastic Anglican missionary who visited the Nilgiris in 1824, was particularly impressed by the healthy-looking European children he met in Ootacamund, who were as blooming as any child in Europe. He went on to suggest the immediate location of a missionary establishment in the Nilgiris, arguing this would be educationally the best place for the children of missionaries, while the missionaries would recover their health in its cool climes. Concern for Christian education and worship among Europeans remained the primary rationale for establishing churches in the hills during the first decade of missionary presence in the Nilgiris.[22]

Placing the Toda in European Pasts

Within a few years, increasing numbers of Europeans arrived in the hills and a new thirty-mile-long road was reported to have immediately resulted in more commercial intercourse between the high and low country. Simultaneously, a local market developed in Ootacamund.[23] The European newcomers produced letters, reports, and surveys describing what they saw, i.e. they named, defined, and classified the Nilgiris with reference to the familiar and thereby 'captured' the place in that deeper sense of the word.

It is interesting to see how both the focus and content of these texts change around 1828, when descriptions of land and people began to have an influence on land rights. The arguments become more aggressive and the descriptions tend to be confined to what needed to be said in order to support a particular standpoint on the land question. For most of the 1820s, however, travellers and other spectators were mostly amazed by the exotic people and natural abundance of the region. They sought to locate this landscape with reference to the history of Europe, biblical texts, and the nature in Britain, accessing the place not only by their physical presence but also by incorporating it into their own past. The present became known and knowable to Europeans by being located in familiar histories.

The general idea was that the Toda had resided in the hills for longer than anyone could remember, and that documentary evidence was not to be found. The history of their origins was a constant subject of debate. Hough seems to have made up his mind to completely distrust historical narratives that located the Toda's roots in South India. In his compilation of articles on the Nilgiris published in 1826, he suggested a historiography that tied them to ancient Rome, thus questioning the Toda's claim that they were aboriginals of the Nilgiris. They could not be aboriginals, he argued, since they had no account of their origins nor any vestige of tradition from which such conclusion could be plausible. The only source of knowledge about their ancestors was to be found in the recollections of the oldest man, whose memory Hough profoundly distrusted. He had heard some Toda relate that their forefathers had been palanquin bearers of Runga Swami, who, according to Hough, was 'the mediatory power of the Hindoos and god of the hills.'[24] But

Hough countered this claim with critical questions about its empirical validation: the story was vague, people hardly knew anything about Runga Swami and, before 1819, palanquins were not to be found in the Nilgiris. The story was therefore said to have been fabricated and conveyed to the Toda either by the followers of Runga Swami or by British civil servants.

Instead of a Toda past with roots in Indian soil, Hough assumed a direct link with Europe. He argued that the Toda doubtless had an ancient origin, having lived on the hills for centuries. Other classes regarded them as lords and had paid tribute to them ever since their own immigration to the hills. Remnants of old munds further indicated that they had once been in possession of the whole region. But having first discarded local memory Hough now claimed to rely on 'native history and traditions' and assumed that the Toda were also immigrants who had fled from Poligar wars in the plains 400–500 years earlier. Most likely, he argued—and after reluctantly accepting that they could not be of Jewish origin—the Toda were the remnants of a Roman colony. Their bodily features, noble manners, and Herculean strength all indicated as much.[25]

Henry Harkness, who made field observations in 1829, completely agreed with Hough's conclusions:

> The appearance of the Tudas, who may be considered the original inhabitants of the hills, is certainly very prepossessing. Generally above the common height, athletic, and well made, their bold bearing, and open and expressive countenances, lead immediately to the conclusion that they must be of a different race to their neighbours of the same hue, and the question naturally arises, *who can they be?* ... A large, full, and speaking eye, Roman nose, fine teeth, and pleasing contour; having occasionally the appearance of great gravity, but seemingly ever ready to fall into the expression of cheerfulness and good humour, are natural marks, prominently distinguishing them from all other natives of India.[26]

The claim to Roman heritage was occasionally questioned by other European visitors to the hills, but remarkably often only to replace it with similar suggestions placing Toda roots far away from the Nilgiris, usually in Europe. So, with their imaginative conclusions about the Roman noses of the Toda, this makes Hough and Harkness representative of most accounts of the Nilgiris from this period. During the first decade of European settlement in the hills, narratives of present and past seem to have served the purpose of placing the author and the community he represented in relation to the place. There were descriptions of both distance and similarities, but in either case they served to tie bonds between Europeans and the Nilgiris, the Nilgiris also became a European place.

Attitudes within narratives of the early encounters between Europeans and people in the Nilgiris were ambivalent, particularly in relation to the Toda. Polyandry and female infanticide were constant topics of debate. The killing of girl children was detested but explained by the need to reduce Toda family size. Some initiatives were taken to compel the Toda to desist. Toda family organisation, in which several brothers shared one wife, was similarly seen as an objectionable custom in need of termination. Missionaries, in particular, objected to polyandry. Thompson learnt about the system when he visited a Toda mund near Ootacamund:

> When I made an excursion to some of their huts, I had some little communication with them, one of the circumstances relating to their habits which attracted my peculiar notice was this, that ... 5 men live with one woman as their wife. Undoubtedly this must be a very old practice among them, for they informed me that it was the case everywhere among their tribe. This strange habit perhaps may account for their very small number, there being as I am told only 80 families on the whole extent of the Western hills ...[27]

In an earlier letter Thompson relates how 'that horrid custom of polyandry' seemed to disappear as '[h]appily they seem to be now thoroughly ashamed of it'.[28] The model for marriage was naturally the monogamous heterosexual union of one man and one woman, and for a number of missions it came to be a requirement for baptism. Over the years, very few Toda actually converted. All the same, missionary journals occasionally published photographs of Toda before and after conversion. The first would show people in putkuli shawls, women with corkscrew curls, and men with bushy hair and long beards; the second people in European clothes, men shaved and with short haircuts, women with their hair in a tight bun.[29]

The unfamiliar Toda family structure was discussed simultaneously in terms of organization and moral values, and polyandry interpreted as an undesirable expression of women's liberty. It was seen as a form of romantic harem, of the known gender order turned upside down whereby women were 'allowed [a] plurality of husbands'. In 1819, after a brief excursion into the hills, the French naturalist Leschnault de la Tour wrote: 'It is common enough to see two or three brothers with but one wife between them, who dispenses her favours *selon son gre*. Independent of this peculiar privilege of the women, they are allowed a cicisbeo of their own choosing, with whose advantages no husband would think proper to interfere.'[30]

In this context we may reflect on British interpretations of and reactions to the matrilineal system of the *tharavadus*, the influential landed matrilineal households in the neighbouring region of Malabar. This was often described as a system of polyandry, or of Nayar women's 'polyandrous sexuality', and British administrators did not acknowledge the women of the tharavadus to be married in the legal sense. In her study of matriliny in Malabar, G. Arunima finds no evidence of Nayar women having more than one man at the same time, while remarriage (serial monogamy) was allowed. Husbands were not 'the "visiting husband" phenomenon as the prototypical marital form among the Nayars', described in anthropological works such as that of Claude Lévi-Strauss (1996). More significantly, though, marriage did not alter women's property rights in their tharavadus. The important change which Arunima observes in the early colonial period is the emergence of a gendered redefinition of property and of a patriarchal figure in the eldest male of the household, which had implications for property, legitimacy, and gendered status.[31]

Two images from 1834 and 1856 serve to illustrate the ambivalent attitude to Toda polyandry.[32] Both are included in a government publication, *Ootacamund. A History* (1908). The earlier picture (Ill. 1) is titled 'St. Stephen's church Ootacamund' and shows a church consecrated three years earlier. The landscape is barren except for a small shola forest next to the church, and the church is enclosed by a wall. A man in European dress can be seen in front of the entrance. Nearer the spectator and walking towards the church is what appears to be a Toda family: father, mother, and child. The European monument is the main focus of attention while the Toda group represents the place.

Ill. 3 Ootacamund on the Neilgherries, 1856, drawing by Private Fraser
(Reproduced courtesy British Library.)

The later picture gives an overview of the European settlement in Ootacamund and the surrounding landscape. This time a Toda family is placed in the centre of the picture, the man holding a stick and watching over a seated woman and a small child who leans on the woman's knee. The group seems a spitting image of compositions depicting Joseph, Mary, and Jesus, the man portrayed as male patriarch, keeping a protective eye on his family. To the left, slightly hidden, is a Toda temple, with a priest standing inside the temple yard with his back towards the spectator. Further down the slope a Toda man, looking away, can be dimly seen. In the distance to the right, approaching the viewer, are a man and a woman, arm in arm, dressed according to the European custom. They appear to be strolling through the landscape and the man points towards the little family, as if guiding the woman.

Significantly, neither of these images seeks to suggest the Toda as practising polyandry, but associates them instead with monogamous marriage. Considering the fact that both pictures show the families as consisting of a mother, a father, and one or two children, they are also images of the nuclear family. However, it would be a mistake to assume the nuclear family became a norm actively imposed and prevalent among the Toda, even by the mid-nineteenth century. Just as all the other components of these images are idealized, so too are the gender relations and family norms within them. Among Europeans too, in fact, there was a difference between norms and practice. Up to that point the Anglo-Indian family, like its British counterpart, functioned socially and culturally as an extended family. Finn describes the 'Imperial family' as a household family of co-residence with instrumental relations between family members, as a lineage family linking husbands and wives to influential centres of power. These were lineages of race that did not equate simply with colour, but acknowledged national and religious difference. It resembled a circle of kin, including social 'mothers' and 'fathers' in the institution of wardship.[33]

Though Romantic in representation, both are images of the British project of transforming the Nilgiris into a developing European society. The first lithograph places the Toda family in immediate relationship to the Christian church, the second shows the Toda within a landscape prominently displaying the developing market and cantonment of Ootacamund in the background. The Toda were exotic but domesticated, a people to be viewed by tourists whose leisure consists in refreshing walks.

The form of historiography which Hough and Harkness represent, pointing simultaneously to similarities and differences between the Nilgiris and Europe, contrasts with many texts produced later, when Ootacamund, Conoor, and Kotagiri had developed more firmly into European settlements. Already in Harkness's oft-quoted work there is a remarkable absence of European interaction with native society. This captain of the Madras army was a curious explorer, taking the reader on months of travel through the beautiful landscape of the hills. But, in spite of his own obvious presence, Europeans are almost completely absent from his narrative. He is deeply impressed by what he experiences, and the various 'tribes' are portrayed in a positive light, with a detailed description of their social interrelationships. Apart from narrations of his conversations with people he met, there is however very little to go by on how he gathered his information. It remains a rather loosely kept travelogue.

While Hough observes the promising Nilgiris 'developing' through increasing interaction with the plains, Harkness is absorbed by its nature and people. In Hough's accounts the integration of the Nilgiris into the South Indian economy plays an important role. He relates that grain merchants had begun taking the route through the hills for their markets, rather than travelling via Palghat to the western coast. Large villages had begun to form along this route, with bazaars at which merchants travelling up to 80 miles sold grain and other commodities.[34] In contrast Harkness is the interested ethnographer who closely observes native settlements, customs, and rites, while remaining the distant spectator. Harkness's account, with all its hypothetical assumptions, remains one of the most detailed ethnological works of the period, but the European and Indian encroachments on people's lives and livelihoods are hidden in his texts.[35] One of his concluding remarks is significant in relation to how he located the Toda in history and place. Having attended a funeral and described how people came in their finest clothes and jewellery, he observes:

> [T]he character of every thing connected with the scene passing before us, was so totally different from any thing else of the present day, either in this, or perhaps in any other part of the world, that it required no

> great force of imagination to suppose, that what we were witnessing, were relics of forms and ceremonies handed down traditionally through countless generations, of a people who, except this poor remnant, have long since passed away.[36]

The Nilgiri Hills in Regional History

The trope of the Nilgiris as a secluded enclave, isolated in the hills and cut off from the economy and politics of the plains, has remained strong in scholarly works. Not until Anthony Walker's *The Toda of South India. A New Look* (1986) was there any serious criticism of labelling the Toda as a never-changing community, defined in essentialist terms, and living aloof on a distant hilltop. Walker develops the argument that Toda society is better understood within the context of the larger South Indian 'Hindu civilization', and that it has been far from static. He argues that the Nilgiris had developed into a distinctively different society but that the region was never sealed off from the surrounding civilizations. It was included in South Indian empires and states from the Hoysala (twelfth century BCE) onwards.[37]

With this argument Walker critically positions himself in relation to a broad variety of works, from David G. Mandelbaum, the anthropologist who from 1937 chose to focus much of his research on the Kota community; and Nurit Bird, who in a study of the Kurumba and Naiken communities questions the supposedly closed tribal system of the Nilgiris yet argues the region's pre-British isolation; to Lucile H. Brockway, who uses the Nilgiris as one of her examples in a worldwide study of plant transfers in the British empire.[38] More directly, he critically positions his study in relation to W.H.R. Rivers' magnum opus *The Todas* (1906). Rivers (1873–1919), one of the founders of the British school of anthropology and among the first to emphasize the importance of gathering data through experience in intensive and well-structured fieldwork, explicitly applied an anthropological and scientifically exact method of kinship studies to the Toda. He considered the genealogical method he had developed to be his best instrument.[39] However, Walker identifies an unfortunate legacy of Rivers' otherwise seminal work in its synchronic perspective, and from within this criticism he develops his own argument.

The work of Rivers was a first step away from evolutionism towards a functionalist perspective more fully developed by two of his students,

Bronislaw Malinowski and A.R. Radcliffe-Brown. George Stocking finds Rivers' standpoint moving ambivalently between these two perspectives, with failed evolutionary assumptions leading to conclusions about unique customs and religion. Rivers' detailed search for Toda genealogy, cult, passage-rite customs, ceremonies, and so on came to form an image of a social organization that maintained and reproduced a unique society, and ultimately he 'binds all these beliefs and practices into a whole so that they constitute the Toda religion'.[40] His study thus portrayed a culture unaffected by change, i.e. the notion of change was not made part of the enquiry. In Walker's reading, Rivers represented Toda society as small-scale, bounded, and essentially closed.[41] In line with Rivers' thesis, academic works throughout the twentieth century continued on the whole to project the Toda as an isolated, non-Hindu, and pastoral people living in a polyandrous society and occasionally practising female infanticide. A brief survey of popular science, modern media, and tourist information will suffice to show that, even now, this image remains solidly in place in popular representations of the Toda.

Walker's contribution to what has occasionally been termed 'Toda studies' arrived at a time when anthropologists were debating the phenomenon of culture as a shared system of meaning. It was questioned whether culture should be understood primarily as a value system, an ideology, and a shared set of beliefs, or whether it has an ontological core, an essential and almost unchanging element specific to every particular culture.[42] Walker does not explicitly engage in this debate, but his study gives indications of where his sympathies lie. He describes a situation in which a distinct people is slowly adjusting to modern society. 'The modern Toda' still constitute 'a distinctive cultural entity', according to Walker. They are 'a unique people', with their own language, dress, and material culture, and have through the ages adapted economically to the specific environmental conditions of the Nilgiris.[43]

However, while arguing that the Nilgiris were never cut off from surrounding states and societies, Walker also claims that there is a 200-year gap in the historical documentation. The two missing centuries occur between 1603 and 1812, when no European eyewitness reports on the Nilgiris were written—at least no reliable ones. The reports produced by British revenue surveyors in 1800 were dismissed as early as 1819 by Sullivan as mere falsifications based on hearsay.[44] Two reports are selected to mark the beginning and end of the 'dark period', and neither of them is particularly extensive. In 1603 an Italian Jesuit priest, Father Fenicio, entered the hills in search of a Thomas Christian community among the Malabar mountains. His short visit resulted in a detailed letter to the Vice Provincial of Calicut, which includes a description of a visit to a Toda mund.[45] In 1812 the assistant revenue surveyor William Keys wrote a brief report on the physical and geographical condition of the Nilgiris and made some notes about the people living there.[46] During the 200 years between these dates, writes Anthony Walker, 'our window on the community [the Toda] closes.'[47]

Interesting and well worth noting is the very notion that there is a 200-year gap in the record and the way in which this is reinforced in the academic literature. Even more noteworthy is the fact that only reports of European origin are considered when this claim is made. Occasionally, the lack of information is taken as proof that nothing in particular changed in the life and livelihoods of the people of the Nilgiris over the period. The descriptions written in 1603 and 1812 look far too similar, and counter-arguments to this assumed continuity have not been forthcoming. Such conclusions are an example of the 'ethnographic trap' that arises when a local population is analysed discretely and as separate from social history. We may safely assume that the substantial impact of early ethnographic writings and the early anthropological works that followed contributed significantly to this lack of grounding not only of people's social lives but also of a proper social understanding of the region.

If, for example, we focus on transactions in kind at the local level, described in many ethnographic and anthropological works, we find indications of fundamental changes in the seventeenth and eighteenth centuries. The early ethnographers were intrigued by the system of exchanging goods and services, Harkness more than Hough. It was described as marking social hierarchies and centred on the giving of *gudu*. The system was said to be fairly closed, tying the Toda, Badaga, and Kota communities together. The Toda contributed dairy produce, while the Badaga produced agricultural crops, and the Kota, who were artisans, provided the necessary implements. Irula and Kurumba hunters and gatherers were described as not formally included in this social system, but as supplying honey, wax, and other small forest products to the local economy. Anthropologists working in the Nilgiris all observed this system. However, it tends to be portrayed as ancient and static, with no acknowledgement of transformations that may have occurred alongside the historical changes of immigration and colonial rule. As Nurit Bird points out, early accounts of social organization and ethnographic observation of the people living in the Nilgiris tend to be more contradictory and variegated than twentieth-century anthropological models and cultural maps of 'pastoralist Todas', 'agriculturalist Badagas,' 'artisan Kotas', and 'food-gathering sorcerer Kurumbas', in line with Mandelbaum's model of 1941.[48]

Walker writes that the Badaga community were 'pivotal in the economic life of the Nilgiri people'.[49] His argument aligns with the commonly accepted assumption that the Badaga community arrived from the north in the late sixteenth century—the name Badaga meaning 'northerner' (Tamil *vaṭa, vaṭakku* 'northern'). This places the immigration immediately before Father Fenicio's visit to the Nilgiris. In line with Hockings' argument, Walker states that, as a consequence of Badaga immigration and the subsequent cultivation of land under Toda authority, the socio-economic system typical of the region developed. If this assumption is correct, the transformation of local society in the Nilgiris after 1600 must have been radical, and the situation was far from one of unchanged continuity until 1800.[50] By the time Rivers published his account of the Toda in 1906, British imperial power was deeply rooted in Indian soil and society, and land relations and resource use had changed dramatically for people native to the Nilgiris. However, Rivers remained blind to the effects of his own presence as a European, acting within the premises of the British empire. Comparing Fenicio's report of 1603 with his own observations in 1906, he concluded that Fenicio's information, however meagre, was 'sufficient to show that there has probably been little change in the Todas and their surroundings in the three centuries which elapsed between his visit and mine'.[51]

Allen Zagarell vigorously questions the notion of a historically isolated Nilgiri enclave, but does so from a very different point of view than Walker's, and applying a longer time frame. Partly in criticism of Walker, Zagarell uses archaeological evidence to argue that state authority in the eastern and central Nilgiri Hills was exercised periodically, through revenue assessment, extended agriculture, or military operations, from at least the eighth or ninth century to the seventeenth to eighteenth centuries. His findings question the assumption of historical continuities. Toda pastoralism was not simply a more complex social organization of Neolithic forms of pastoralism that may have existed earlier in the region. Arguing against any historiography that places the Toda in a timeless past as the relics of 'a people who, except this poor remnant, have long since passed away'—to quote Harkness's words from 1832—he states: 'The actual social history of the region stands opposed to an improbable, imagined evolutionary scheme, in which the past is viewed as just a less complex form of the present.' Comparing hero-stone reliefs in the upper and lower Nilgiris, the majority of which date from the twelfth to the seventeenth centuries, Zagarell finds that they depict orthodox Saivite themes in similar ways, indicating that people in the Nilgiris embraced the religious cosmologies of larger South Indian states. However, differences between hero stones found at the lower and upper elevations reveal access to skilled craftspeople nearer the plains, while stones at the higher elevations are more crudely worked and portray women in roles generally associated in the lower regions with male images, such as involvement in armed combat. Whether this reflects actual differences in gender relations or represents a more idealized gender order in either of the regions is hard to determine.[52]

Zagarell's study thus helps to open the window which Walker found closed on the pre-British history of the region. Being located in the lands facing east and north from the hills, extending to the lower elevations towards the Coimbatore plains and the Moyar river, it connects hill societies to larger states, most prominently Vijayanagar (1336–1565), followed by the expanding Mysore state, which grew from a tributary state of Vijayanagar to become independent and the strongest challenge to the EIC in South India in the eighteenth century. Similarly, to deepen our understanding of social organization in the Nilgiris, we need to look westwards to see the influence of political centres of power at the lower altitudes and on the plains to the west of the hills. Occasionally, early-nineteenth-century documents refer to socioeconomic relationships between Toda munds, in particular munds close to the Pykara river, which cuts through the upper plateau from north to south, and the rajas of Wynad. Especially during times of conflict with the EIC administration, the Nilambur raja's name appears. The domain of his authority was part of the socio-political order of the Malabar tharavadus or matrilineal spheres of territorial power of Nair/Nayar and Samanthar castes, some of which claimed royal status.[53]

In the wars between the EIC, often allied with the Kottayam royal house in north Malabar, and the Mysore state, supported by the French East India Company,[54] the Malabari tharavadus were squeezed between the two opposing forces. Depending on the fortunes of the wars, rajas could switch allegiance to remain on the safer side and, at times, they entered into agreements with both, while remaining the ultimate losers. The region was looted several times and rebellion severely punished.[55]

In the first two Anglo-Mysore wars, Haider Ali and his successor Tipu Sultan gained the victory and, between 1784 and 1792, the whole of Malabar was under Mysore's control. But in the following two conflicts British troops were reinforced and, in 1792, Malabar was conquered by the EIC. Simultaneously, EIC troops were closing in from the south, through the Kongunad plains which became Coimbatore district, and from the east, through the hills and plains of the Eastern Ghats. Seven years later, in 1799, armies under the EIC and the nizam of Hyderabad captured Srirangapatam, the capital of Mysore, and Tipu Sultan was killed. As long as the social order of Malabar was not under external pressure, it maintained a certain stability in the region. However, in the transition from regional to colonial rule during the four Anglo-Mysore wars, the system began to collapse. As early as 1792, when a British commission investigated revenue and judicial administration, land control and tenurial systems were redefined.[56]

In spite of the geopolitical boundary later drawn by the British administration between the Wynad and Nilgiri districts, the western part of the Nilgiris is in fact the upper part of Wynad, historically and ecologically speaking. The close historical connection between the Nilgiris and the lands lying immediately east of the hills, which is sometimes assumed to have been the dominant focus of interaction between the hills and the plains, derives mainly from an uncritical reading of Sullivan's reports from 1829–30. At that time, the boundary between the Malabar and Coimbatore districts was vigorously disputed within the EIC. Sullivan, whose administration was under critical scrutiny, was anxious to keep the entire Nilgiri plateau within his own domain of the Coimbatore district, while the Board of Revenue, together with the collector of Malabar, argued that a large portion of the Nilgiris should fall under the Malabar administration (and later went on to include a much larger portion than just the Wynad section). When Sullivan left office in 1830, most of the Nilgiris were transferred to the Malabar district.[57]

In today's historiography Sullivan's verbose minutes are generally taken as descriptions of actual facts. However, there is convincing evidence of close contact between Toda society and the political centres of Wynad, some of which were linked to the royal house of Kottayam in Malabar. Most parts of Malabar and Wynad were under the control of the Kottayam ruling family, and authority over the region was divided between family members. Wynad fell under the western branch of the Pazhassi (Pychi) region. Nambalacotta (which had affinal links to the Kurumbranad raja of the Kottayam family) and Nelliyalam (under the Nilambur raja) were old centres of political authority in the western part of the Nilgiri plateau, which also included lands on the upper western slopes. Their spheres of influence were certainly limited in size and yet substantial in the regional context.

During the Anglo-Mysore wars Wynad also got caught up in the turmoil—first when the Mysore ruler wanted to secure control of the region, and later when British troops sought to consolidate territories they had wrested from Mysore. As a consequence of the politics of war, Nambalacotta and Nelliyalam battled and, after the British conquest of Mysore, the right to collect tax in Wynad, including the division of Todanad in the Nilgiris, passed from Nelliyalam to Nambalacotta and was to remain in its hands at least until 1830.[58]

As early as 1787 Tipu Sultan had ordered Kottayam to hand over the division of Wynad to Mysore, but the head of the Pazhassi division refused to cede control. The EIC for its part tried to ally itself with Pazhassi against Tipu. However, during the last Anglo-Mysore war, tension between the Malabari rajas and the EIC swelled to rebellion. Insensitive and harsh collection of taxes by the British, which disregarded the significance of Malabari land laws and the sovereignty of the tharavadus, caused conflicts. The British assumed that rajas who submitted to British overlordship did so in the hope that the plan (generally adopted in the Malabar province) of reinstating the rajas expelled by the Mysore rulers would also be carried into effect in Wynad. In this way they would retain limited autonomy, while simultaneously reinforcing the regional social order of old. But the rajas decided differently. While some of the Malabari rajas chose to negotiate, the Pazhassi raja rebelled. When the latter's uncle, the raja of Kurumbranad, assumed authority over some of his lands and entered into a treaty with the British, it strengthened the Pazhassi raja's decision to revolt.[59]

The British had no intention of preserving a class of independent rajas and, in 1796, war broke out between the EIC and the raja of Pazhassi. The fact that it lasted almost ten years can be explained in large part by the difficult terrain and guerrilla-like strategies of the raja's forces once they moved into Wynad. At the time of the fall of Mysore, a small group of British and Indian officers of the EIC was sent to Wynad to proclaim British overlordship and secure the rajas' surrender. While most of them surrendered, the Pazhassi raja suggested through intermediaries an agreement by which he would acknowledge EIC overlordship but remain the tax collector and sovereign of his own domain. The British officer in charge reported that he had no hope that 'anything short of marching a detachment into Weinaud will give us the possession of it'.[60] Three years later the British officer was close to giving up, suggesting that the whole of Wynad would be better traded to the reinstated raja of Mysore in exchange for some other land. When the Pazhassi raja was killed in 1805, he had refused throughout the conflict to collect taxes for the British, thus honouring his duties as ruler, and was seen by the British as a serious threat to their claim to sovereignty. During the final years of the rebellion, when he was on the run from a British search party, he occasionally moved between Toda munds in south Wynad.[61]

In view of the turbulent war years, the emergence into view of a Nilgiri-authored document, purportedly a bamboo document, is particularly important. It was created in 1783–4 (the year 959 ME[62]) and collected in 1829 by a British officer from the Nambalacotta administration.[63] The document is a 'deed of promise'. It begins by naming four Toda men residing on lands belonging to the Paradevatha temple. In the English translation provided by the officer it reads:

> Peshamoorry or Deed of Promise, executed by Todawara Karekel Manthil Kenan Todawan, Yerrootendenarnad Manthil Aria Todawan, Kembalan Todawan, Yellyket Todawan, the Jenm–Koodians of the Wettekoroo magan Barathinatha residing on the Jenm lands belonging to the Barathewatha Devassom Situated on the West side of the Piakara river.
>
> Whereas we, the jenm Koodians of the Barathewatha, have not, during the last eight years, supplied to the Barathewatha Devassom the 60 guindies of ghee and 120 old fanams which ought to have been furnished by us annually according to the custom which has obtained from time

> immemorial, by reason of our having been obliged to quit the country and remain absent from it in consequence of the disturbance which prevailed in it. We now promise to tender to the Barathawatha Devassom from and after this day, the 20th Toolam 959, according to the ancient custom, 60 guindies of ghee and 120 fanams per annum. That we may enjoy the blessing of Barathewatha and the favour of the Raja, and that our children may prosper we execute this Dead of promise and submit it to the Waranoor Tambooraw, and to the execution here of the undermentioned persons are Witnesses, Goodaloorattil Pathew Badoogan, Charamatha Badoogan, Kataril Walia Moondan, and Pangan Kottan. Dated 20th Toolam 959, the signatures of the four persons above named.[64]

This document was filed as part of a major investigation to determine the correct boundary between the Malabar and Coimbatore districts, an investigation which drew together many different types of evidence, including correspondence with the district collectors, depositions by Badaga and Toda *monigars*,[65] formal surveys, and a search for pre-British documents which resulted in the document above. The British officer's purpose in referring to the deed of promise was simply to prove that Sullivan was wrong in the boundary conflict and to show that the inhabitants of the Nilgiris could just as well make their way to the district headquarters of Malabar to present themselves to the court when the need arose. The officer who transferred the document to the Madras government affirmed that it proved beyond doubt the Nambalacotta raja's proprietary right in the land west of the Pykara river.[66]

To us, however, it reveals a number of issues pointing to people's relationships with the wider world. While the officer's purpose was simply to determine the boundary, the document itself speaks of relationships across that boundary and beyond. First of all, it confirms that the Pykara river, 21 kilometres west of Ootacamund, formed a boundary with lands under one of the Wynad jenmi landlords, 'rajahs' or heads of matrilineal ruling households. The document was drawn up by the Nambalacotta administration controlling jenmi lands in the name of the Paradevatha *devasam*, or temple trust.[67] Toda munds thus paid annually, in cash and in kind, for the right to reside on the western side of the Pykara. Other documents included in the 1829 investigation confirm this information. A *sheristadar*, Kulpully Karoonagara Menon, was part of a search party into Wynad to seize the Pazhassi raja's minister when he met Toda who grazed their cattle on either side of the river. They explained that they were accustomed to paying a certain sum for the use of the pasture ground to the Nambalacotta 'Bara Deevom (a temple so called)'. At the time, they were residing on the eastern side of the river, owing to the rebellion in Wynad. The Paradevatha (literally, the chief or original goddess) of the Paradevatha temple, Sri Porkali Devi, was also a chief goddess for the Pazhassi raja.[68]

During the investigation, inhabitants in the territory explained to the surveyor that the Nambalacotta raja had the right not only to elephants and sandalwood within his territory, but also to tax on Toda land south-east of the Pykara and to the medicinal root called *waymbam*, grown in the Tarnadmund region. These were rights that the British had continued to respect.[69] Depositions taken from Badaga monigars during the investigation of 1829 further confirm the boundary line, by reference not to the river but to nearby peaks. And in other depositions Toda witnesses stated that the Nelliyalam (Nilambur) raja, too, was well aware of the boundary along the Pykara river. Sullivan unintentionally corroborated this information by stating that the Toda in these munds lived on the western side of the river during the northeast monsoon and on the eastern side during the south-west monsoon. And in earlier correspondence with the government, before the boundary conflict appeared on the agenda, Sullivan described the 'intimate connection that has always subsisted between the Neelgherries and Wynaud'.[70] It may also be noted that, contrary to British assertions, the Toda handled money prior to the establishment of markets in the hills as a result of European immigration. 120 fanams, whether in gold or silver, was a fairly large amount of money to be paid as a lump sum once a year.[71]

Secondly, the agreement recorded that the deed of promise had existed 'since time immemorial', i.e. for as long as anyone could remember. Being fixed in written form, one may assume that it must have been in force for at least three generations, or throughout the eighteenth century. The formal arrangement of the deed should be noted, with four witnesses present at its execution, two of whom were members of the Badaga community, one of the Kota, and one of the Malayali Moondan community.

Thirdly, the document assigns the land as *jenmi*, which means that the raja's rights in the land and his tenurial relationships to the Toda were defined according to the legal terminology of Malabar. The Toda are termed leaseholders, 'jenm-koodian' or *kanakaran*,[72] and thus contracted within the logic of the jenmi system. Arunima makes the important observation that, in the process of settling land rights in Malabar, the British reinterpreted the locally varied tenures that had previously existed, replacing them with a narrow definition of absolute property under jenmi landlords: 'it marked the transition from the flexibility of the pre-colonial period, where rights or tenures were not rigidly interpreted, to a stage where, in the last instance, the colonial state was to remain the final arbiter of indigenous tradition.'[73] A very clear example of such a reinterpretation of land relations appears in Sullivan's argument in support of Toda absolute rights in land: 'The intimate connection that has always subsisted between the Neelgherries and Wynaud, and their proximity to the western coast where private property in the land is universal ... Having no doubt whatever myself that the Todavurs are to all intents and purposes, as much proprietors of the soil here, as the *Nairs* and other classes are of the adjoining District of Wynaud.'[74]

Kanam (lease or mortgage), too, was shaped by the context within which it had been created, but, as a result of British land and revenue settlements, the different forms were collapsed into a homogeneous category, suitable for revenue purposes.[75] We should not, therefore, understand the relationship between the Nilambur raja and the Toda who grazed cattle and resided on his land as one between a private property holder and a tenant. Ultimately, local conditions shaped the specific forms of tenure that existed.

Finally, the Toda had been unable to pay their dues for eight years when they had fled the place owing to the wars, which would be from 1775/6 to 1783/4, coinciding with the second Anglo-Mysore war. Evidently, these 'disturbances' affected not only Wynad rajas in western Nilgiris and the upper catchments of the western slopes, as was narrated in several imperial gazetteers and reports, but also a number of Toda munds, owing to their incorporation into the realm of the Wynad economy.

This is one of the few documents from pre-British times in the Nilgiris that remains in British colonial archives. It shows that the region was in no way isolated, but connected with events originating far outside the hills. In an interesting way, it also shows how social organization in the Nilgiris, which is often defined as a fine balance of mutual relationships between the Toda, Badaga, and Kota communities, was woven into larger social networks and polities. The document thus contributes to a more complex understanding of what otherwise tends to be a temptingly simplistic version of the *jajmani* system.

The Refugee and the Entrepreneurial Burgher

As is evident from the discussion above, the many studies of Nilgiri nineteenth-century history which have been entirely dependent on colonial historiography need to be read critically against recent studies of medieval and early modern South Indian history. British colonial visions of transforming the Nilgiri landscape shaped not only their general ideas of the hills as a location and abode for ancient herders, but also their view of the specific history preceding their own arrival there. To set their transformative visions in motion, British officers specifically targeted the cultivating community, the Badaga. We shall therefore return to the question of the immigration of cultivators into the Nilgiris.

The Toda, being so strongly identified with a buffalo economy and dairy produce, were totally dependent in the early nineteenth century on Badaga cultivators for foodgrains. It has generally been assumed that this dependence was of long standing, indicating early contacts between them and cultivating communities. There is in addition a strong and often repeated assumption that the Badaga community immigrated into the Nilgiris from the north, arriving as refugees from the chaos of warfare. The fact that the name Badaga means 'northerner' is treated as proof of their origin in the Mysore plains. At times, the harsh rule of Mysore under Hyder Ali and Tipu Sultan is referred to, but for the most part the collapse of the Vijayanagara empire in 1565 is cited to account for the flight of people from the plains. A word of caution may be in place when it comes to more routine assertions about cultivators from the plains fleeing from oppression into the forests and hills to form tribes. Such claims tend to echo early racial theories about people in the south escaping from a superior Aryan onslaught, thus serving to mystify regional histories.

Combining oral documentation from his field visits in the Nilgiris with nineteenth-century colonial reports, Hockings puts together a more varied set of sources on past migrations. He describes a continuing immigration from both the Mysore and the Coimbatore plains and argues that people arrived over a somewhat longer period of time, both before and after the fall of Vijayanagar. The assumed 'anarchy' following the collapse is said to have caused heavier migration, but he finds the beginning and end of such a period difficult to date. The immigrants thus formed a community once they arrived in the Nilgiris and hypothetically, therefore, 'northerner' may apply to a cultivator arriving from the outside, whether from the north, the west, or the east. Hockings' assumption that the many references to the sixteenth century in the colonial reports are a sign of solid evidence for dating the migration is open to question, since these reports are most likely interdependent, resting ultimately on the testimony of a few European visitors to the Nilgiris in the 1820s. More importantly, however, he combines a comparative search for the different religious affiliations of Badaga clans with their own legends of their pasts. Maintaining a more open hypothesis of long-term immigration thus provides a more plausible regional social history.[76]

It is also useful to establish the relevant research questions not just from within the Nilgiris as a region—i.e. not only to observe a single community living in the region, such as the Badaga, and trace where they came from—but to define a larger region and search for historical transformations in which the Nilgiris, too, were involved. The archaeologist Kathleen Morrison draws important conclusions about the relationship between the extension of swidden agriculture and the incorporation of the Western Ghat forests into long-distance trade as far back as the first centuries BCE. As a point of departure, she argues that '[a]s far back as we can trace, forest peoples have always been integrated in some way into larger political structures'. Using pollen data and soil evidence, she notes that the clearing of forests for cultivation had begun and an upland savannah created during this early period. Further, soil evidence shows that permanent fields were established in the Nilgiris some three or four hundred years earlier. Compared with Hockings, she draws less dramatic and yet far-reaching consequences from the Vijayanagara influence on the region, arguing that agriculture expanded at the expense of forest because of tax incentives, which accelerated in the sixteenth century—and claiming that land clearance incentives were extremely common in the Vijayanagara period.[77]

In addition, Portuguese colonial trade, with its enormous demand for forest products such as pepper, ginger, and cardamom, resulted in changed production patterns in the hills. Pepper and cardamom grew on mid-elevation hill slopes, below the Nilgiri plateau. When the demand for these spices escalated, Morrison observes, people's livelihood changed from a mosaic of practices of swidden cultivation, hunting, and gathering of products both for trade and subsistence, to a specialization of production for the sake of trade, with forest communities cultivating the required spices. The changed pattern of production, from collecting wild pepper and cardamom to cultivating them, probably limited both the cultivation of other crops and the spatial scale of gathering and hunting among these communities.[78]

Along similar lines, Zagarell suggests an even more gradual settlement of cultivators in the hills, arriving from lower elevations north of the plateau. As noted earlier, he convincingly argues that from the twelfth to the seventeenth century the lower Sigur and Moyar regions of the Nilgiri Hills were under state domination and administrative control. Towards the end of the period, irrigated cultivation was under the control of the Lingayat priestly caste. In the Vijayanagara period, in particular, the state intervened through taxation, administration, and raids into the highlands. From the twelfth century onwards, people from the north settled in the highlands, and 'by the sixteenth century many of these came to make up the so-called Badaga community within the highland Nilgiri area'.[79] It is possible that these cultivators were trying to escape taxation and state control, but they may also have moved in search of new land for cultivation. Zagarell argues that over a period of a thousand years prior to British rule, people in the Nilgiris 'operated in a world of episodic state authority, stratification, taxation, and organised military activities', which in turn created the conditions for 'classical Nilgiri social relations'.[80]

But when the British began to explore the past and present of the Nilgiris, the narrative on Badaga cultivators turned rapidly into the singular tale of a cultivating caste from the plains, fleeing oppressive rulers into the hills. It is interesting to examine the package of assumptions within which the British reports delivered this narrative.

It must first be remembered that the British had no written accounts of the Badaga community. Their version of it was basically a hypotheses based on what they encountered in the hills, and on how they organized their new knowledge to form their narrative understanding of Indian history. Harkness's claim that the Badaga was 'in every respect the Sudra cultivator of Mysore, [who] ... migrated to these hills, together with the other classes of this tribe, about six generations ago' is quite representative.[81] Even before his work was published, similar statements had been made, though Harkness has mostly been referred to as the authoritative source. In the reports, the Badagas were generally described as the entrepreneurial small farmers of the plains who arrived in the hills with skills lacking among the hill communities ('tribes'). In Harkness's words, 'they brought with them the knowledge and improvements resulting from a superior state of civilisation.' These skills soon made them welcome visitors and resulted in a 'conventional arrangement' between them and the other communities.[82]

As noted in many studies, the notion of 'lack' was often used to position a people or society on a scale of development. Without deeper insight into socio-economic or political organization, colonial explorers could thereby identify the absence of certain predetermined criteria for developed or civilized societies. In the Nilgiris, the Toda were observed to lack skills of entrepreneurship inherent in settled cultivation, while historical narratives depicted the Badaga as having once been an entrepreneurial class of cultivators. Interestingly, with only one exception this community was never referred to as 'Badaga' in colonial government files. That name was only used in ethnographic studies. Throughout Hough's work, they are spoken of as 'Buddagurs', and articles in the *Asiatic Journal and Monthly Register* use the same name. Harkness translated and explained the meaning of 'Buddacars' and 'Vaddacars' as 'north', while noting that the tribe was known by 'the general term Burgher'. A search of more than 400 government documents (Madras government, revenue and military files, Madras despatches and Board's collections) from 1815 to 1845 uncovers only one use of the name Badaga ('Buddagar') by an EIC officer. Significantly, in all other cases they were referred to as 'Burghers'.[83]

It is not immediately evident how the term Burgher came into use. However, it may be noted that the exceptional report in which the Badagas were referred to by the name they used for themselves is one where the reporting officer was writing about individuals—'Buddagars and Toders'—with whom he had developed personal relations when they accompanied him in the hills in 1829. Apart from this document, the Court of Directors once, also in 1829, quoted a report describing the great natural and medical advantages of the Nilgiri Hills. It was written by the surgeon Annesley and, as a text, may be assigned to the ethnographic category. Of all the vegetables, fruits, and grains grown, Annesley observed, the 'Budigars' cultivated the red poppy in abundance, using it to make opium. Considering the different types of texts involved, it appears that the term Burgher was used for administrative and policy purposes.[84]

Harkness continued to speculate about late-sixteenth-century Mysore and the inconvenience suffered by the Badaga as they left the civilized life of the plains behind, and with it their mechanics, barbers, and washermen. To make up for the loss of their services, the Badagas were assumed to have ensured 'the good neighbourhood' of the Kota and Kurumba and agreed to pay them to carry out these tasks, while themselves reaping other 'advantages' from the agreement. Thus, the social organization which Harkness witnessed in the Nilgiris was assumed to have come about as a form of contract between essentially fixed communities.[85]

The perception of the lost civilization of the Badaga emerges even more clearly when Harkness writes:

> The subversion of the Hindu governments, however, brought about another change, and from that period up to the present, the different tribes have continued much on their original footing one with another; the Burghers having multiplied to a great extent, and spread themselves over almost every part of the hills; and looking back with regret to the time when they hoped to establish themselves not merely independent of their neighbours, but superior to them ... their dread of the power of evil spirits, while it acted as a check to their cupidity, was at the same time an obstacle to the attainment of the many benefits which must otherwise have resulted to them from their superior industry.[86]

This narrative depicts the downfall and subordination of a 'caste' to a 'tribe'. Occasionally, the Badaga were described as dirty and filthy, making 'immoderate use of opium' and producing only simple crops. Hough also declared that they were an inferior race to the Toda, being 'very diminutive'. But the Europeans obviously projected onto them the idea of the superior civilization they themselves were keen to promote in the Nilgiris and, from within this vision, the British historical narrative was produced. The prospects of transforming the Badaga into settled cultivators were deemed to be good.[87] Yet Hough, Harkness and Sullivan simultaneously argued that, at the time of their arrival, the Badaga were forced to establish a relationship of dependence with the Toda. Members of all communities acknowledged the Toda as the 'lords of the soil' to whom the Badaga, too, paid tribute in the form of a share of their harvest. Interestingly, in the Toda language the name for the Badaga community makes no reference to their immigration, but means 'labourer'. As is quite common, the word the Toda use for their own community means 'men' or 'human being'.[88]

The descriptions of the Badaga that we find in the colonial reports from the early period of European settlement in the Nilgiris are surprisingly different from the dominant notion of shifting cultivators presented in other historical works on Indian colonial history. The sweeping, negative judgements about this 'wasteful', 'primitive' form of cultivation, which have been thoroughly researched in many studies, are almost absent from the Nilgiri reports.[89] Jacques Pouchepadass's study of British attitudes to shifting cultivation in South Kanara from 1800 to 1920 is an interesting point of reference in this regard. As Kanara was located in the Western Ghats, north of the Nilgiri Hills, and administered within the Madras Presidency, it would be reasonable to assume a uniform treatment of shifting cultivation in both Kanara and the Nilgiris. However, throughout the nineteenth century the shifting cultivators of Kanara were described as primitive tribes, far removed from the entrepreneurial small farmers that the British saw hidden in their Nilgiri counterparts. From the early 1820s shifting cultivation in Kanara was already beginning to be acknowledged as part of the land revenue system and divided into two separate legal forms: shifting cultivation settled directly between the individual and the government (*sarkar kumri*) and shifting cultivation under local large landowners who were taxed on their estates (*warg kumri*). Subsequently, from the 1840s, warg kumri began to be seen as a problem. Until then, forest clearance had tended to be encouraged for the sake of preventing fever and, more importantly, because as yet the government had sufficient supplies of timber from other forests where valuable species were more prominent.

Consequently, Thomas Munro's policy of non-interference with native agrarian systems, for the sake of keeping the peace, had been upheld.[90]

The 1840s appear to have seen a turn of the tide in South Kanara. Increasingly harsh restrictions on shifting cultivation began to be enforced in order to protect the forests from clear-felling and thereby secure the supply of timber. In addition to this concern for timber, the question of ownership was given priority. As in the general debates on the ryotwari revenue system, the government wanted to curb the authority of middlemen who pursued interests that conflicted with its own. Under the rubric of warg kumri, the area under shifting cultivation increased after British annexation, perhaps even quadrupled or quintupled according to Pouchepadass's estimates, owing to a transformation of the social base for kumri cultivation in the region. As this further increased the influence of large landowners, the government responded by denying them absolute property rights. At the same time, deprecatory judgements of shifting cultivation gained prominence, and negative opinions on the cultivators' morals, intellectual capacity, and uncivilized way of life coloured the reports.[91]

Consequently, what may at first glance seem to be a difference in attitudes to shifting cultivators in the Nilgiris and Kanara ought rather to be seen in the light of the government's way of reading and relating to local social organization, and of its natural resource requirements. In Kanara, shifting cultivators had a form of tenureship in which they were dependent on *wargdar* landlords, while the Badaga—Toda relationship was economically less hierarchical. As the wargdars' influence grew with the expansion of warg kumri, they began to be seen as a threat to government control of land. The Toda never aspired to become landlords in a similar way, and until the mid nineteenth century the Nilgiri forests did not produce significant amounts of timber. However, in both regions, the means of suppressing landlords was to deny them ownership, be they lords with tenurial rights or pastoralists who were locally acknowledged as 'lords of the soil'. Attitudes hardened only after 1840, when competition for land increased, threatening both timber supplies and government sovereignty. Before that, the policy towards shifting cultivation was relatively relaxed in Kanara, just as it was in the Nilgiris.

In the Nilgiris, in spite of their appreciative attitude to the Badaga, the British were not satisfied with the state of hill cultivation. In 1829, by when more and more members of the Madras government had begun to settle in the Nilgiris for the hot season, complaints began to pour in about the lack of goods for consumption. In a president's minute sent to the Court of Directors, a bold suggestion was made to ship small farmers from Europe to the Nilgiris to serve as a model for the native inhabitants. Deploying the watchword of the times, the government argued that they would bring 'improvement' to the region. These 'scientific and enterprising' European farmers were assumed to be 'of hardy, persevering and industrious habits.'[92]

The note gives a vivid description of the kind of society the Madras government wanted to see in the hills. The immigrants were to be acquainted with agriculture and irrigation; they were to know about the management of cattle; and, ideally, they would include master workmen who knew enough to set up manufacture: 'We do not want labourers, but directors of labour, small capitalists, agriculturalists and manufacturers; with a very trifling assistance from the Government one or two dozen of such settlers would find abundant means for their prosperous establishment on the hills, and their skill, enterprise and industry, if properly directed, would soon develop the latent resources of this most extraordinary and interesting country.'[93]

The governor believed that this plan offered a perfect solution, since the only assistance the European immigrants would need was their passage out and the free allotment of suitable sites in the Nilgiris. Not only was their exact route through Malabar suggested, but also the equipment the immigrants would need to bring with them from Europe: a few sheep, an English stallion and bull, two or three cows, a supply of seeds, carpenter's tools for rough work, spades and pickaxes, a selection of sieves for corn and flour, a small hand corn-mill, and one or two fowling pieces with powder and shot. The success of these model farmers was assumed, there being no fear of 'attacks from predatory hordes of wandering savages or of distress from drought'. The entire plan was typical of European expansionism from the seventeenth century on. Similar projects to send out groups of settlers with livestock and provisions had been undertaken with varying degrees of success by various European expeditions. Note that the Nilgiris and their people were said to have *latent* resources that could be developed under the proper direction of British capitalists and manufacturers. In keeping with the classical Orientalist idea of India—once a prosperous civilization with good prospects for development, but now at a standstill owing to violent interruptions, not least by Muslim conquerors—the Nilgiris, too, were assumed to have dormant resources. Perhaps unsurprisingly, in 1830 the Court of Directors declined to support the idea.[94]

The vision of transforming the Nilgiris into an idealized European landscape encompassed every aspect of life, including diet. British officers deplored the 'coarse grain' which the natives consumed. Clearly, they failed to see the connection between their food habits and muscular appearance. It was described as a great improvement when the Toda began to replace locally grown millets and 'other small grains' with imported rice. Except during the south-west monsoon, rice was now imported from Wynad. The otherwise vegetarian Toda even occasionally ate roast buffalo. Now they also preferred to sell their dairy produce, rather than barter it for clothes and grain. And, to European chagrin, they had learnt the trick of raising prices. Even the gentlemanly luxury of smoking tobacco had been introduced among them.[95]

Not everyone took an unfavourable view of the Toda diet. The Anglican missionary Thompson was overjoyed by what he saw in the Nilgiris when he visited his dear and admired friend John Sullivan. He immediately perceived it as the most prosperous place not only for sick missionaries, but also for the conversion of natives. The Toda—these 'harmless, good-natured ... unprejudiced children of nature', with huts resembling tabernacles—appeared defenceless in their poverty.[96]

> I am told they are plain and harmless. But how long they may continue so, seeing the communication with the plains since the first settling of Europeans on these hills (about 5 years ago) becomes daily more and more pregnant, is very doubtful. Hitherto their place of abode and their ignorance have screened them from various vices prevailing among the rest of the natives in this country; but any cunning race from below is now come in a more close contact with them, and consequences may easily be foreseen. This circumstance calls upon the friends of humanity for a speedy relief. (I shall add, that the appearance of the Todas indicates a robust constitution and flourishing health, no doubt an effect from their simple and sober diet, and the salubrity of the climate.)[97]

A constant source of debate within the administration was the extent to which the Toda actually controlled extensive lands in the Nilgiris. As discussed in Chapter 4, such claims had very significant implications for the settlement of land rights. But this issue is also important from the perspective of Badaga immigration or settlement in the hills. Before land rights became an issue, European visitors had generally assumed that the Toda were originally in possession of the whole range. That conclusion was only logical, given that the immigration of Badaga cultivators would imply that there must have been a period before their arrival when the Toda were the only people on the plateau, living there with unquestioned authority.

But many eyewitness reports—in letters, surveys, and studies undertaken by private initiative—show that when the Europeans and Indians began to settle, the Toda had a rather limited portion of land under their control. It just so happened that this was also where Europeans settled. Assistant surgeon R. Orton noted that the Toda inhabited only Todanad, and Hough that they 'chiefly' occupied Todanad and Malnad, i.e. the central portion of the plateau.[98] In 1829, when land rights had appeared on the agenda and the tone had begun to change, Sullivan said the scanty Toda population should not lead to erroneous conclusions. He claimed that, originally, the Toda had been in possession of the whole range, and that it was only with their permission that the Badaga had settled and cultivated the land. More importantly, though, Sullivan warned of the consequences of Badaga expansion: 'The cultivation and population in their nauds, are rapidly increasing, and in a few years, the Bergers if left undisturbed, will occupy all the best descriptions, and many of the inferior soils.'[99] By 1829, according to Sullivan, the Badaga had already taken over most of Todanad and Kondanad, and all that was left for the Toda was the small portion of Todanad called Malnad, and another portion of Kondanad. Of these, only Malnad was completely free from cultivation—until the Europeans arrived, that is.[100]

At the time when Sullivan wrote these two reports, he was deeply involved in land disputes and argued the case for Toda property rights. In 1835, when he again reported on the state of the Toda, he had less need to put forward arguments in support of such rights, resulting in a somewhat less categorical narrative, although still with no indication of how he gathered his information. Now he dated the first immigration of Badaga to 450 years earlier, in the late fourteenth century. The first colony of immigrants was said to have arrived from the Malasal Hills, thirty miles south of Mysore. Within the 'contract' then agreed on, which was still 'religiously observed', they rendered the Toda a proportion varying from one-tenth to one-eighth of their produce, known as 'godoo', in acknowledgement of their being the original proprietors. Sullivan compared gudu to the *marah* of Arcot.[101] The Badaga and Lingayat were said to have gradually spread over the hills and, at the time of the report, they occupied land in Peringanad, Todanad, and Maiknad, while the Toda had 'gradually withdrawn' into Malnad, retaining exclusive occupation of that area until the Europeans intruded. Although the Badaga cultivators paid tax to the government, they still continued to pay gudu to the Toda on all lands in the Nilgiris.[102]

While acknowledging the weak substance of these observations in matters of detail, it has to be said that they lend further confirmation to there having been a long-term transformation in the Nilgiris, beginning long before the British arrival, whereby shifting cultivation came to occupy more and more land. This was a change which possibly also shortened rotations. If this assumption is correct, the realm of Toda supremacy must accordingly have decreased over time. However, the implications of such interdivides in the Nilgiris have only occasionally been dealt with in academic studies. By and large, the social organization prevalent in the limited Malnad region has been taken to account for the entire Nilgiris. Bird-David rightly points out that the stereotyped idea of the typical, singular Nilgiri 'tribal system' has been exaggerated owing to the many accounts that concerned themselves with it. While each account was based on references in previous studies, taking these as evidence, the cumulative effect of such 'evidence' provided further generalizations—like 'Winnie the Pooh in search of the Heffalump'. However, while Bird-David suggests the existence of two kinds of 'intertribal worlds' in the Nilgiris, one in Nilgiri-Wynad and the other on the Nilgiri plateau, documentation with a broader historical reach suggests a more fluid, continuously changing socioeconomic organization.[103]

The situation Sullivan reported on illustrates how the imagined wilderness of the Nilgiris and wildness of its people, together with the transformative visions of British officers, had come into collision with the realities they faced. Officers dealt with this by relying on their vision. The landscape overwhelmed them, not least by its familiarity. From the moment they perceived it, they grasped it and understood it via ideas of progress and improvement. On encountering the 'robust and lordly' Toda, the observers were sure that these people must be of European origin, and that, with proper training, the cultivators—the Burghers—ought to catch up with development and return to the efficient, settled cultivation they had engaged in on the plains from which they came. It followed logically that the only solution to the problem of securing enough goods to meet the consumption requirements of the British officers was to import European model cultivators for the locals to imitate.

In these ways the general interest of the British in the Nilgiris differed in character from their interest in hill regions where, in the first instance, a demand for valuable timber or security concerns defined the framework for intervention. These important differences point to the need not to lump people in forest and hill tracts as 'tribals', and to assume a common trajectory for their precolonial past as well as the impact of colonial intervention.[104] In the early-nineteenth-century Nilgiris, the administration perceived a settled agrarian society as the norm, according to which the value of land derived from its cultivation. Until the late 1830s or even the 1840s, when the plantation economy increased in scale, the aim was to turn the hill cultivators of the region into settled small farmers: hence the projection of the large Badaga community as entrepreneurial Burghers. In the Nilgiris, shifting cultivation was not outlawed until 1862. Deborah Sutton has chosen to emphasize the government's hostility and aggressive policy towards curbing this 'undeveloped' form of agriculture, which it claimed promoted only fraud and laziness. However, this did not emerge as a change in policy until the 1850s. Analysing the process, Sutton puts forward important arguments for the role of the advancing land market and the competition for land experienced by the Badaga population as a result of expanding plantations. At this point in time, in terms similar to those applied to the Toda, the Badaga were no longer described as the entrepreneurs of modern agriculture, but as 'wretchedly poor', indolent, and lacking any initiative for progress. Simultaneously, in the late 1850s, when the demand for timber for the railways had grown and the Mudumalai forests leased from the Nilambur raja (or Tirumalpad) were practically emptied of teak by order of the Conservator of Forests, Hugh Cleghorn, people in the Nilgiris were required on a large scale for occupations other than agriculture. At that time, however, it was members of the Kurumba community who were hired as carriers of timber; and neither the Toda nor the Badaga were involved in the trade.[105]

Notes

1. Field notes, Kandelmund, November 2001, and Manjakalmund, December 2002. See also Sutton, 2002, 'Horrid Sights and Customary Rights. The Toda Funeral on the Colonial Nilgiris', 67, for a discussion of the display of 'Toda tribal culture' in exhibitions and museums at the end of the nineteenth century.
2. John Sullivan was the son of John Sullivan (senior), who was appointed to the Madras Civil Service in 1765 and, among several influential parliamentary and EIC positions, held the post of parliamentary commissioner on the Board of Control for more than twenty years. The uncle of J.S. senior, Laurence Sullivan, was EIC director for ten years and deputy director for five during the period 1758–86. Thomas Munro, governor of Madras, 1820–7, was appointed governor in 1819. OIOC, MRP, 2–17 September 1822, From the Secretary to the Board of Revenue, 2482–3; OIOC, European Manuscripts, Thomas Munro Collection, vol. 92, Letter book (from Munro) 1820–6, to John Sullivan, 24 June 1821. Philips and Philips, 1941, 'Alphabetical List of Directors of the East India Company from 1758 to 1858'; Stein, 1989, *Thomas Munro. The Origins of the Colonial State and His Vision of Empire*, 25–6, 30, 180.
3. OIOC, European Manuscripts, Thomas Munro Collection, vol. 28, Letters to Munro from John Sullivan 1815–19, From Sullivan to Munro, 8 January 1819. Mackworth, 1823, *Diary of a Tour through Southern India, Egypt and Palestine in the Years 1821 and 1822*, 127.
4. Sir Walter Scott (1771–1832). In the early nineteenth century, 'Anglo-Indian' denoted British residents in India. Margot Finn, lecture at Uppsala University, the Department of History, 6 April 2006. Finn, 2006, 'Colonial Gifts. Family Politics and the Exchange of Goods in British India, *c.* 1780–1820', 218, 226–7. For an elaboration of how affection and nostalgia combined with British middle-class ambitions to structure perceptions of and relationships to Indian landscapes, see Arnold, 2005, *The Tropics and the Traveling Gaze. India, Landscape, and Science 1800–1856*, 54–61.
5. Raffles, 1999, '"Local Theory". Nature and the Making of an Amazonian Place', 324, 327, 333–4; Ingold, 2000, *The Perception of the Environment. Essays on Livelihood, Dwelling & Skill*, 189, 194.

6. Hough, 1829, *Letters on the Climate, Inhabitants, Productions, &C., &C., of the Neilgherries, or, Blue Mountains of Coimbatoor, South India*, 54–5.
7. Schama, 1995, *Landscape and Memory*, 547, 555–6, 559.
8. Jervis, 1834, *Narrative of a Journey to the Falls of the Cavery; with an Historical and Descriptive Account of the Neilgherry Hills*, 45–7.
9. Arnold, 2005, *The Tropics and the Traveling Gaze. India, Landscape, and Science 1800–1856*, 75.
10. Ibid., 2000, *Science, Technology, and Medicine in Colonial India*, 76–8. Arnold, however, notes a report of 1843 in which it is argued that temperate hill stations, too, were unsuitable for permanent settlement. Ibid., 2005, *The Tropics and the Traveling Gaze. India, Landscape, and Science 1800–1856*, 47–9.
11. See, for example, one of many reports of the Medical and Physical Society of Calcutta in *Asiatic Journal and Monthly Register for British India and Its Dependencies*, vol. 25, January–June 1828: 225–6.
12. Within a few years, the benefits of the Nilgiris were on the agenda of the Medical and Physical Society of Calcutta and, in 1829, the Government of Bombay recommended its officers to place their furlough in the hills. Ibid., and vol. 27, January–June 1829: 631; *Madras Government Gazette*, 13 March 1821, Extract of a letter from a correspondent on the Nilgherry Mountains, 3 March 1821, and 13 June 1822, Extract of a letter from Mr Assistant Surgeon John Jones to the Military Board of Bombay, 7 July 1821; OIOC, European Manuscripts, Thomas Munro Collection, vol. 28, Letters to Munro from John Sullivan, 1815–19, from Sullivan to Munro, 26 June 1817.
13. Grove, 1993, 'Conserving Eden. The (European) East India Companies and Their Environmental Policies on St. Helena, Mauritius and in Western India, 1660 to 1854', 322; Metcalf, 1994, *Ideologies of the Raj*, 171; Arnold, 2000, *Science, Technology, and Medicine in Colonial India*, 76.
14. Arnold, 2005, *The Tropics and the Traveling Gaze. India, Landscape, and Science 1800–1856*, 54–7.
15. Metcalf, 1994, *Ideologies of the Raj*, 92–112.
16. Mackworth, 1823, *Diary of a Tour through Southern India, Egypt and Palestine in the Years 1821 and 1822*, 125; Hough, 1829, *Letters on the Climate, Inhabitants, Productions, &C., &C., of the Neilgherries, or, Blue Mountains of Coimbatoor, South India*, published in the *Bengal Hurkaru* under the pseudonym Philanthropos, Coimbatoor, 3 November 1826, 65–6.
17. Ibid.

18. Ibid., 73–4.
19. Harkness, 1832, *A Description of a Singular Aboriginal Race Inhabiting the Summit of the Neilgherry Hills or the Blue Mountains of Coimbatoor, in the Southern Peninsula of India*, 8.
20. Shortt, 1868, *An Account of the Tribes on the Neilgherries*, 10.
21. Harrison, 2002, *Climates & Constitutions. Health, Race, Environment, and British Imperialism in India, 1600–1850*, 118–19.
22. BUL, Special Collections, Church Missionary Society, Rev. Marmaduke Thompson, 4, Letter from Thompson to D. Coates Esq., Nilgherry Hills, 10 August 1824; 6, Letter from D. Rosen to Coates, Nilgherry Hills, 7 October 1824. D. Rosen is noted as the author, but the handwriting, abbreviations and the way the letter has been filed suggest that the writer was in fact Thompson.
23. OIOC, European Manuscripts, Thomas Munro Collection, vol. 72, Letters from George Canning, John Sullivan, *et al.* 1818–26, from Sullivan to Munro, 30 January 1824.
24. Ranganatha or Rangaswami is one of the names for Vishnu. In the Nilgiris, it is generally associated with Irulas worship at a Vishnu temple on the Rangaswami Peak, located in the north-eastern part of the plateau.
25. Hough, 1829, *Letters on the Climate, Inhabitants, Productions, &C., &C., of the Neilgherries, or, Blue Mountains of Coimbatoor, South India*, 59–60, 63–6, *published in* Bengal Hurkaru *under the pseudonym Philanthropos, Coimbatoor, 3 November 1826.*
26. Harkness, 1832, *A Description of a Singular Aboriginal Race Inhabiting the Summit of the Neilgherry Hills or the Blue Mountains of Coimbatoor, in the Southern Peninsula of India*, 6–7, emphasis in the original.
27. BUL, Special Collections, Church Missionary Society, Rev. Marmaduke Thompson, 6, Letter from D. Rosen to Coates, Nilgherry Hills, 7 October 1824.
28. Ibid., 4, Letter from Thompson to D. Coates Esq., Nilgherry Hills, 10 August 1824.
29. For a comparison of missionary organizations' attitudes to non-monogamous marriages, see Berge, 2000, *The Bambatha Watershed. Swedish Missionaries, African Christians and an Evolving Zulu Church in Rural Natal and Zululand 1902–1910*, 64–6, 91–3, 232–4.
30. Hough, 1829, *Letters on the Climate, Inhabitants, Productions, &C., &C., of the Neilgherries, or, Blue Mountains of Coimbatoor, South India*, 7, Extract of a letter from Mons. Leschnault de la Tour, dated Pondicherry, 5 July 1819.

31. Lévi-Strauss, 1996, 'Introduction', 1–7; Arunima, 2003, *There Comes Papa. Colonialism and the Transformation of Matriliny in Kerala, Malabar, c. 1850–1940*, 11–13, 52–3.
32. Illustrations 1 and 2. Ill. 1 also published in Baikie 1934.
33. Margot Finn, lecture at Uppsala University, the Department of History, 6 April 2006.
34. Hough, 1829, *Letters on the Climate, Inhabitants, Productions, &C., &C., of the Neilgherries, or, Blue Mountains of Coimbatoor, South India*, 44–5, published in *Bengal Hurkaru* under the pseudonym Philanthropos, n.d.
35. Harkness, 1832, *A Description of a Singular Aboriginal Race Inhabiting the Summit of the Neilgherry Hills or the Blue Mountains of Coimbatoor, in the Southern Peninsula of India.*
36. Ibid., 160.
37. Walker, 1986, *The Toda of South India. A New Look*, 1–9, 294.
38. Brockway, 1979, *Science and Colonial Expansion. The Role of the British Royal Botanic Gardens*, 134 (quoting Rivers, 1906); Walker, 1986, *The Toda of South India. A New Look*, 240; Bird, 1987, 'The Kurumbas of the Nilgiris. An Ethnographic Myth?' 174; Mandelbaum, 1989, 'The Nilgiris as a Region', 4; Ibid., 1989, 'The Kotas in Their Social Setting'.
39. Rivers, 1906, *The Todas*, v, 11; Rivers, Firth and Schneider, 1968, *Kinship and Social Organization.*
40. Rivers, 1906, *The Todas*, 442.
41. Walker, 1986, *The Toda of South India. A New Look*, 7–9; Stocking, 1995, *After Tylor. British Social Anthropology, 1888–1951*, 189–93.
42. For two broader explorations of core issues in the debates, see Hall, 1994, 'Cultural Studies. Two Paradigms'; Ortner, 1994, 'Theory in Anthropology since the Sixties'.
43. Walker, 1986, *The Toda of South India. A New Look*, 61, 286.
44. OIOC, MBRP, 15 March 1819: 3279–82.
45. Walker, 1986, *The Toda of South India. A New Look*, 20–1. Father Fenicio's letter is quoted in translation in Rivers, 1906, App. I. See also Walker 1998: 1101–14.
46. 'A Topographical Description of the Neelaghery Mountains', report by William Keys to W. Garrows, Collector of Coimbatore, 1812, in Grigg, 1880, *The Manual of Nilagiri District*, App. 17.
47. Walker, 1998, *Between Tradition and Modernity and Other Essays on the Toda of South India*, 160.
48. Hough, 1829, *Letters on the Climate, Inhabitants, Productions, &C., &C., of the Neilgherries, or, Blue Mountains of Coimbatoor, South India*, 59–60;

Harkness, 1832, *A Description of a Singular Aboriginal Race Inhabiting the Summit of the Neilgherry Hills or the Blue Mountains of Coimbatoor, in the Southern Peninsula of India*, 18, 108, 110.; Bird, 1987, 'The Kurumbas of the Nilgiris. An Ethnographic Myth?', 177, referring to Mandelbaum, 1941, 'Culture Change among the Nilgiri Tribes', 19–26.

49. Walker, 1986, *The Toda of South India. A New Look*, 25.
50. See, for example, Hockings, 1980, *Ancient Hindu Refugees. Badaga Social History 1550–1975*, 136.
51. Rivers, 1906, *The Todas*, 694.
52. Harkness, 1832, *A Description of a Singular Aboriginal Race Inhabiting the Summit of the Neilgherry Hills or the Blue Mountains of Coimbatoor, in the Southern Peninsula of India*, 160; Zagarell, 2002, 'Gender and Social Organization in the Reliefs of the Nilgiri Hills', 78–9, 81, 103.
53. Most new tharavadus were established with the oldest female member as the head of the household, Kottayam being an important exception. Arunima, 2003, *There Comes Papa. Colonialism and the Transformation of Matriliny in Kerala, Malabar, c. 1850–1940*, 32–4.
54. After 1664: the Compagnie des Indes Orientales.
55. Frenz, 2003, *From Contact to Conquest. Transition to British Rule in Malabar, 1790–1805*, 11, 72.
56. Arunima, 2003, *There Comes Papa. Colonialism and the Transformation of Matriliny in Kerala, Malabar, c. 1850–1940*, 44–5; Frenz, 2003, *From* Contact to Conquest. Transition to British Rule in Malabar, 1790–1805, 11, 110–13; Menon, 2004, 'Colonial Constructions of "Agrarian Fields" and "Forests" in the Kolli Hills', 320.
57. OIOC, MRC, 1 February 1830, To The President and the Members of the Board of Revenue, from Pl. Coll. of Coimbatore J. Sullivan, and 1 March 1830.
58. Francis, 1908, *Madras District Gazetteers, the Nilgiris*, 102–3, 369–71; Hockings, 1980, *Ancient Hindu Refugees. Badaga Social History 1550–1975*, 38. Apart from secondary sources, Hockings refers to Barber, 1830, 'Journal of a Route to the Neelghurries from Calicut', 314–15; Ouchterlony, 1848, 'Geographical and Statistical Memoir of a Survey of the Neilgherry Mountains, under the Superintendence of Captain J. Ouchterlony, 1847', 82.
59. TNA, CDR, vol. 591: 35–7, To the Board of Revenue, from William Macleod, Collector, 27 October 1799. Ibid., App. 8: 42, Letter from Venket Row, at Weinaud, to Captain Macleod, 12–13 October 1799; Innes, 1908, *Madras District Gazetteers. Malabar and Anjengo*, vol. 1: 77. Arunima, 2003, *There Comes Papa. Colonialism and the Transformation*

of Matriliny in Kerala, Malabar, c. 1850–1940, 35; Frenz, 2003, *From Contact to Conquest. Transition to British Rule in Malabar, 1790–1805*, 112.

60. TNA, CDR, vol. 591: 35–7, App. 9: 56–8, To Dear Colonel from William Macleod, 2 December 1799. Ibid., App. 8: 42, Letter from Venket Row, at Weinaud, to Captain Macleod, 12–13 October 1799.
61. Ibid., To the Board of Revenue, from William Macleod, Collector, 27 October 1799. Ibid. App. 8: 42, Letter from Venket Row, at Weinaud, to Captain Macleod, 12–13 October 1799; Innes, 1908, *Madras District Gazetteers. Malabar and Anjengo*, vol. 1: 474. OIOC, MRC, 1 February 1830, App. B, no. 1: 1598–1600, The Arzee of Kulpully Karoonagara Menon Sherishtadar of the Survey Department; Frenz, 2003, *From Contact to Conquest. Transition to British Rule in Malabar, 1790–1805*, 115–25.
62. Malayalam Era.
63. The document was translated and transmitted together with the original (later to be returned to the Nambalacotta Waranoor) by W.E. Underwood, Act. Principal Collector of Canara, who surveyed the lands west of Ootacamund in order to determine the correct boundary between Coimbatore and Malabar districts. He calls it a 'Bamboo document' but it could well have been a palm–leaf document. OIOC, European Manuscripts, Walter Elliot Collection, Aboriginal Caste Book, vol. II, 15 January 1830, D318: 444, From W.E. Underwood, Act. Principal Collector of Canara to the Principal Collector of Coimbatore.
64. Ibid., App. 1: 445–6, From W.E. Underwood, Act. Principal Collector of Canara to the Principal Collector of Coimbatore.
65. The lowest-level government official, who represented a link between the colonial administration and an individual revenue village.
66. OIOC, European Manuscripts, Walter Elliot Collection, Aboriginal Caste Book, vol. II, 15 January 1830, App. 1: 444, From W.E. Underwood, Act. Principal Collector of Canara to the Principal Collector of Coimbatore.
67. On devasam, see also Frenz, 2003, *From Contact to Conquest. Transition to British Rule in Malabar, 1790–1805*, 18. OIOC, MRC, 1 February 1830, App. A, no. 1: 1594–7, Information given by four chetties ... inhabitants of Nabolacottah.
68. The word 'Menon' indicates that the sheristadar was a village accountant. Today, the temple is administered by the Nilambur temple association. Field notes, C.R. Sathyanarayanan, September 2005. OIOC, MRC, 1 February 1830: 1598–1600, B, no. 1. To W. Sheffield Esq., Pl. Coll. of Malabar, The Arzee of Kulpully Karoonagara Menon Sherishtadar of the Survey Department, 11 June 1829.

69. Ibid., App. 1, 'Information given by four chetties ...': 1594–7. Barber, 1830, 'Journal of a Route to the Neelghurries from Calicut', 314–15.
70. OIOC, MBRP, 23 October 1828: 10687–9, To the President and Members of the Board of Revenue, from John Sullivan, para 11. OIOC, MRC, 1 February 1830: 1585–93, To The President and the Members of the Board of Revenue, from Pl. Coll. of Coimbatore J. Sullivan, 31 December 1829, para 2; OIOC, MRC, 1 February 1830, App. 8, Translation of a Declaration given by Oochagounden aged 60 years late manigar of Toonary in Todanud on the Neelgherry Hills, 31 July 1829: 1610–13, and App. 7: 1609–10, Translation of an urzee addressed by the undermentioned inhabitants of Todanaud and Makenaud on the Neelgherries.
71. A less likely interpretation of the document would be that the sum was contributed as payment in kind equivalent to the sum of 120 old fanams. If so, it indicates that Toda produce was measured in monetary terms. As the original document is lost, the words, which have been translated into 'old fanams' cannot be traced.
72. See Frenz, 2003, *From Contact to Conquest. Transition to British Rule in Malabar, 1790–1805*, 17.
73. Arunima, 2003, *There Comes Papa. Colonialism and the Transformation of Matriliny in Kerala, Malabar, c. 1850–1940*, 47.
74. OIOC, MBRP, 23 October 1828: 10687–9, To the President and Members of the Board of Revenue, from John Sullivan, paras 11, 13.
75. Arunima, 2003, *There Comes Papa. Colonialism and the Transformation of Matriliny in Kerala, Malabar, c. 1850–1940*, 48.
76. Hockings, 1980, *Ancient Hindu Refugees. Badaga Social History 1550–1975*, 11–39.
77. Morrison, 2002, 'Pepper in the Hills. Upland-Lowland Exchange and the Intensification of the Spice Trade', 110–11, 114–15, 118.
78. Ibid., 119–21.
79. Zagarell, 2002, 'Gender and Social Organization in the Reliefs of the Nilgiri Hills', 80–1.
80. Ibid., 78–9.
81. Harkness, 1832, *A Description of a Singular Aboriginal Race Inhabiting the Summit of the Neilgherry Hills or the Blue Mountains of Coimbatoor, in the Southern Peninsula of India*, 105.
82. Ibid., 106.
83. See, for example, Anonymous, 1828, 'Medical and Physical Society of Calcutta'; Hough, 1829, *Letters on the Climate, Inhabitants, Productions, &C., &C., of the Neilgherries, or, Blue Mountains of Coimbatoor, South*

India, 7; Anonymous, 1832, 'The Neilgherry Hills'; Harkness, 1832, *A Description of a Singular Aboriginal Race Inhabiting the Summit of the Neilgherry Hills or the Blue Mountains of Coimbatoor, in the Southern Peninsula of India*, 19.

84. OIOC, MRC, 1 February 1830: 1600–3, App. C, no. 1, To W. Sheffield Esq. Pl. Coll. of Malabar, from B.J. Ward, Captain, Surveyor in Malabar, 8 June 1829. OIOC, MD, no. 43, 10 November 1830: 449–64, para 3, Report of Surgeon Annesley, 19 July 1829.
85. Harkness, 1832, *A Description of a Singular Aboriginal Race Inhabiting the Summit of the Neilgherry Hills or the Blue Mountains of Coimbatoor, in the Southern Peninsula of India*, 108.
86. Ibid., 111.
87. See, for example, Sullivan's long minute of 1835 to the Board of Revenue. OIOC, MRC, 6 October 1835, Sullivan's Minute, 20 August 1835, para 17. On Badaga use and cultivation of opium, see *Asiatic Journal and Monthly Register for British India and Its Dependencies*, 'Medical and Physical Society of Calcutta', vol. 25, January–June 1828: 225–6, and OIOC, President's Minutes of the 6 September 1829, Written in the margin of the minutes for OIOC, MD, 10 November 1830, no. 43, Fort St George Public Department para 2: 451–4.
88. Toda: marvs = 'labourer'. Hough 1829: 59–60, published in *Bengal Hurkaru* under the pseudonym Philanthropos, Coimbatoor, 3 November 1826; *Asiatic Journal and Monthly Register for British India and Its Dependencies*, vol. 25, January–June 1828, 225–6; OIOC, MRC, 6 October 1835, Sullivan's Minute, 20 August 1835, para 16.
89. See, for example, Pratap, 2000, *The Hoe and the Axe. An Ethnohistory of Shifting Cultivation in Eastern India*.
90. Pouchepadass, 1995, 'British Attitudes Towards Shifting Cultivation in Colonial South India. A Case Study of South Canara District 1800–1920', 140–1.
91. Ibid., 128, 146–7.
92. OIOC, President's Minutes of 6 September 1829, Written in the margin of the minutes for OIOC, MD, 10 November 1830, no. 43, Fort St George Public Department, para 2: 451–4.
93. Ibid.
94. For an example of an early British expedition for settling a colony on Madagascar in 1645–6, see Foster, 1912, 'An English Settlement in Madagascar in 1645–6'. The expedition eventually failed, a large number of people died of illness, starvation and hostile attacks from native neighbours. Less than a dozen of the 140 settlers returned to Britain.

I am grateful to Karen Middleton for drawing my attention to this study. OIOC, MD, 10 November 1830, no. 43, Fort St George Public Department, para 2, Letter from Court of Directors, 27 October 1830: 449–64, and President's Minutes of 6 September 1829: 451–4.

95. Hough, 1829, *Letters on the Climate, Inhabitants, Productions, &C., &C., of the Neilgherries, or, Blue Mountains of Coimbatoor, South India*, 74–5, published in *Bengal Hurkaru* under pseudonym Philanthropos, Coimbatoor, 3 November 1826, OIOC, MRC, 1 February 1830: 1585–93, To The President and the Members of the Board of Revenue, from Pl. Coll. of Coimbatore J. Sullivan, para 9.
96. BUL, Special Collections, Church Missionary Society, Rev. Marmaduke Thompson, 4, Letter from Thompson to D. Coates Esq., Nilgherry Hills, 10 August 1824; Ibid., 6, Letter from D. Rosen to Coates, Nilgherry Hills, 7 October 1824.
97. Ibid.
98. *Madras Government Gazette*, 13 June 1822, A medical report on the Nilgiri mountains, R. Orton, Asst. Surg. Madras, 2 January 1822; Hough, 1829, *Letters on the Climate, Inhabitants, Productions, &C., &C., of the Neilgherries, or, Blue Mountains of Coimbatoor, South India*, 59–60, 63–6, published in *Bengal Hurkaru* under pseudonym Philanthropos, Coimbatoor, 3 November 1826.
99. OIOC, MRC, 1 February 1830: 1585–93, To The President and the Members of the Board of Revenue, from Pl. Coll. of Coimbatore J. Sullivan, 31 December 1829, paras 20–1.
100. Ibid., paras 48–50.
101. Certain fees collected from produce in the mirasi system.
102. OIOC, MRP, 26 February 1835: 2237–43, no. 1, To the Principal Collector of Malabar, from John Sullivan, formerly Pl. Coll. of Coimbatore, 16 January 1835, paras 4–6.
103. Bird-David, 1997, 'The Nilgiri Tribal Systems. A View from Below', 17.
104. See, for example, Saravanan, 2006, 'Economic Exploitation of Forest Resources in South India During the Early 19th Century', 2–5.
105. Report of the Conservator of Forests, Madras Presidency, Annual Reports, 1859–60, para 3, App. E, Mudumalai, 1861–2, para 6, Nilgiri Forests, 1897, 8–9, The Mudumalai Range. Sutton, 2001, publicly available 2066, *Other Landscapes. Hill Communities, Settlers and State on the Colonial Nilgiris, c. 1820–1900*, 92–5.

3 *Negotiating Law*

There are no *pattas* (titles) for Todas, I am told, only permits. As the saying goes: if a Toda man gets a patta, he will immediately sell the land, which is not good for him or for the Toda community. Consequently, the Toda have permits that allow use of the land but prohibit its sale.

In Marlimund there is very little land and only a few sacred buffaloes. Government wastes that were earlier used for grazing are now planted with blue gum, pine, and eucalyptus, and buffalo rearing is greatly reduced. The road leading to the mund winds for part of the way through dense eucalyptus forest. On our way we pass small groups of women carrying large bundles of eucalyptus leaves, and further down in the valley below the mund a greyish wreath of smoke reveals the place where leaves are heated to produce oil.

Kaasi, who cultivates his father's three acres, is frustrated by the fact that it is so difficult to extend the area cultivated. In the last fifteen years, as chemicals and new seeds have replaced dung and old seed varieties, he

Ill. 4 Mr Kaasi in Marlimund
(Photo by the author.)

has seen yields decline and crops attacked by pests hitherto unknown. But chemical fertilizers and pesticides are expensive and the market is unreliable, so people are searching for more sustainable solutions that can be managed with limited means.

The Melgash patriclan tried another approach when they began to put some of their 65 acres of additional grazing land under the plough. The colonial government's decision to secure land to the munds, and not to individuals, proved to be to this patriclan's disadvantage, since they have only 4 munds. In all, they have permits to cultivate 27 acres of land, which must meet the needs of 64 families living in the 4 munds. However, a large portion of this area is uncultivable waste, and for a century one of the munds has largely been a major tourist attraction, located as it is at the top of the Botanical Garden in Ootacamund.

The patriclan's efforts are now focused on Porshe, a mund further south. Here there are 65 acres of grassy slopes for grazing, of which the Forest Department has planted two with acacia. The department's move is understood by the people as a slow and quiet extension of the reserved forest. They speak of the Forest Department as an unstoppable force against which arguments are of little use. Six months ago, when the Melgash men had taken things into their own hands and were making a boundary through the land for the purpose of cultivation, department officials arrived and stopped them. Since then, the matter has rested with the collector. People shake their heads in resignation.

'When the government agrees to do something for the people, other people in between cut in, so nothing comes of it.'

There are mixed feelings about the British colonial administration. No one can now formally take Toda land, since the British once wrote it into the documents as 'Toda patta'. But Kaasi explains that, once the British left, the land was sold to strangers even though it once belonged to the Toda.[1]

Competing for Conquered Territories

At times, the establishment of colonial rule has been described as the coming of troops and revenue collectors, the conquest of land with gunpowder and assessments. The enforcement of colonial law has been taken for granted. However, in the Nilgiris the trajectories of legal codification of land rights were characterized, rather, by negotiation. The administration may occasionally have been heavy-handed, but just as common were decisions made on the spot. These gave local administration a slightly arbitrary character. This situation was particularly characteristic of the first decade of British administration in the hills, when Europeans were both exploring the region and seeking to secure a bargain for themselves.

These explorations were not lawless—at least not in the sense that those who claimed land or resources did not care about the legal implications of their claims. On the contrary, Europeans secured what they believed to be legal status for their land claims from the district administration, which is why the district collector John Sullivan obtained an enclosure for himself of the nearly 2,000 acres he claimed to have purchased from the Toda through a decision of the governor.[2] But the legal principles on which people relied differed. Broadly speaking, some claimants looked on the Nilgiris as virgin land—*terra nullius*, land free of ownership, owing to the lack of permanent labour on it. Such empty lands were assumed to be up for grabs for anyone wanting to cultivate them. Others were concerned to establish whether there were ancient rights in the possession of the native population. In the latter case, if possession could be established since time immemorial, it would become a birthright. The administration's uncertainty about existing rights is well illustrated by voluminous correspondence on the subject. Time and again, reports were sent back for further enquiry, arguments were passed back and forth between government departments and district offices, and landholders, local people of influence, shifting cultivators, and pastoralists were called in to be questioned on the subject.

To understand the situation in terms of negotiation by no means implies that the different parties to land disputes had equal influence in the proceedings. Power relations were highly unequal, access to information was unevenly distributed, and, what is more, different notions prevailed as to what constituted a right. And yet all the people involved, including pastoralists and shifting cultivators, had *some* kind of influence over the codification of law. It is possible to argue that this was a 'zone of anomaly', to use Sivaramakrishnan's term: an ecological-political space in which the colonial administration had not yet secured or consolidated a unified polity. This would imply a situation in which regulations had been passed to reorganize the economy of a particular region, but their implementation had been thwarted; from the perspective of the colonial government, things were never in order.[3] Broadly speaking, it was a region in which colonial rule was still uncertain and questioned, and the term 'zone of anomaly' facilitates an understanding of social and ecological factors that shaped the idea of a political frontier in forest and hill tracts. As I will argue, it is in this broad sense that the term can be applied to the situation in the Nilgiris; a more specific use could give rise to a number of methodological problems.

Sivaramakrishnan writes that zones of anomaly emerged 'at different stages in colonial statemaking', which means that his term is founded within the notion of the colonial state, i.e. in the end result and the leading theme of the history he is investigating. Such zones were *not yet* fully part of the colonial state, but were constitutive of processes that led to its establishment. That is, although the term zone of anomaly should be seen as an argument against teleological and chronological models, it derives at the same time from a study of the larger process of state-making. Conceptually, the colonial state is thus taken for granted. There is therefore a risk of re-reading a consolidated colonial state and the situation that formed the basis for its durability back into earlier history, in much the same way as we, living in the twenty-first century and knowing that such a state came to be established, may make inferences about earlier history based on this knowledge. However, at the heart of the term lies a contradiction on which the term itself builds: namely, the anomalous situation in which people may not have foreseen a colonial state as either desirable or possible. They may not have thought of British officers as representatives of a (future) state, and many EIC officers themselves may have perceived the building up of a state-like administration as a threat to their own trade, and therefore tried to counteract its establishment. My point is not to question the analytical use of the term zone of anomaly in the rear-view mirror of history, but to draw attention to the blinkers that it may put on an understanding of people's acts and perceptions, which are unlikely to have been guided by the notion of a future colonial state at all.

It is certainly a challenge to find priorities other than the establishment of colonial rule in the colonial administrative documentation, which at every point had the aim of securing power in a specific situation—be it for the sake of a trade agreement, a land settlement or a military conquest. However, as will become apparent, owing to the character of the conflict over land within the administration and the endeavour to settle it according to the principles of law, ethnographic surveys and depositions taken for the purpose of collecting information about 'native' ideas of rights piled up over the years. As both sides in the conflict between the district and government administrations had substantial resources with which to pursue their causes, the interests they represented filtered through into the investigations. They were, so to speak, searching for different answers in support of different interests. And while people may not have understood or bothered about the biases in questionnaires, they explained their motives and claims over and over again from different points of view, in the hope of securing what they believed to be their rights. Furthermore, as people in the Nilgiris were in a sense also competing for land within the boundaries of existing social arrangements, the Badaga cultivators, in particular, appear to have found an avenue to secure land through the British. For the historian, this has left a variety of documentation in the form of highly detailed accounts and correspondence.

Until recently, most historiographies of the Nilgiris tended to focus on Sullivan, either as villain or hero, but always as a strong man. Casting Sullivan as the main character has often given land conflicts the appearance of a vendetta between headstrong individuals. However, a consideration of the interests which he defended (interests that were not merely personal) reveals deep rifts in the colonial settlement of land. In the first instance, these were conflicts about ultimate authority in the Nilgiris. In principle, the bureaucracy of the EIC did not allow for private initiatives by its administrators. The process of decision-making was hierarchical and clear. But day-to-day implementation, in particular in the newly conquered regions, required a good deal of improvisation and left room for solutions that could eventually benefit individual officers, not least those who took advantage of the situation.

The Nilgiris were no exception. Since the territory had no strategic military importance and the forests on the plateau were of little commercial value, it mainly drew the attention of entrepreneurs seeking agricultural land or adventurers who came to experience the climate, landscape, and 'exotic' people. This situation resulted in the first decade being one of slightly lax hierarchical control, allowing the district collector and the commander of the hills, who came to reside in the Nilgiris, to take decisions on land, revenue, and the construction of minor buildings quite independently. From the late 1820s, however, complaints began to turn up in the administration files in Madras about mismanagement and lack of attention to the administration of the district as a whole, particularly as Sullivan preferred to stay in the hills rather than in the district headquarters on the Coimbatore plains. His defence is a manifestation of local politics. He angrily explained to Thomas Munro that he worked hard for a man of weak constitution and why he wanted to prevent the critical officers from visiting the Nilgiris.[4]

By the end of the decade, with different European interests in the region beginning to collide, the faultlines began to show and the district, presidency, and central administrations of the EIC began to defend their interests. They all found cause to claim authority over the Nilgiris as a legal entity, but on quite different grounds. The district administration argued that its expertise in the region should give it the final say on the settlement of rights. The Madras government claimed sovereignty as rulers and called on the district administration to fall in line with its decisions. Soon, as the conflicts reached the highest echelons of the Company and the Court of Directors intervened, the focus of the debate had shifted to more profound ideas about rights in property and how to govern the new British subjects of the Madras Presidency. Before moving on to processes of legal codification of rights in the Nilgiri Hills, we will therefore look more closely at the major dividing lines in these legal debates that set the agenda for many discussions about specific local rights.

From 1799 when the EIC seized the Mysore state and the Nilgiris were made part of Coimbatore district, until around 1820 when Europeans began to settle in the Nilgiris, the main purpose of the Madras administration was to secure peace, land, and revenue. Even before the Mysore state had finally fallen, revenue assessments were organized in the conquered territories in which Mysore had progressively lost control. In the settlement of the region that was to become Coimbatore district, the superintendent of revenue Alexander Read tried out a revenue system intended to get to grips with a situation in which income was urgently needed but in which the Mysore *amildar* revenue officers had lost all credibility among the population. The system was therefore based on a direct relationship between the cultivator and the revenue administration. On paying an annually fixed assessment, the cultivator received a title (patta) to a particular plot of land. This system formed the foundation for the ryotwari system elaborated by Thomas Munro, and which came to have a strong proponent in Sullivan. It bypassed all the supposedly corrupt middlemen who, he complained, were swarming all over Coimbatore district. In 1816, after two years on a mission to sort out revenue assessment in the district, Sullivan wrote to Munro: 'I find they [the amildars] have been sitting at their Causbas [revenue villages], making the settlement with the Curnams and Monigars [village accountants and administrative servants], and taking no notice whatever of the means of the Ryots to pay it—scarcely a Pattah has been given away in the districts hence all is uproar and confusion.'[5]

The ryotwari system under Munro as governor of Madras provided district collectors with direct control over land. Munro also bestowed far-reaching judicial authority on the collectors, and the combination of judicial power and direct control over revenue suited Sullivan's independent way of administering the Nilgiris once he had taken to living permanently in the hills from 1822. As collector he was expected to survey the land and establish land relations, and his posthumous reputation has made him known as a defender of Toda rights. But before 1828 no customary rights were ever questioned in the Nilgiris. Until then the Toda and their buffalo economy and authority over land had been considered merely for their ethnographic interest. The land required for European or Indian buildings had been made available by Sullivan with little in the way of official procedure. By the late 1820s, though, the government was wanting to assume control over the granting of land, and Sullivan responded by requesting a limit to European expansion into Toda land, arguing that the Toda had immemorial rights. This was an argument that immediately tied the Nilgiris into the British legal debate.[6]

During this period in Britain, many customary-based common rights disappeared and manorial wastelands were defined as private property as the process of enclosure reached its climax. The notion of custom, the rights of common, and common law were fundamental to the British legal system and, as has been well shown, this transformation of man–land and ruler–subject relations was riddled with conflict. However, the situation was not carried over lock, stock, and barrel into the Indian debate. On the contrary, both proponents and opponents of customary rights in land pointed to the differences between the British Isles (mostly implying England) and India. The arguments advanced for upholding such rights did, though, emphasize the authority of legal principles within the growing British empire. When Britain became greater, incorporating new territories, the number of subjects under British jurisdiction also increased. It followed that all subjects should enjoy the same rights, irrespective of where in the empire they lived. Arguments against respecting customary rights in India also referred to differences, but with the conclusion that such differences should be bridged not by law but by progress. To those critical of customary rights, custom represented an irrational judicial confusion which complicated and, for the most part, made impossible progressive legal reform.

In the general legal debate, there was a strong concern with territory. At the level of principles, territorial expansion on other continents became a theoretical and philosophical problem of combining seemingly irreconcilable rights, the chief one being the rights of conquest. How could the right to establish an empire avoid violating the liberty of the conquered? As long as the empire was established only over the seas, the freedom of commerce maintained the fine balance between imperial expansion and the liberty of all. But once the claim and right to territory, *dominium*, included expansion on land, it infringed the rights of others, their *libertas*, requiring justification. Roman law being the basis of British law, the notion of the Roman imperium had a profound influence on the British legal debate. David Armitage has noted that the Roman legacy of imperium to early modern Europe and, ultimately, to the British empire was a combination of three founding notions: one denoted independent authority or sovereign rule and jurisdiction, another described a territorial unit, and the third provided a justification for these claims in history.[7]

However, before sovereign rule could be established over a particular territory, it had to be ascertained whether or not there were indigenous populations who could prove rights of possession in the land. Alan Frost has pointed out three ways in which, according to theory, a European state could acquire land in the mid eighteenth century. Two of these acknowledged indigenous rights of possession. The indigenous population could either be persuaded to submit to European overlordship, or else the right to settle on part of the land could be purchased from local inhabitants. If it could be established, though, that no person was in permanent occupation of the land—this being proved by cultivation, enclosure, or sovereign government—the land was assumed to be empty of rights. The land did not have to be without people to be without rights, but according to this logic rights were tied to permanent labour on the land. Consequently, people who were not permanently settled, such as pastoralists or shifting cultivators, were by definition without rights in land. Such land became *terra nullius*, literally 'no person's land'; in effect land without ownership and territory that could be justly claimed by a state or a person who intended to establish permanent labour on the land.[8] As is so often the case, however, the discrepancy between theory and practice is demonstrated by the many examples of native inhabitants who were subjected to crude force and less-than-noble elaborations of legal principles. In practice, European land claims were often a matter of finding the means to establish occupation and property.

Returning to the specific debates about the Nilgiris, British agrarian transformation had implications for the principles that were argued among Company officials in India, at board meetings, in investigations and reports, and in the British Parliament. We may distinguish two major contradictions that were common in these debates, one concerning rights in land and resources, the other relating to the utility of nature.

In the fundamental debates about rights, the arguments put forward contrasted the local with the national, or the vernacular with the universal. On the one hand the exclusive rights of subjects according to native custom were guarded against intrusion. Such rights derived from having dwelt in a particular territory in unquestioned authority for longer than anyone could remember, i.e. time immemorial. Land was in these circumstances a birthright. The counterposition rested on the principles of government and sovereignty. Irrespective of whether a subject could prove a particular right in land, such rights were considered subordinate to the superior principle of sovereign government. As will be explained, ascertaining governance in a specified territory according to this principle implied subduing a whole range of rights under a sovereign.

Following logically from this discussion is the question of the value and utility of nature. In practice, it became a matter of defining to whom the preferential right of deciding on such issues belonged. Which group or interest had the ultimate right to determine land and resource use? One position focused on 'aboriginal' livelihoods and native use of land and natural resources, the other put the case for the 'public need' as this was defined by the colonial government.

As a rule, proponents of aboriginal rights and the importance of respecting native custom were to be found within the district and local administrations of the Company, while the Madras government argued forcefully in favour of utilizing nature and organizing the landscape in accordance with 'the public good'. However, disagreements were not restricted to the question of the vernacular *versus* the universal, or the aboriginal *versus* the new progressive British subject. They also extended to who those aboriginal or native subjects were. If we continue to define the extreme positions and focus on the Nilgiris, both rested on racial conceptions of people. The former used ethnological arguments to prove the Toda's aboriginality and lordship. They could thereby defend absolute rights in land for the Toda, and the racial argument was used in an inclusive way. The latter used ethnological arguments in an exclusive way to prove Toda subordination and subjecthood to Company rule. By this logic, the Toda would only be granted user rights under Company sovereignty.

Asserting Legal Rights

As was touched upon in Chapter 2, just before Sullivan left office as collector of Coimbatore district in 1830 there was a heated dispute between his administration and those of the Madras government and Malabar district on the correct boundary between the two districts. The government and the Malabar collector wanted the boundary moved further east, cutting into the Nilgiri territory of Coimbatore district. In a firmly worded note from the government to the revenue board, among other arguments designed to disprove the Coimbatore claim is a statement about the Toda. It was intended to demonstrate the weak substance not only of their claims to land, but also to any involvement in decision-making on their part. Surprisingly, in spite of all the government investigations in which the Toda had been key informants on account of their knowledge,[9] the government now concentrated on their lack of such knowledge and, furthermore, on their society and form of livelihood as disqualifications:

> These poor men are continually migrating from one part to another, have no fixed habitation, no settled rules of life, no written laws, no taste for agricultural pursuits, no population which presses on their means of subsistence, and no taxes which cannot be paid with the greatest ease; and if there is any class of people to whom a more free and enlarged intercourse with the inhabitants of the adjoining countries, and with settlers in their own, can be beneficial, it is surely those who will receive knowledge, clothing, and [be] better supplied, in the place of ignorance, nakedness and discomfort.[10]

Representing as it does the views of one of the parties in the dispute about authority over land settlements, this statement reflects several of the core principles that were contested in the legal debate. These 'poor men' were, in effect, claimed to be subjects of a benevolent British government. They were said to have great freedoms, light taxes, and plentiful resources. But they had as yet failed to realize the benefits of submitting to the care of government. In the eyes of the government, they still lacked the most essential features of civil life: sedentary agricultural labour and written laws. Reminiscent of the political and ideological justification for conquest in North America and Australia was the Madras government's argument that land was plentiful. The Toda could therefore share it with cultivators, particularly as buffalo herding was considered to be an inefficient use of land. In what Thomas Flanagan terms the 'agricultural argument' (in his study of the ideological rhetoric of conquest over Native American land), land was looked upon as a common property resource just waiting to be enclosed for cultivation. European appropriation was considered just on the grounds that Native Americans did not need all the land; they neither used all of it nor owned it since they were hunters, not agriculturists. This argument resembles a core element of the Madras government's position in 1830.[11] 'If there is any description of people by whom, more than by others, the occupation of a small portion of land by strangers should be regarded as a matter of indifference and not as an object of jealousy, it is the wandering herdsmen of the Hills.'[12] And the secretary went on to state that Sullivan 'set up a preposterous claim on the part of a small body of herdsmen to the absolute proprietary right in the soil ... no part of which they have ever brought under cultivation, and whose rights, if they ever had any, he was the first to violate when he deliberately applied to Government for sanction to enclose 500 Bullas or 2,000 acres of waste land on the Nilgherries.'[13]

The Toda had, in effect, forfeited their rights in land by not putting the plough to the ground. In the Nilgiris, the arguments put forward, whether in support of the district or the government position, rested on this notion of property. As an ideological principle the right of personal security, liberty, and property was forcefully argued both in Britain and in their dominions overseas. It was, from one point of view, the baseline of common law as indirectly referred to by district and local interests, and from the other an absolute right of a sovereign government. This also indicates that the notion of property was unclear and could be referred to and claimed on very different grounds. Some references remind us of 'allodial' tenure without an overlord, referring however not to a feudal lord but to a government or state. Other references speak, rather, of property as tenure in a commercial economy. Robert Gordon's reading of the general political rhetoric of the eighteenth century leads him to conclude that the different historical sources on the ideology of property converged 'sloppily' in the modal form of property as dominion. Its claim to be an absolute individual right expanded beyond the private possession, disposition, and alienation of land to include any type of potentially valuable expectance and, ultimately, political rights. In the American Revolution, liberty itself was property—or meant having a freehold.[14]

Furthermore, during the agrarian transformation in Britain, in which land relations were fundamentally changed, there were competing jurisdictions that recognized conflicting rights in the same property. There were also discrepancies between legal arguments, which pursued a certain logic, and the multifaceted realities of privileged access to land and resources. As Gordon argues, the limited sphere of absolute dominion rights in Britain was riddled with ambiguities and conflicts that would disrupt any project to enforce a singular system of property rights. Needless to say, there was no single British policy on property that could be implemented in India. It is therefore no surprise to find administrators at different levels in the EIC bureaucracy seeking to protect property using arguments that appear to have been drawn from opposite ideological ends of the legal spectrum—as indeed they were.[15]

This situation highlights the problems that arise when a government or a state claims sovereignty over a specific territory by means of universal principles and codes. According to the logic which has been theoretically argued by James Scott for high-modernist authoritarian states, and empirically explored in India—for example in the many studies of scientific forestry—a modern state searches for singularity and simplification through large-scale schemes. The British colonial state is often referred to as the obvious case of a state attempting to implement a singular law and bureaucracy over large territories comprising different regions with different histories, polities, and legal systems.[16] To the extent that this endeavour is evident before the restructuring and strengthening of state institutions in the 1860s, such policies tended to collide with complex realities. At the level not only of legal practice but also of legal principles, laws had to be regionally renegotiated. During the legal codification of rights in landed property, native custom had to be negotiated against universal principles.

Neeladri Bhattacharya's study of the fundamental debates about and codification of customary law in Punjab clearly illustrates the complexity of the British legal elaboration of Indian 'tradition'. Bhattacharya shows how the legal debate changed over time by comparing Orientalist discourses of the late eighteenth century with imperial debates of the late nineteenth. Throughout the nineteenth century there remained the two opposing strands of, on the one hand, a search for an authentic Indian legal tradition and, on the other, a progressive utilitarian move to replace dysfunctional native law with a new social order systematized into a single universal code, enacted by government. According to Bhattacharya this opposition did not disappear under the British imperial government, but the methods for establishing tradition changed. While in the late eighteenth century ancient texts had been the medium of access to immemorial Indian custom, a hundred years later information from surveys and local Punjabi informants had long been established. This was now read against common law theory. And yet, although custom remained a significant structuring principle under imperial rule, emphasizing the specificities of region (as Bhattacharya shows, colonial perceptions of Punjabi tradition varied significantly from those of Bengali tradition), the concepts and categories of the surveys reveal the systematic logic of the imperial government: 'Beneath the audible voice of the preserver [of tradition and custom] was the hidden transcript of the Utilitarian reformer.' Thus, while there was a profound change towards the universal principles of legal codes in the late nineteenth century, the notion of custom and tradition, which made legal codes relative to colonial understandings of regions and people, remained in place.[17]

The contrast between those who advocated acknowledgement of customary and traditional rights in property and those who argued for universal principles of property was therefore not a matter of custom *versus* reason. In one way or another, native custom had in practice to be accommodated, even within utilitarian-informed principles. When the Madras government, seeking to deny the native population of the Nilgiris proprietary rights in land, remarked that the Toda had no written laws, it may be seen simply as the intent to label them uncivilized. However, in a stricter sense, it was designed to establish their lack of a legal position from which to negotiate with the government. Regardless of the traditions the Toda or, for that matter, the Badaga could refer to as the basis for asserting absolute rights in land, the government argued back that they had no inscribed set of codes against which their claims could be assessed.

Protecting Subjects' Rights against Absolute Rule

Bhattacharya's point is important for any study of the legal settlement of rights in early-nineteenth-century India. At times, the terminology in historical studies of conflict in forest and hill tracts becomes a bit blurred when 'custom' or 'customary law' is discussed. Almost without exception, the term custom is used to denote systems of indigenous or tribal rights, in contrast with colonial law. Despite the fact that British property law rested to a large extent on the notion of custom, the term is used as a counterpoint to a British legal system of administration, which is assumed to be guided by enlightened reason and utilitarian ideas.

Prior to the introduction of Cornwallis's system of administration in Bengal in the late eighteenth century, the EIC policy was one of non-interference with indigenous institutions. The reason was more practical than ideological. And although a change in administrative terms could be seen earlier than this, it was with Cornwallis that a system of government based on English bureaucratic principles was introduced in law reforms and administration. Without going into the details of the Permanent Settlement of 1793 and the ryotwari system, we may note that both sought to correct faults caused by what was thought of as native political practice. Cornwallis's system instituted bars against the 'Oriental despotism' adopted by the EIC. This was effected by separating civil and military powers, thereby preventing government abuse. The powers of government were to be reduced and counterbalanced, and order was to be secured in the freedom of landed property. In contrast, the ryotwari system removed all zamindari and other 'feudal' middlemen from the administration of land and revenue. In the Munro doctrine, government was to rest on trust among the native population, which would be gained by uniting the 'liberal policy of a European state' with Asiatic monarchy. In the Fifth Report of the Select Committee on EIC affairs, Munro argued from his experience of settling the Ceded Districts that the ryotwari system was in effect an expression of Indian custom and that no other system could be permanent.[18]

Rooting the ryotwari system in custom reflected the fundamentals of common law. Custom being deeply rooted in the legal discourse and common rights in Britain, legal practice varied from place to place depending on locality, landscape, and nature. According to common law, both the lord's absolute right in land and the tenants' right to use the commons were protected by the king. As common rights were granted in return for labour services and rent, these rights were appendant to the land and land could not be sold or partitioned without them. It was generally agreed among all shades of political opinion that the right of property could only be alienated by consent and that all British subjects were entitled to have their property regulated by common law. However, this principle became a cause of great concern when viewed in an imperial perspective. As P.J. Marshall observes, British legal authorities doubted that all aspects of common law were applicable to the colonies, not least when such rights were claimed for subjects of non-British origin.[19] This situation explains why the regulation of land rights in a region as limited as the Nilgiris came to be so widely observed and required such extensive elaboration. When the logic of common law was argued for a group of pastoralists it was, in effect, argued for British subjects and could have repercussions for subjects elsewhere within the empire. As will become clear, in the Nilgiris arguments in support of Toda rights were founded on the notion of property as a birthright and on the strong rights of lords, secured in common law.

But even if common law was expected to protect 'real' rights, such as specific landholdings, the legal system also reflected changes in an increasingly commercial economy in which the rights of the landed elite were affected. David Lieberman dates the transformation of land law due to the impact of commerce much earlier than the commonly discussed market capitalism of the nineteenth century. But for our purposes it suffices to conclude that, in the appropriation of new territories on other continents, British merchants and EIC officers were unable to firmly invoke an unquestioned body of land law. At the same time, the situation allowed them to elaborate the implications of the law for their own purposes.[20]

Furthermore, British legal culture was internally diverse. It encompassed the fundamentally different traditions of Scottish and English law, and the distinctly different but coexisting structures of manorial, customary, equitable, common law, and statutory courts. The common law system was fiercely defended as a bulwark against absolutism—an argument that fed into Orientalist criticisms of Indian Oriental despots. But rhetorical forcefulness should not be taken as a description of actual situations, as these were arguments voiced in a situation of diversity.[21]

This means that there was little political scope to question common law on an ideological basis or to claim it was invalid. At the same time, through practice, common law was continuously being adjusted to meet the new requirements arising from major economic and political transformations. From the late eighteenth century, in the heyday of enclosure, the English courts increasingly decided against user rights derived from custom, since they stood in the way of 'improvement'. Much potentially rich land would lie waste unless labourers were made available to cultivate it, and this could only be achieved if common rights were detached from land. Jeanette Neeson notes that critics of the commons wanted to develop the British nation and change the structure of rural England. In this agrarian transformation, 'lazy commoners' were targeted for their 'beggarly independence'. User rights once permitted to commoners—with their local variations depending on the ecology, land types and wealth of the region—allowed common people an income and livelihood in addition to what they could derive from labour and from such land as they possessed. Consequently, in regions where pasture was abundant, such as forests, fens, marshes, heaths, and coastal plains, there were also large numbers of commoners. These lands were now increasingly coming into focus from the standpoint of the progress that was assumed to be inherent in closing and fencing them, thus detaching common rights from the land and making the right of common illegal. What was legally protected as common land and common rights in specific lands was gradually being redefined. Over time, wastelands ceased to be accessible to commoners, but came into the realm of either the public—a domain defined by the state—or the private. Without established ownership in such land, it became free for purchase. David Armitage notes that land defined as vacant (*vacuum domicilium*) was a standard basis for dispossessing indigenous peoples in Britain from the 1620s, and became a regular legal argument for doing the same on other continents well into the nineteenth century.[22] Neeson argues that economic growth on a broad front was the ultimate aim of the proponents of transformation. People who were not available for farm labour, and who were relatively independent of wages, implied a threat to such an agrarian economy, and only the exclusive enjoyment of property would create a proletariat and ensure economic growth.[23] As John Brewer and Susan Staves observe, 'property rights are rights "against" other people, rights to exclude them from the use and enjoyment of the things owned'. Accordingly, property is necessarily relational, 'conceivable only in the context of communities of people', and its introduction is a process of exclusion.[24]

Reflections of debates on British land rights can be seen in the correspondence from the Nilgiris. The rights of pastoralists and shifting cultivators could either be supported by reference to the free and independent English peasant, or be opposed by invoking the image of the commoning peasant wastefully draining public resources. Different interests could be protected, without dismissing common law, by relying either on the logic inherent in the rights of commoners or on the protection of individual property. Critics who sought to discredit common rights took their line of reasoning to another level in both countries. Referring to the agrarian transformation in England, the importance of introducing private individual property has been stressed also for the introduction of capitalist relations in India. Interestingly, Neeson identifies a different argument advanced during the enclosure process. It justified enclosure on the grounds that 'improvers', enclosers, and critics of the commons were advocating social restructuring for the sake of the nation, i.e. to improve society and the agrarian economy. In order to achieve such progress, an attack on the individual became possible. Neeson argues that this was not a celebration of the individual above the community, but a process whereby individual property rights became subordinate to the 'national interest'. Peasants exercising common or customary rights in land through gleaning and grazing could now be accused of selfish individualism, of being thieves threatening the national interest. The individualist was, in fact, robbing the state of resources that ought rightfully be redistributed to meet public needs as defined by the government. Ultimately, the legitimation of enclosure did establish private property rights and produce a labour force, much to the benefit of the enclosers, but in order to achieve this end the common rights economy had to be denigrated.[25]

This argument in support of the nation developed alongside the European wars of the late eighteenth century. The mechanism for enclosure—Private Acts that enabled enclosers to avoid negotiating with landless users of commons and evade most compensation payments—was already established in the early eighteenth century but became most useful in the 1790s, during the wars, when Parliament sensed the urgent need to cultivate the country's wastelands.[26] Many of the statements in these parliamentary debates bear a strong similarity to comments about the lazy Toda cattle herder watching over his buffaloes day in day out, cultivating nothing and producing no revenue. But in contrast to the British rhetoric, those who argued against Toda property rights in India did not envisage a nation or a national interest. It was not contended that people in the hill tracts of South India were part of an extended British nation. The ground for rejecting Toda property claims was argued as the public duty of government, a core argument among utilitarians. Representatives of the Madras government mostly framed their arguments in terms of the public good. In view of the public, 'a small body of herdsmen' had no rights.

Deploying this logic, H.J. Chamier, secretary to the Madras government, criticized Sullivan for misrule. Sullivan had not ensured 'the just protection of the Todawars and other classes of the people in the enjoyment of all the rights to which they are really entitled in the manner most conducive to the public good'.[27] He went on to instruct the collector of Malabar, who was in charge of the region after it became part of that domain:

> This is a point of such importance to all the salutary objects intended in forming a settlement upon the Hills that the Right Honourable the Governor in Council cannot permit any further alienation of the Company's wastes or woods without further information, and ... the Right Honourable the Governor in Council desires that his [the Malabar collector's] special attention may be directed to the opinions of Sir Thomas Munro that he may be the better enabled to give to the Hill people more correct notions of what they are entitled to than they appear to have received from Mr Sullivan.[28]

Large tracts of land controlled by people with no interest in cultivation and unavailable for public purposes were not conducive to the public good. Nor would such tracts secure the enforcement of Company sovereignty, which was supposed to protect Indian subjects from misrule by indigenous masters.

The overall mechanism for this supposed redistribution of resources for the public good in India was land revenue, which of course depended on the existence of landholders able to pay it. In the Nilgiris, one of the purposes of many subsequent surveys was to establish the existence of specific rights in particular lands. Munro saw that the prevailing and uncodified legal system based on custom obstructed the successful operation of the ryotwari revenue system. Law based on custom implied local differences and irregularity. In contrast, revenue assessment required regularity, fixed categories, and general applicability; anything else would have been inefficient. In Britain, the law secured property, not revenue; so the fact that in India law was made for the sake of revenue was itself anomalous.[29] However, in the Nilgiris the question was not so much of revenue income as of land rights. During these early years the amount of revenue that could be obtained from the pastoralists and cultivators in the hills was never large. Therefore the imperative was to establish absolute control of nature as property.[30]

In the wider perspective of large-scale revenue systems designed to address the question of financial income for Presidency governments, such as the ryotwari and permanent settlement systems, a brief look at studies of early colonial administration in other regions is useful. In his study of ecological transformations caused by the enforcement of the permanent settlement in deltaic Orissa, Rohan D'Souza emphasizes the devastating effects of introducing capitalist market relations and private property in land. He contrasts flexible revenue administrations under Maratha and Mughal rulers, which were sensitive to local agricultural conditions such as seasonal changes and agrarian regimes, with an inflexible British revenue system. Under the latter, cultivators faced non-negotiable rent payments and zamindars' taxes were fixed by contract. D'Souza argues that while the Mughals and Marathas were embedded in rural society, letting the agrarian economy work through a system of rural alliances, the EIC needed to turn land into a commodity from which to extract revenue; they treated it as a purely economic form.[31]

It has been quite common to emphasize the economic aspect of the deep transformations that took place when the EIC consolidated its rule. In consequence, aspects of political power or governance have been somewhat downplayed or treated as a byproduct of the former. Since the Nilgiris were so obviously a poor source of revenue, the nature of governance here stands out more clearly; it may even be argued that establishing revenue was a tool of governance. The ryotwari system was first tried out in Coimbatore district during the last Anglo-Mysore war in the 1790s, when this southern part of Mysore state had been conquered. The long-term ecological effects of the introduction of land titles for small farmers in the Coimbatore highlands can certainly be compared with the logic of transformations arising from the new revenue system in Orissa. In Coimbatore district, the dominant producers were cattle breeders who did not use land in the manner of a cultivator dependent on the soil alone. But over the following generations, increasing numbers of small farms generated by the ryotwari settlement caused partial deforestation and the region became increasingly dependent on irrigation from deep wells.[32]

However, the ryotwari system was not completely insensitive to the situation in Coimbatore district. The *bhurty* or shifting system reflected the existence of both shifting cultivation and pastoralism in revenue assessment categories. This allowed a cultivator to hold up to five times the area of land shown in his patta. The *ayan* or grass allowance was a low-taxed piece of land not exceeding one-fifth of a person's holding. The grazing patta referred to land to which the holder had a preferential right. Such land was granted at a fourth of the usual assessment and could be held until required for cultivation.[33]

The idea of separate categories for shifting cultivation and pasturage was applied in the Nilgiris, too. As late as 1842, the Board of Revenue warned the Malabar collector against changing the system, since low-country practices were found to be unsuitable and premature for the hills. The board was 'averse to sanctioning an innovation which would be very unpalatable, merely for the sake of effecting greater regularity of Revenue management'.[34] In the hills, sensitivity to local custom was thus given priority over the needs of regularity for the sake of an efficient revenue system.

In spite of what appears to be forceful rhetoric, and what became forceful methods of implementation, British debates on South India emphasized the role of trust. Securing the consent of people or, rather, of patrons in India was one of Munro's major concerns. The Toda were definitely not such patrons. While one party in the EIC administration referred to the need for consent, arguing that they represented Toda rights, their opponents did not consider such consent necessary since they claimed to know already what was best for pastoralists. However, during the conflicts that arose in the 1830s from European immigration and claims to land in the Nilgiris, the Court of Directors found cause to remind the government of Madras of the importance of maintaining legal principles for the sake of securing the confidence of subjects in just government.[35]

Munro's concern not to provoke discontent among people under British control is evident in his communications. For example, his suggestion for keeping the Bhils of West India under control is clear in this regard. The Bhils were a people with substantial sovereignty, claiming kingship status, who raided the plains and whom the British were attempting to pacify. Though he described them as 'a miserable race, poor and few in numbers', Munro asserted: 'I see no reason to expect disturbances from any of the native states now surrounded by our territory ... well treated, they will in a few years become as quiet as any of our other Indian subjects.'[36] In 1826 Munro circulated John Malcolm's instructions to his assistants and officers. These instructions were intended to strengthen feelings of patriotism among Indians in relation to the benevolent government of strangers. The watchwords were tolerance, justice, and wisdom. The moral defects of the natives were 'to be referred to that misrule and oppression from which they are now in a great degree emancipated'. The text is a piece of classical Orientalism: Malcolm argues that Hindu institutions, particularly caste, which raised society in 'a remote period' had also kept it stationary at that point of early advancement. To inspire confidence and trust, British officers were now instructed to consider Indians as equals, though preserving European manners among themselves, 'for to adopt their manners is a departure from the very principle on which every impression of our superiority that rests upon good foundation is grounded'.[37]

These concerns were certainly pragmatic in nature—discontent may cause rebellion, and Munro was anxious to ensure the safe consolidation of the British territories—but they also had an ideological resonance deriving from Scottish political thought. Among Munro's contemporaries in India were Mountstuart Elphinstone and John Malcolm. Having reached high military ranks and been appointed governors of Madras and Bombay, they were among the most successful middle- and upper-ranking Scots who made a career in the Company.[38] In her study of the influence of Scottish Enlightenment ideas on the thinking of Munro, Elphinstone, and Malcolm, Martha McLaren describes the three as an important and progressive leadership cadre that shared a Scottish school of thought on Indian government: their ideas were 'a clearly articulated system of political economy on lines specified by Adam Smith, David Hume, and other Scottish writers.'[39] A more common interpretation of British rule in India in the early nineteenth century is to describe the exercise of power as authoritarian and label it as exercised by a military state. David Washbrook points to the deviation, even departure, from the civil government of Cornwallis once Munro, Malcolm, Metcalfe, and Elphinstone returned from the battlefields and came to dominate provincial governments. He argues that military imperatives dictated economic policy, backed by an extremely powerful state economy based on land revenue. The role of government that he describes is one which, without hesitation, adopted the principles of Oriental despotism.[40]

McLaren by contrast states that Munro, Elphinstone, and Malcolm saw military rule as a necessary but temporary system of government.

It was only by securing the 'good-will of the people' that the empire would survive. Despotism would in addition inhibit economic growth, which could be ensured by a certain autonomy of the subject *vis-à-vis* the government and via private property. The guiding idea of Oriental despotism was indeed adopted by the colonial government, but it was eventually expected to be replaced by the idea of European authoritarian monarchy. That position should not be mistaken for democracy, but it was nevertheless a clear rejection of absolutism. In India, too, there was to be a balance between authority and liberty. Liberty implied the protection of person and property from arbitrary and absolute power by an enlightened sovereign government, and authority rested on a bond of consent between the government and Indian elites, as expressed in Hume's 'First Principles of Government'.[41] From what can be seen of the implementation of such a political philosophy in the Madras Presidency, there is good reason to ask if Munro illustrates the fact that principles of government need not be reflected in their implementation. Contrasting the two studies cited, McLaren's intellectual history focuses on principles of rule in which philosophical logic is sought before political realities: she emphasizes the coherence of ideas. Washbrook, who researches the implementation of government policies, stresses the pragmatism of the colonial government and points to a despotism made permanent when Munro centralized civil, military, and judicial powers into the hands of the sovereign (i.e. the Company): 'British-Indian law became less a tool of liberty than an instrument of despotism.'[42]

Munro belonged to the generation of Company officers who were transforming a company of merchants into rulers. For this they needed information. Unlike the Orientalists, who searched classical Hindu texts for knowledge of Indian society, men like Munro looked for facts about actual polity, administration, and law in order to establish functioning rule. In contrast with the utilitarian position, which argued for law to establish a new social order, Munro searched for indigenous practice. A colonial administration shaped according to traditions of the place was expected to be more comprehensible to Indians. It would encourage them to co-operate with the EIC, thereby ensuring societal stability under sovereign rule. McLaren notes that Munro turned to a 'rough common sense empiricism', as was favoured by the Scottish moral philosophers. However, as Jon Wilson points out, when officials searched for the 'real state of things', they constructed those things that they found administratively useful. Burton Stein makes a similar point regarding Munro's settlement of the Kanara district: 'Munro constructed a history in order to justify a level of revenue assessment … which could be collected without promoting opposition from its ancient, dominant landholders.'[43]

Interestingly, Neeladri Bhattacharya finds a similar logic for the colonial administration of a later period in Punjab. Having contrasted the Orientalist aim of finding the customs of India in their pure form—purged from foreign influence and practices that had distorted their origins—with the utilitarian positivist disdain for tradition and custom, Bhattacharya concludes that neither of these perspectives was exclusively applied in late-nineteenth-century Punjab. Here, the colonial administration's relationship with native traditions was ambiguous and varied. On the one hand, the laws applied in colonial courts were based on principles of common law, where custom was seen as embodied in practice; in that sense, law was contextual. But to establish what sort of custom existed in Punjab, officials used surveys, civil code manuals, and case law. The framework for interpreting custom therefore came to be founded in Victorian anthropology and common law theory rather than in Punjabi practice.[44]

Early Attempts to Protect Toda Rights

When Sullivan submitted a report to the revenue board in 1827 on the alarming situation among Toda pastoralists resulting from the immigration of Europeans into the Nilgiris, he seemed unaware of the adverse response he was to receive from the board and the government of Madras. In view of the rapid increase of settlements at Ootacamund, Sullivan suggested rules that would protect Toda proprietary rights in the soil. He argued that the central division of the Nilgiris, Malnad, which was entirely pasture, had been in the possession of the Todas 'from an antiquity remote beyond the reach even of tradition. They are the most ancient inhabitants of the Mountains, and are recognized as the proprietors of the soil by the people of more recent origin, the Bergers, (the agricultural class) who pay them annually as such, fees in kind.'[45]

Sullivan's description of Toda rights and the rules he suggested were well in line with similar assertions of land rights earlier put forward by Munro. A decade earlier Munro had acted to protect the jenmi rights of Malabar landlords against the EIC monopoly in timber. Increasing demand from the navy and the Bombay docks had heightened the pressure on Malabar teak and, in order to secure the supply of timber, legislation had been passed in 1805 placing the forests of Malabar and Kanara under the complete control of the Bombay government. Thus, when EIC sovereign rights were proclaimed in these forests, influential landowners lost rights which in colonial eyes had been permanent, heritable, and saleable. Stressing the role of trust, Munro had argued in favour of securing private property against monopoly. He questioned the moderation of the government, which had promised 'reasonable assistance' in getting hold of non-private timber, as 'there can be no reasonable assistance where Government interferes; and this slight beginning with reasonable assistance has now grown into a wide and oppressive monopoly'. By re-establishing jenmi rights the free market would serve to regulate timber yield without destroying the owners' trust in government, and guarantee the security of colonial rule.[46] However, Munro's plans came to nought. In 1824, a year after the Company's monopoly in timber was banned, the collector of Malabar reported that there had been a rush into the market which cleared it of timber felled for public purposes and left the government empty-handed. In 1840 the collector claimed that Munro's high opinions of the owners' concern for forest conservancy had been 'utterly disproved by the last 17 years experience', when large tracts had been clearfelled.[47]

In his report of 1827 Sullivan described how a large share of Toda land was now occupied by houses, the woods were rapidly disappearing, and large herds of untaxed cattle belonging to Europeans were grazing on land for which the Toda paid revenue to the government. He therefore suggested three rules to prevent the Toda from being adversely affected by the settlement of Europeans. First, the limits of European settlement should be fixed, beyond which no houses were to be built or land appropriated. Second, land that was occupied by houses and gardens should be taxed and the revenue paid to the Toda. Sullivan added that only arable lands had so far been surveyed, while grazing grounds (the major part of the land) were still to be measured. Finally, the cattle that were grazing on Toda land should be taxed for the benefit of the Toda, and public woods subjected to government regulation. Sullivan sought in short to ensure that the Toda would be 'abundantly remunerated, for the encroachments that have hitherto been made upon their property'.[48]

In response to Sullivan's letter the government immediately ordered a survey to determine the enclosures already made, their legal status, and the remuneration paid to the Toda, as it believed that the claims were often unreasonable. However, Sullivan could only report four enclosures, two of which were his own, and it remains unclear whether anyone but Sullivan himself had paid for their land. Apparently, Europeans had settled in the central Nilgiris with a minimum of paperwork on the part of the district collector.[49]

In addition to his argument that the Toda had immemorial rights, Sullivan compared Toda land rights with those prevailing in Wynad. The intimate connection between Wynad and the Nilgiris, and their proximity to Malabar, 'where private property in land is universal', made it reasonable to assume the same property in the soil in the Nilgiris, too. Sullivan also brought the phenomenon of gudu into his argument. Gudu, as we saw earlier, was a kind of social tribute or gift within a socio-economic-ritual system of interdependence between communities in the Nilgiris. It was mostly given by Badaga shifting cultivators as a share of their produce to the Toda, who held authority over the particular piece of land they cultivated. Sullivan, however, compared gudu with the payment of rent, and described how Badaga cattle could be killed unless it was paid promptly. According to Sullivan, the Toda were in fact as much proprietors as the Nairs of Wynad. In addition, he submitted information about his own payment and the amount of tax paid by the Toda, so that the revenue board could calculate future payments for Toda land. This would turn unenclosed pasture into cultivated land and, in effect, into revenue.[50]

The revenue board distrusted Sullivan's information. It suggested that the government go ahead without further ado, since 'there can be no doubt that the latter [the Toda] would be willing to compromise any right they might be found to possess in respect to the appropriated space on very easy terms'. The government decided accordingly, ordering the district collector not to survey the pastoral land in Malnad and refusing to enter into a discussion on Toda proprietary rights. The more urgent decision was to settle the terms on which individuals should be permitted to occupy land in the hills. And, with a sarcastic hint at Sullivan's laudable anxiety to protect Toda interests, the government made the amount of his payment the norm for the 'compensation for the *usufruct* of the land which they (the Todawars) have hitherto enjoyed'. Within months of the decision, applications for land grants began to reach the Madras government.[51]

Two details merit special attention in this exchange of letters. First, the government was keener to regulate European occupation of the land than to determine claims made by or on behalf of the native population. Pastoralists or shifting cultivators in the hills were not seen as a potential threat to government sovereignty, while a European society, however limited, could not be allowed to develop outside government control. Furthermore, in the disputes between the district and presidency administrations, 1828 is when the question of usufruct first appears on the agenda. In the government's view the Toda lost their rights to use the land for pasture when enclosures were made. These were rights which they possessed by custom. Enclosing the land was both correct and necessary in the eyes of the government and, in the process, temporary users such as graziers or gatherers should be compensated for their loss of usufruct.

The strong emphasis on usufruct in 1828 can also be seen in the light of a change of government. Munro died suddenly in 1827 and was succeeded by Stephen Rumbold Lushington, whose policies were truly utilitarian and lacked all concern for incorporating Indian native custom in law and administration. The difference of policy between these two governors can however be exaggerated, for Munro too had sought to establish government sovereignty in the Madras territories, and if native custom stood in the way of government sovereignty, he was likely to secure the latter. However, Sullivan had been left relatively undisturbed during Munro's governorship, and they had maintained a close relationship in correspondence and opinion. For most of the time, with the government's attention concentrated on settling other regions, the Nilgiris had remained low on the agenda. But by the time Munro died and Lushington took up the governorship, government policies of consolidation and coherence in administration had reached the hills. From this period onwards the tone of correspondence between the government and revenue board in Madras and the Coimbatore district administration grew tense.[52]

A year later, when the question of proprietary rights had become entangled with the boundary conflict between Coimbatore and Malabar, Sullivan's correspondence with the revenue board had intensified. On the day after he left office as district collector, Sullivan wrote a thirty-paragraph-long defence of keeping the Nilgiris within Coimbatore (now arguing the case for its historically intimate connection with that district) and ensuring that Toda proprietary rights in the soil were as clear as those of the *mirasidars* of Malabar. In response, Chamier burst out with a lengthy reprimand for having to waste time with yet 'another of those disquisitions'. The two letters clearly contrast the opposing positions on rights in land—both argued by officers of the EIC.[53]

The district collector first laid down that hill people *had* rights, while the secretary to government stated that hill people were poor and itinerant and therefore could not possibly hold more than insignificant portions of land. The collector, in contrast, asserted that the Toda held proprietary rights in the soil equal to jenmi rights on account of being original settlers in the hills. This was the assertion of a birthright founded on native custom. It was in line with the logic of common law and with Munro's position that the law should be based on custom, and 'no fanciful theories founded on European models' should be incorporated into law in India.[54] The Badaga were claimed to possess property in all the lands they occupied, owing to their payment of a fixed quit rent to the Toda. The latter claim was a significant strengthening of Badaga rights, which had earlier been explained more in terms of tenancy under Toda sovereignty. In contrast, the secretary argued that all claims for Toda proprietary rights were unsupported by documents or other valid proofs. Additionally, 'It is universally acknowledged that the absolute property in the soil in India is vested in the Sovereign who is entitled to the rent and may transfer and assign it a right of occupying the cultivated lands, *on the condition of keeping up the cultivation so as to produce rent of revenue to the state* is allowed to the Ryots, but always subservient to and dependent upon the *absolute* proprietor.'[55] Whereas the collector argued that no part of the land under the property of hill people could be cultivated without the consent and remuneration of the proprietors, the government dismissed all property claims made on behalf of people who occupied the land on a migratory or temporary basis. In addition, it firmly established that the rights inherent in settled cultivation were subordinate to the absolute proprietor, i.e. the state.[56]

The dispute regarding the boundary between the Malabar and Coimbatore districts became deeply intertwined with the conflict over property rights. Starting off as a collision of views along bureaucratic lines, it developed into a tool to limit Sullivan's exercise of power. In 1830 it was finally decided that two-thirds of the Nilgiris, including the entire hill establishment, were to be transferred to Malabar district, and the remaining portion was attached to a taluk in northern Coimbatore district. All in all, 136 members of staff (of whom 85 were peons) were transferred to Malabar district.[57]

Preferring Cultivation to Pastoralism: The Case of Ketti

In view of the principles for determining existing land rights and the legal principles adopted for assigning rights to people, the case of the government farm Ketti (spelt Kaity) is interesting. The farm occupied 127 acres.[58] It was in a valley close to Ootacamund. In 1833 it was established that almost three-quarters of the land had earlier been used by nine Badaga cultivators and that, most likely, they had a valid claim on these lands. After four years of investigation the government decided to provide compensation and, by that time, only two claimants remained; the others had been declared dead, had left the Nilgiris, or were not considered to possess valid claims.[59]

From the outset the government observed that the Badaga had a 'prescriptive right of occupancy' that was equal to a form of tenancy. If such land was taken by the government, and as long as the cultivator paid rent, the loss of land must be compensated for. Having the aim of treating the Badaga liberally, the government considered compensating them for the loss of the profit which the land would have yielded had it been available to them. It also offered other lands, equally large, in exchange for the Ketti land. The Badaga claimants, however, estimated the loss at almost twice the amount suggested by the government and refused to accept the new lands. They would rather have the rocky piece of land on which the farmhouses were built than the good-quality land offered to them. Obviously, the quality of the land was of less importance than their demand that the only buildings on the land, the government farmhouses, should be taken over or demolished. The government officer reported that he failed to understand the logic of their request, since the only purpose for which they would receive any land would be for renewed cultivation.[60]

The utter confusion about the nature of hill agriculture marked both the ensuing inquiry and the legal outcome. A detailed memorandum set out each holder's lands and their sizes, rate of revenue, and assessment for the five years preceding the establishment of the government farm in 1831 (when the Badaga had been denied access). However, to us it also clearly reveals that these were small plots of land under shifting cultivation with a rotation of two to three years. A particular piece of land is noted to have been 'left waste', 'increased', or 'decreased' after, at most, three years. In his final report the officer remarked that none of the Badaga claimants, monigars and carnams among both Toda and Badaga, local government officers, tahsildars or other 'interested' Badaga from neighbouring villages, who joined him at the disputed site were able to state firmly the exact extent of cultivated land and waste prior to the setting up of the government farm. All boundary marks that may earlier have existed on the ground had disappeared, and it had become almost impossible to establish exact boundaries for small plots of land that had been cultivated under short rotations four to nine years earlier. Estimating the amount of monetary compensation for loss of profit therefore became an intricate task of calculating the lands that Badaga claimants would actually have used, considering their 'custom' of leaving the land fallow after a few years. No such land would then be considered eligible for more than three years' compensation. This exercise can surely be seen as a collision of two opposing norms of land value and land use.[61]

In parallel with this, an investigation was carried out regarding lands claimed by two Toda settlements. These were lands appropriated by the military cantonment in Ootacamund. In this case too the government wanted to establish exact boundaries and holdings, and to negotiate an agreement with the Toda in which the latter relinquished all land claims. (This particular conflict will be discussed in Chapter 5.) However, in the context of the disputed lands in Ketti, a statement by the officer investigating the Toda claims is noteworthy. Only a month after the amount of compensation for the Ketti land had been decided, the officer took pains to note that, although the Toda would be compensated in money, this did not mean that the government considered them the equals of permanent cultivators:

> it would appear that Government consider that lands so assumed are cultivated in perpetuity, but I beg to state that so far from this being the case, lands so taken up are commonly retained for a few months, a year or more as suits the convenience of the parties, but with few exceptions occupied for any considerable time so that such lands on being abandoned revert to the Todas who have the same enjoyment of them for pasturage as formerly.[62]

Observable here is the fact that the officer noted that land was returned to the Toda after it had been cultivated for a few years. In spite of a vigorous effort to prove that the Toda had no legitimate claims to land because there was no permanent labour on it, this is one of several instances in which Toda authority over non-cultivated land in the central Nilgiris was still recognized. In the case of Ketti, however, there was no recognition of the Toda's loss of grazing ground during the years the land had been occupied by the government farm. In contrast, the Badaga shifting cultivators, with their equally non-permanent labour, were compensated for their loss of profit—on the basis that their land had been under temporary, not permanent, labour. The government's preference for cultivation over pastoralism could not be more clearly illustrated.

The dispute over the land occupied by the Ketti farm and the cantonment did not end here; the 1830s were years of prolonged disputes between parties claiming conflicting rights in the same land. The legal elaboration of these claims could not be resolved until 1843, when the first regulations on land rights in the Nilgiris were passed: Rights of the Todawars, and Rules for grants of land on the Neilgherries.[63] The limited size of the Toda population compared with the strength of the EIC would suggest that rights would have been rapidly settled to the advantage of the government. But the strong interest in securing individual property as British subjects now combined with effective local politics—in which not least the Toda participated, to ultimately ensure that legal codification became the arena in which the battle over land rights was fought. When the 1843 regulations were passed they made manifest the sovereign rights of government, the baseline being government's absolute rights in uncultivated land: 'From a consideration of the universally acknowledged rights of the Government in respect to uncultivated lands, as well as to the peculiar circumstances of the case under discussion, we cannot admit the existence of any such proprietary right in the soil on the part of the Todas, as can in any way interfere with the right of Government to permit parties willing to pay the full assessment to bring it under the plough.'[64]

Both jenmi and mirasi rights were taken as examples to prove the point. In Malabar, the government asserted, a man was only allowed to keep his land waste if he paid a tax equal to that paid for cultivated land. Land under mirasi tenure could be disposed of by government to parties willing to cultivate it, after the mirasidar had first been given the option of paying the full assessment. The fact that the Toda paid tax for their land therefore did not assure them of permanent rights in the land, since their payments were on the 'nominal' level of grazing tax, which covered no more than wasteland. The only matter remaining to be determined was consequently whether or not they 'possessed a right to be compensated for the abridgement of the grazing privileges which they have exercised' and, if found to have such a right, to decide the principles for the compensation for the loss of those privileges. The title advanced on the part of the Toda was that of 'immemorial occupation'. The only advantages ascribed to such occupancy were those of pasturing their herds and the Badaga's payment of gudu. However, the government did not expect there to be any imminent loss of grazing land on a large scale. Long before settled cultivation might seriously have begun to interfere with their need of land for pasture, the government hoped that they would have been influenced by settled habits and begun combining pastoralism with cultivation of the soil.[65]

Once the specific title to land and its implication for rights had been established, the regulations went on to determine the principles for paying compensation to the Toda. Here the pencilled notes in the margin of the document expand. As soon as the government began to elaborate on the payment of money, an officer signing himself 'A.S.' raised objections. Since losing the income of gudu was considered a cause for compensation, the government suggested that the payment should equal the amount of gudu which the Toda received from the

Badaga. Obviously, any social commitment associated with gudu had entirely escaped the government. However, A.S. writes: 'This is all very right if indeed it were ascertained that the Todawars have a property in these lands—but until this shall be ascertained surely we cannot assign to them any payment for that would be to admit a *title* the existence of which is not ascertained.'[66] Having to deal with reports from surveyors who spoke of ownership, landholders and the purchasing rights of the Toda had been a constant headache for the revenue board. The legal crux was how to avoid the transfer of money for land which could in any way resemble a purchase of rights, since that would imply the existence of an owner.

To further control the exchange of rights to land in the hills, the government declared that individuals who had purchased rights in land from the Toda could not claim to possess other rights than those the Toda had possessed, i.e. 'the right of occupying the land for purposes of pasturage'. Any other use, such as cultivation, would be liable to full assessment. Over the ensuing months, a manual of instructions concerning land grant procedures was compiled. Here it was laid down that all land for which an application for a land grant was submitted must be offered at public auction and sold to the highest bidder. The requirement to obtain a land grant had been announced as early as 1828, but it took many years for the decree to have any effect. In 1837, when the government was pursuing the question of establishing grants for itself for the Ketti farmlands and the cantonment, letters from worried Europeans began to reach the collector's office. These hill residents had often invested considerable sums of money in their land on the assumption that they held it as freehold property.

Sullivan had surely been instrumental in reinforcing such impressions. Now their land, too, had to be put up for public auction, since they did not hold grants. Occasionally, they were the second or third holders of the land and the purchase had been administered by the district administration. In spite of this, they risked having to buy the land a second time or losing it to a higher bidder.[67]

The manner of paying compensation for Toda land was itself an implemented act of government policy. The government recommended that such payments should be added to the assessment of the land, so that a fund could be set up. The annual yield from this fund could subsequently be made available to assist Toda who wished to undertake agricultural operations. The government advised against paying a lump sum directly to the Toda, as it was assumed that the money would be dissipated by this 'simple race' instead of being invested in the desired activities.[68]

The 1843 regulations became a landmark in the legal codification of Toda rights in land and resources. The only portions of land remaining under their absolute control were munds and 'spots appropriated to religious rites.' The former referred to the limited lands on which their houses were built, the latter to their temple munds. Hills of religious importance and routes for the dead to reach the afterworld were not included in what the government thought of as spots for religious rites. Regarding the lands immediately surrounding the munds, the advice given was that they should not be sold. It was hoped that the Toda would eventually be influenced by settled habits and bring these under cultivation.[69]

***

There were two major contradictions in the debates about the principles governing rights in land and resources, one relating to the question of rights and the other to that of utility. Initially, these were primarily general ideas applied to broader issues, such as large-scale revenue systems and the principles of government. In the Nilgiris, once such principles were directly linked to interests in land, they were rhetorically voiced in more polarized forms, becoming almost polemically stereotyped the deeper the conflicts grew. Whether preference should be given either to the local and the vernacular, or to the national and the universal, was a major dividing line in the dispute over legal principles. Once the formalization of land rights appeared on the revenue board's agenda, it consistently argued for the latter. The overall goal was systematizing governance in order to establish a uniform administration for the whole presidency. No other principle was assumed to secure sovereign government.

However, such absolute principles were unable to sustain the confrontation with local realities. In the 1843 regulations the government of Madras insisted on the universal application of the principle of sovereignty but was at the same time careful to adjust legal ideas applying to the vernacular to those that applied to the universal. The government could not remain insensitive to principles that were considered legitimate by its subjects—be they Indian or European. In the legal text, the notion of immemorial right was borrowed from common law, but narrowed in its implications for the specific rights of the Toda. In a sense Toda rights were still birthrights, but only an account of 'immemorial occupation' due to their 'privilege' of using the land to graze buffaloes. These were no longer property rights laid down by common law.

Throughout the dispute the government gave national or public interests priority over local interests. Nonetheless, specific local conditions could not be entirely bypassed. Even the Court of Directors was keenly aware of the importance of protecting 'this interesting race' from threats to its specific livelihood. The Madras government was therefore careful to emphasize that it had only the best interests of the Toda in mind, and gudu was even made part of the form in which compensation was paid. The fact that the implications of gudu thereby changed dramatically was dismissed as irrelevant. In the regulations gudu was said to be an unexplained term, for it had never been ascertained if these 'donations' were made for the sake of property or on superstitious grounds, or simply to prevent the Toda from molesting the Badaga. Ultimately, for anyone claiming land in the hills, the government decided that rights could not be allowed to remain with a holder if the use to which the land was being put was seen by government to be detrimental to the public interest.[70]

The government also went a long way in determining the needs of its subjects. With regard to the Toda, however, those needs were defined only from the point of view of an economic livelihood. Social or political aspects of the Toda economy were left unrecognized. This is particularly clear in the way gudu was treated. Here the government's difficulty in dealing with local notions of rights, embedded in mutual systems of social, political, and ritual authority and exchange, gave rise to profound contradictions. After first dismissing the entire notion of gudu as incomprehensible, it went on to establish gudu as the principle by which compensation payments should be determined.

The situation clearly reveals the hybrid and contextual nature of the process of codifying legal rights in land and resources, both at the fundamental level of legal ideas and in their practical implementation. At times, in historical studies, a view of the immediate impact of ideas on British law in India as based on European enlightenment and utilitarian political thought remains unproblematized. British law then comes to be seen as a taken-for-granted part of imperial policy. However, with legal rights in land in Britain in a state of profound transformation, and different interests colliding at both the normative level and the level of implementation, it was such conflicts—rather than any uniformity of colonial legislation—that came to be reflected in legal settlements in the South Indian hills. The conflicts were not simply transferred to a new arena; disputes over land in India, which were deeply contextual, were at the same time legally argued using a rhetoric fuelled by British debates.

In a narrow sense, debates on sovereignty and property in the Nilgiris reflected the transition in EIC rule in the Madras Presidency. The government's attention shifted from a primary concern with military security over dispersed areas to administrative consolidation and sovereign rule. Accordingly, the government sought to achieve a certain uniformity of administration, the aim being to bring administration in the hills closer to that prevailing in the plains. Law and bureaucracy were instrumental arenas in facilitating this transformation. In contrast to later histories of north-east India, where the hill regions became regions of difference, the South Indian hills were slowly integrated into the dominant administrative principles of an agrarian economy. Flanagan's conclusion is relevant in this context, too. He asserts that we need to raise our attention above the level of individual property—where European agriculturists were competing with native pastoralists or shifting cultivators for land—to the level of the state: 'The real issue ... was not private ownership but public sovereignty; for sovereignty carried the underlying title to the soil that allowed the sovereign to convert common resources into private property.' Or, as noted by Armitage, it was ultimately a matter of *imperium*, not *dominium*.[71]

Notes

1. Field notes, Marlimund, 26 September 2003.
2. OIOC, MRP, 17 September 1822: 2422–3, To the President and Members of the Board of Revenue, from P. Still, Secretary to Government.
3. Sivaramakrishnan, 1999, *Modern Forests. Statemaking and Environmental Change in Colonial Eastern India*, 30.

4. OIOC, European Manuscripts, Thomas Munro Collection, From Sullivan to Munro, 22 April 1825.
5. See Sullivan's correspondence with Thomas Munro, 1815–16, for further details of the confusion in the collection of revenue. OIOC, Thomas Munro Collection, vol. 28, 15 April 1816, From John Sullivan to Thomas Munro. Monigar, see Chapter 2, note 65. See also Stein, 1989, *Thomas Munro. The Origins of the Colonial State and His Vision of Empire*, 187.
6. OIOC, MBRP, 3 January 1828: 324–5, To the President and Members of the Board of Revenue, para 2.
7. The philosophical argument of unchallenged liberty at sea should be seen against the existing situation of international and national territorial rights at sea. Armitage, 2000, *The Ideological Origins of the British Empire*, 30, 33, 42, 121, 124–5, 143–5.
8. Frost, 1981, 'New South Wales as *Terra Nullius*. The British Denial of Aboriginal Land Rights', 514–15. This argument also served as a legal justification for the notion of 'wasteland'.
9. See, for example, OIOC, MRC, 1 February 1830, App. 1–3: 1594–7.
10. Ibid., 1 March 1830: 2603–14, To the President and Members of the Board of Revenue, signed H.J. Chamier, Secr. to Government.
11. Reynolds, 1987, *The Law of the Land*, 31–5; Flanagan, 1989, 'The Agricultural Argument and Original Appropriation. Indian Lands and Political Philosophy', 590.
12. OIOC, MRC, 19 February 1830: 2603–14, Extract from the Minutes of Consultation.
13. Ibid.
14. Gordon, 1996, 'Paradoxical Property', 95; Lieberman, 1996, 'Property, Commerce, and the Common Law. Attitudes to Legal Change in the Eighteenth Century', 144–7.
15. In the process of the English enclosure, customary usage could be extinguished from common law by the Court of Common Pleas. In spite of this, usage could still be claimed as a local right by custom of a manor or village. Thompson, 1991, *Customs in Common*, 143; Gordon, 1996, 'Paradoxical Property', 95–7.
16. Scott, 1998, *Seeing Like a State. How Certain Schemes to Improve the Human Condition Have Failed*, 11–22; Rajan, 2006, *Modernizing Nature. Forestry and Imperial Eco-Development 1800–1950*, ch. 3.2.
17. Bhattacharya, 1996, 'Remaking Custom. The Discourse and Practice of Colonial Codification', 22–7, 40.
18. Stokes, 1959, *The English Utilitarians and India*, 1–5; Washbrook, 1999, 'India, 1818–60. The Two Faces of Colonialism', 399. OIOC, Parliamentary

Papers, The Fifth Report from the Select Committee on the Affairs of the East India Company, 28 July 1812: 18, and App. 31, 'Extract from Report of Principal Collector of the Ceded Districts; dated 15 August 1807': 943. Stein, 1998, *A History of India*, 212–14.

19. An old established principle allowed for conquered peoples to retain their laws unless the conqueror decreed otherwise. This principle made possible the denial of rights based on common law. Marshall, 1996, 'Parliament and Property Rights in the Late Eighteenth-Century British Empire', 530–1.
20. Lieberman, 1996, 'Property, Commerce, and the Common Law. Attitudes to Legal Change in the Eighteenth Century', 144–7.
21. Finn, 2000, *Law, Debt, and Empire in Calcutta*, 7, 18, 21–2.
22. Armitage, 2000, *The Ideological Origins of the British Empire*, 97.
23. Neeson, 1993, *Commoners. Common Right, Enclosure and Social Change in England, 1700–1820*, 22–34, 72.
24. Brewer and Staves, 1995, *Early Modern Conceptions of Property*, 3.
25. Neeson, 1993, *Commoners. Common Right, Enclosure and Social Change in England, 1700–1820*, 44–5.
26. Ibid., 19, 44.
27. OIOC, BC, 7 April 1826, Parts of Sir John Malcolm's Instructions, OIOC, MRC, 1 March 1830, To the Board of Revenue from H.J. Chamier.
28. Ibid.
29. I am indebted to David Washbrook for a discussion of this issue.
30. In 1830, the revenue board complained that assessments had fallen to half the level at which revenue had been collected prior to Sullivan's administration of the Nilgiris. Sullivan explained that previously a rack rent had been exacted on valuable goods saleable in the low country, and that a new system had been introduced. However, a new survey would increase assessments as the area of cultivated land would simultaneously increase. It should further be noted that in spite of a significantly lower level of assessment on Toda pastoral grounds compared with cultivated land, the small population in relation to the large areas and low returns may in fact have resulted in high revenue costs for the individual munds. Statistics being incomplete, the effects of revenue assessment are difficult to calculate. OIOC, Thomas Munro Collection, Box 75, 1820, Mr Fullarton's Plan. OIOC, MBRP, 8 January 1829: 557–8, To the Secretary to the Board of Revenue from J. Sullivan, 27 December 1828. OIOC, MRP, 18 February 1830, Resolution no. 5. Stein, 1989, *Thomas Munro. The Origins of the Colonial State and His Vision of Empire*, ch. 3; Washbrook, 1999, 'India, 1818–1860. The Two Faces of Colonialism', 407.

31. As several studies have shown, small dam irrigation systems, which were maintained locally with state support in early modern India, tended to disintegrate under colonial rule. In the case of western India, Hardiman regards the introduction of a uniform tax on irrigated land as the major factor in this decline. From nineteenth-century British reports he reconstructs a possible system for the management of these dams during the seventeenth and eighteenth centuries, in which local control was a key component. However, by the 1830s–1850s, this system was in a state of collapse. Taxation of irrigated land, which had earlier depended on the amount of water needed for each type of crop, had now increased substantially on the less valuable but most common crops. Peasants thus ended up in debt and were forced to abandon heavily taxed fields. Deforestation, the decay of community-based control and a lack of interest on the part of the colonial government exacerbated the situation. Hardiman, 1996, 'Small-Dam Systems of the Sahyadris', 197–9, 203–8; D'Souza, 2004, 'Rigidity and the Affliction of Capitalist Property. Colonial Land Revenue and the Recasting of Nature', 237–9, 270.
32. Cederlöf, 1997, *Bonds Lost. Subordination, Conflict, and Mobilisation in Rural South India, c. 1900–1970*, 44–6; Cederlöf, 2003, 'Social Mobilisation among People Competing at the Bottom-Level of Society. The Presence of Missions in Rural South India c. 1900–1950', 344–7.
33. Francis, 1908, *Madras District Gazetteers, the Nilgiris*, 268–9; Cederlöf, 1997, *Bonds Lost. Subordination, Conflict, and Mobilisation in Rural South India, c. 1900–1970*, 45–6.
34. OIOC, MBRP, 10 November 1842, Proceedings, para 1.
35. OIOC, MD, Madras Revenue Department, 10 April 1839, para 49.
36. Gleig, 1830, *Life of Major General Sir Thomas Munro*, vol. 2, 51–2; Hardiman, 1994, 'Power in the Forest. The Dangs, 1820–1940', 106–12; Skaria, 1999, *Hybrid Histories. Forests, Frontiers, and Wildness in Western India*, 135, 155.
37. OIOC, BC, 7 April 1826, Parts of Sir John Malcolm's Instructions, 1, 7–9.
38. Thomas Munro, Governor of Madras 1819–27, Mountstuart Elphinstone, Governor of Bombay 1819–27, John Malcolm, Governor of Bombay 1827–30. McLaren, 2001, *British India & British Scotland, 1780–1830. Career Building, Empire Building, and a Scottish School of Thought on Indian Governance*, 15–21.
39. See further Bryant, 1985, 'Scots in India in the Eighteenth Century', 22–41, for a discussion of the Scots in eighteenth-century India; MacKenzie, 1993, 'Essay and Reflection. On Scotland and the Empire', 714–39, on the Scottish role in the British Empire; and McLaren, 2001, *British India*

& British Scotland, 1780–1830. Career Building, Empire Building, and a Scottish School of Thought on Indian Governance, 79.

40. Washbrook, 1999, 'India, 1818–1860. The Two Faces of Colonialism', 402–4. See also Peers, 1995, *Between Mars and Mammon. Colonial Armies and the Garrison State in India, 1819–1835*, 44–6. Burton Stein notes that two-thirds of the more than two hundred minutes written by Thomas Munro between 1820 and 1824 were on military matters. Stein, 1989, *Thomas Munro. The Origins of the Colonial State and His Vision of Empire*, 252.
41. Thompson, 1991, *Customs in Common*, 86–7; McLaren, 1993, 'From Analysis to Prescription. Scottish Concepts of Asian Despotism in Early Nineteenth-Century British India', 470–1; Wootton, 1996, *Modern Political Thought. Readings from Machiavelli to Nietzsche*, 606; Wilson, 2000, *Governing Property, Making Law. Land, Local Society and Colonial Rule in Bengal, c. 1785–1830*, 80, 103–5; McLaren, 2001, *British India & British Scotland, 1780–1830. Career Building, Empire Building, and a Scottish School of Thought on Indian Governance*, 182–8.
42. Stein, 1989, *Thomas Munro. The Origins of the Colonial State and His Vision of Empire*, 106; Washbrook, 1999, 'India, 1818–1860. The Two Faces of Colonialism', 407.
43. In recent years, a growing body of scholarship has emerged on the place of Ireland in the British empire, in which comparisons are made with India. This work will contribute further to the analysis of questions of ideology, legal regulation and governance in the formation of rights in land under early colonial rule in India. For a broader argument, see Bayly, 2000, 'Ireland, India and the Empire. 1780–1914'; Stein, 1989, *Thomas Munro. The Origins of the Colonial State and His Vision of Empire*, 71; Bhattacharya, 1996, 'Remaking Custom. The Discourse and Practice of Colonial Codification', 22–4; Pels and Salemink, 1999, *Colonial Subjects. Essays on the Practical History of Anthropology*, 85–6, 88–90; Wilson, 2000, *Governing Property, Making Law. Land, Local Society and Colonial Rule in Bengal, c. 1785–1830*, 75; McLaren, 2001, *British India & British Scotland, 1780–1830. Career Building, Empire Building, and a Scottish School of Thought on Indian Governance*, 235–7.
44. Bhattacharya, 1996, 'Remaking Custom. The Discourse and Practice of Colonial Codification', 24–7, 48–9.
45. OIOC, MBRP, 3 January 1828: 324–5, To the President and Members of the Board of Revenue, from J. Sullivan, 2 October 1827.
46. Parliamentary Papers, session 1812, vol. 7, Fifth Select Committee, App. 23, Extracts from reports respecting land tenures and assessments in Malabar, para 179. Gleig, 1830, *Life of Major General Sir Thomas Munro*,

vol. 2, App. XI, Minute on Monopoly of Timber at Malabar, 6 December 1822, paras 3, 4, 15; Kumar, 1982, *The Cambridge Economic History of India. Volume 2, c. 1757–c. 1970*, 221–4.

47. Gleig, 1830, *Life of Major General Sir Thomas Munro*, vol. 1, Memorandum on opening the trade with India to the outports, 1 February 1813: 1386–7, 1390. OIOC, MBRP, 27 July 1840, App. A, para 6. Stokes, 1959, *The English Utilitarians and India*, 39; Grove, 1995, *Green Imperialism. Colonial Expansion, Tropical Island Edens, and the Origins of Environmentalism, 1600–1860*, 399, 417–19; Rangarajan, 1996, *Fencing the Forest. Conservation and Ecological Change in India's Central Provinces, 1860–1914*, 20–2; Washbrook, 1999, 'India, 1818–1860. The Two Faces of Colonialism', 402–3.
48. OIOC, MBRP, 3 January 1828: 324–5, To the President and Members of the Board of Revenue, from J. Sullivan, 2 October 1827.
49. For the first 1,900 acres, or 500 bullas, nothing was reported to have been paid. For a later enclosure of 9 1/11 bullas 100 rupees was paid (which may also have included compensation for the first piece of land), and for the land surrounding his new residence, 47 7/8 bullas, 16 cantaroy fanams, 9–2 (16-9-2 Rs) had been paid. Ibid., 23 October 1828: 10687–9, To the President and Members of the Bard of Revenue, from John Sullivan, paras 5–6.
50. Ibid., paras 4–5, 9–11, 13. Walker, 1986, *The Toda of South India. A New Look*, 25–6; Ibid., 1989, 'Toda Society between Tradition and Modernity', 196.
51. OIOC, MBRP, 13 November 1828: 11914, To the Chief Secretary to Government from D. Eliott, Secretary to the Board of Revenue. Ibid., 27 November 1828: 12229, From the Secretary to the Board of Revenue. Italics mine. TNA, NDR 1827–35, Military, Commandant's Letter Book, Letters sent: 201, 206.
52. OIOC, MRP, 5 November 1828.
53. OIOC, MRC, 2 February 1830, To the President and the Members of the Board of Revenue from J. Sullivan. Ibid., 1 March 1830, To the President and Members of the Board of Revenue from H.J. Chamier, Secretary to Government.
54. Gleig, 1830, *Life of Major General Sir Thomas Munro*, vol. 3: 320.
55. OIOC, MRC, 1 March 1830, To the President and Members of the Board of Revenue from H.J. Chamier, Secretary to Government. Emphasis in the original.
56. Ibid., 2 February 1830, To the President and Members of the Board of Revenue from J. Sullivan. Ibid., 1 March 1830, To the President and

Members of the Board of Revenue from H.J. Chamier, Secretary to Government.

57. The smaller portion of land was transferred to the administration of Danaiguncottah (Devanaickenkota) taluk, which had been the centre of the hill revenue administration under Tipu Sultan. OIOC, MRC, 1 April 1830: 3942, To the Board of Revenue from James Thomas, Principal Collector of Coimbatore, 20 March 1830. Ibid., 6 May 1830: 4991–5, To the President and Members of the Board of Revenue from J. Thomas, 28 April 1830, and 4994, attached list of Nilgherry Sibbendy transferred on to the Collector of Malabar.
58. 96 cawnies or 126.9 acres.
59. OIOC, MBRP, 21 October 1833: 13045–14048, To the President and Members of the Board of Revenue from F. Clementson, Principal Collector of the Malabar District.
60. Ibid., 6 November 1834: 11903–5, Consultation.
61. Ibid., 17 December 1835: 14825–8, To the President and Members of the Board of Revenue from the Collector of Malabar, 14829, Memorandum of Jamabundy Chitta accounts of Makanaud Village in Danayacundottah Talook. Ibid., 12 January 1837: 410–32, Report on the lands composing the Farm at Kaitie; D. Eliott, paras 3, 7, 12, 15, 21. Ibid., 23 January 1837: 730–5, Read again letter from Eliott, paras 5, 8–9.
62. Ibid., 23 March 1837: 3316–21, To the President and Members of the Board of Revenue from Clementson, App. A, To the Principal Collector of Malabar from E. Smith, Sub Collector, para 7.
63. OIOC, MD, Fort St George Revenue Department, 21 June 1843, no. 13: 51–92.
64. Ibid., para 7.
65. Ibid., paras 7–8.
66. Ibid., written in the margin beside para 9, emphasis in the original.
67. Ibid., para 15. OIOC, MBRP, 14 December 1843: 19191–19206, To the Chief Secretary to Government from E.C. Lovell, Acting Secretary, para 3. Ibid., 13 April 1837: 4211–21, Investigation of European land claims, App. A, Enclosures 1 and 2.
68. OIOC, MD, Fort St George Revenue Department, 21 June 1843, no. 13, para 10.
69. Ibid., para 15.
70. Ibid., paras 3, 16.
71. Flanagan, 1989, 'The Agricultural Argument and Original Appropriation. Indian Lands and Political Philosophy', 601–2; Armitage, 2000, *The Ideological Origins of the British Empire*, 98.

4 *Perceptions of Land and People*

Looking out over fields I asked an old Toda man how the landscape had changed during his lifetime: when had fields begun to be ploughed and the eucalyptus planted on the grazing grounds? His answers came in the form of myths of the divine, of playing, fighting, and disputing gods. 'Now he is wandering off into yet another myth', said the female companion who had accompanied me from Ooty to translate from the Toda language into English. It was only later that I learnt that it was in fact my companion who was asking for myths, disregarding my questions.

She lives in one of the munds which for almost two centuries have been most heavily affected by immigrants—European and Indian—and by expanding urban development. Since the nineteenth century tourists have been guided to the mund to see an 'authentic' Toda hamlet in its 'traditional' form. But with the Toda now cut off from their buffalo herds and grazing grounds, and seeing the size of their land titles mysteriously shrink at the hands of the Forest Department, my companion

Ill. 5 A shrine dedicated to Bhavani Amman
(Photo by the author.)

was always in search of fertile soil from the past to let her own roots grow deep again. She argued that re-establishing myths of the creation and afterworld, and the economic and ritual value of buffaloes, would re-establish the authentic Toda, cleansed from the distortions produced by modernity. The ascribed authenticity in tourist guides being reproduced in front of visiting groups was false: 'We are showpieces.' Now she was trying to recapture lost landscapes for their ritual significance, and she asked the old man about the Toda divinity who had walked across the Nilgiri lands since time immemorial. 'Old father, you speak about Ööhn, did Ööhn come from a particular place?' 'No, Ööhn was from the beginning.' Here, in a mund beyond the reach of the tourist trail, she collected stories like gems, creating new soils of identity, eagerly filling her notebook with new narratives.

Simultaneously, my companion visited women's organizations belonging to the Hindutva movement in the plains, where she found support for her growing conviction that Toda religion is an ancient form of Vedic Hinduism which remains untouched over the thousands of years during which human activities have corrupted Hindu worship from its pure form. Today, Toda homes have both Hindu and Christian images side by side with the oil lamp that is to be lit when night falls and the Toda divinity is worshipped. But this is not an uncontroversial change. When a Hindu temple was built in one of the munds, it caused controversy. Such worship is considered a private matter, for the home or for shrines dedicated to Ayyappan and Bhavani Amman along roadsides, not something to be displayed publicly in the mund. Following the change, my friend seemed to want to establish the essence of that which was uniquely Toda and, at the same time, to merge with mainstream society.[1]

Empirical Science Fixing People to Time and Place

From the very earliest accounts, the Toda appear to be trapped in a paradox. On the one hand they have been defined and positioned in relation to the evolution of humankind. On the other the singularity of their existence has been frozen in time and disallowed any notion of change. The early ethnographies, wholeheartedly embraced by Sullivan, declared the Toda's high and noble standards within an unsophisticated way of life. Later accounts deplored their low human status, which was seen as degraded ever since human beings were banished from the Garden of Eden. Administrative measures taken to secure human development in the community were similarly contradictory. The district administration argued for the protection of the Toda from the negative influences of European settlement and development. In contrast, the Madras government initiated—however impotently, for they were always declared failures—programmes of education and civilization for the moral uplift of the Toda. By the 1830s, when the Madras government moved forcefully to secure sovereign rule and uniform administration in the province, the latter view had come to dominate understanding of the Nilgiris.[2]

The contrast between government descriptions of the Toda and Badaga communities in this regard was significant. Early ethnography maintained that the Badaga were subordinate to the Toda in all respects, pointing to their unclean villages, poor clothing and excessive use of opium and liquor.[3] In contrast, as discussed in Chapter 2, the Madras government portrayed the Badaga as the entrepreneurial agriculturists of the plains. By an unlucky turn in history, and despite their superior skills, they had been forced to submit to the Toda in the hills. They could be put back on the track of evolutionary progress with the assistance of exemplary Britain. They contrasted with the Toda who were projected as frozen in a time of non-evolution. As Tim Ingold notes in the debate on ethnography and the awareness of time: 'The ethnographic encounter is, after all, but a moment in the historical unfolding of a field of relationships in which all parties are inevitably bound up. But to represent the people as existing forever within that moment ... is to consign their lives to a time that, in the experience of the ethnographer, has already been left far behind.'[4]

The many detailed ethnographic works on the different communities in the Nilgiris may, intentionally or otherwise, have served to reinforce the notion of closed ethnicities with ancient, unchangeable, and community-specific characteristics. Over the past 180 years the Toda have been by far the group most often represented in ethnographic texts. Studies about the Toda in the 1980s often began with a polite excuse for adding yet another study to the existing pile. Walker begins his 1998 collection of essays by referring to all the excuses already made and shows in an article, 'The Western Romance with the Toda', how professional anthropologists (among others) have fallen in love with them.

Contemporary anthropologists have also come to favour different communities: Paul Hockings the Badaga, Anthony Walker the Toda, David G. Mandelbaum the Kota.[5]

Ingold's statement serves as a reminder not only for present-day anthropology but also for our reading of its nineteenth-century disciplinary predecessors who, in an instrumental way, projected ancient history onto both 'herders' and shifting cultivators. However, in contrast with the notion of stagnant Toda pasts, the notion of past times attached to the racial construction of the Badaga was transformative. The difference between the two became an important argument in the administration of the region, which was to be elaborated in relation to questions of revenue and property.

The importance of ethnographic accounts in the history of the Nilgiris cannot be overestimated. Ethnological surveys and ethnographic observations were key elements structuring perceptions of the past and present on which colonial administration was based. Whether arguing a high or low racial position for the Toda, it was possible to find legitimate support in scientific work. Simultaneously, scholars of natural history found empirical evidence for their racial theories in the writings of travellers and surveyors.

The work of Johann Friedrich Blumenbach, a leading scholar of medicine and natural history in the late eighteenth and early nineteenth centuries, explored the rational logic of the organization of nature as it was derived from its ultimate origin: God's creation. Working in the Linnaean tradition, he organized his findings within a single scheme that embraced humans, animals, plants, and minerals. All had their original and undisturbed form, according to the intention of the creator; however, they could all degenerate or deviate from this given standard. Two of Blumenbach's more prominent works, *A Manual of the Elements of Natural History* (first German edn 1779) and *The Institutions of Physiology* (first Latin edn 1787), elaborated in detail the functioning of the human body and the location of humanity within an overall system of nature. Critics of sweeping claims regarding the hegemony of a monolithic body of European Enlightenment thought—heard at times within the more extreme arguments about European or Western otherness—have argued that scholars in the natural sciences such as Blumenbach represented an Enlightenment fold characterized by contingency, variety, and complexity, not by coherence and mechanistic uniformity. These eighteenth-century scholars presupposed that nature had a complex history. However, while the singularity of the Enlightenment has been greatly overstated, sometimes transforming post-Enlightenment scholarship into stereotypes, it should be remembered that Blumenbach was searching for the organizing principle of nature.[6]

The question of degeneration caused the translator of the English edition of *The Institutions of Physiology*, published in 1820, to comment that the term implied no reference to inferiority or superiority, but was merely indicating the deviation of a race from its given standard. However, three decades earlier Blumenbach had been quite clear about the hierarchies within the human species as it degenerated into all the different races. While acknowledging the many incomprehensible differences caused by innumerable transitions since the original creation of man, he nevertheless distinguished five races: the Caucasian (including 'the inhabitants of the world known by the ancient Grecians and Romans'[7]), the Mongolian (including most other Asians[8]), the Ethiopian, the American, and the Malayan.[9] 'The Caucasian', he said, 'must, on every physiological principle, be considered as the primary or intermediate of these five principal Races. The two extremes into which it has deviated, are on the one hand the Mongolian, on the other the Ethiopian.'[10]

When James Cowles Prichard published *The Natural History of Man* in 1843, he stood firmly on the foundations laid by Blumenbach's work. His elaborations of the human species were however more methodologically and hierarchically fixed. Prichard, too, argued for the biblical origin of nature. Around the turn of the nineteenth century a biblical explanatory model had become predominant as an antirevolutionary reaction within British scientific debates on humanity. However, to Prichard it became even more important to defend the foundations of civilization than to trace its origins.[11] He was particularly interested in how variations of humans had appeared and influenced the physical and moral agencies of the different 'tribes of the human family'. His scheme is thus considerably more detailed than Blumenbach's. Where the latter's distinctions between the human races were based on physical features in the most general sense, Prichard had begun to make detailed measurements of human complexion and anatomy.

Not entirely content with the precision of his results for the classification of human varieties, Prichard went on to propose definitions based on historical evidence, the most 'authentic' being those of language. Descending from the Adamite family, humanity had been divided by language at the tower of Babel, and degeneration had followed from the ensuing migration into less hospitable environments. Referring to contemporaneous scholars who claimed that the history of nations, termed ethnology, was to be found in the relations between their languages, Prichard maintained that his ultimate object was to investigate the tribes of men whose affinity languages tended to illustrate.[12] More forcefully than Blumenbach, Prichard emphasized the great diversity within a single human variety: All the diversities which exist are variable, and pass into each other by insensible gradation; and there is, moreover, scarcely an instance in which the actual transition cannot be proved to have taken place.'[13]

What carried over in a more systematic way from these debates into the ethnographies of the people of the Nilgiris were ideas about the origins and level of development of the 'aboriginal' or 'barbarian' tribes, and the difference between them and the Hindus—who were defined as belonging to the Aryan race. It had come to be widely acknowledged at this time that the languages spoken by people from the Ganges to the British Isles had a common origin. Prichard preferred to speak of these as the Indo-European 'nations', hence emphasizing the ancient historical roots connecting British society or civilization with those of the Hindu. True to the position of classical Orientalists, people of the Deccan and South India were claimed to constitute a distinct race, different from the Aryan, and understood to be relics of an ancient population conquered by the Aryan Brahmins. The combined study of languages and classical Hindu texts, it was argued, confirmed this position.[14]

In the 1843 edition of *The Natural History of Man*, Prichard made a civilizational distinction between people, or races, inhabiting hilly countries and those who lived in the plains. He referred to the former as 'mountaineers', a term that encompassed 'all the tribes who live remote from cities and cultivated countries, and maintain a savage existence amidst woods and forests.' He considered ethnology yet too imperfect to determine the relationship among these savages and between them and the 'civilized nations' neighbouring on their lands. Their internal divisions could possibly be derived from climatic and other local conditions. Three regions were considered to host aboriginal tribes: the Vindhya mountains, the Gondwana mountains, and the Nilgiri Hills. In the case of the last, the Toda, Badaga, and Kota were specifically noted as three distinct tribes based on physical appearance and manners.[15]

When Prichard first published his magnum opus in 1843, these scientific debates had been coloured by the processes of colonial and imperial consolidation on other continents as well as received important influences from the ethnographic and administrative documentation of new British subjects. In subsequent editions of Prichard's work an important change appeared. Where Blumenbach had established the general hierarchy of the five human races, and Prichard had gone on to distinguish specific aboriginal or savage hill tribes, an introductory note to the 1855 edition of *The Natural History of Man*, published six years after Prichard's death, shows a changing discourse. Edwin Norris of the Royal Asiatic Society of Great Britain and Ireland here wrote: 'The Adamite family was what we now term civilised: it was composed of tillers of the ground, who had a settled habitat, and were guided by a systematic polity… We would call this the state of nature, and all other states degraded.'[16] He went on to explain how this single family had multiplied and small communities had departed from 'the great stock', and how some of these may have continued to exist as smaller centres of population with 'the extreme case of separation of single families producing mere savages'. These savages were assumed to be incapable of co-operation, subsisting on 'spontaneous productions of the earth' and wild animals. Larger bodies of savages could retain domestic animals and live as 'pastoral tribes'. In contrast, Norris asserted, 'the original stock, remaining together, would thereby preserve their original social condition, as an agricultural people, living in settled communities.'[17]

In his Introduction Norris framed Prichard's work firmly in civilization theory. Civilization was here constituted as an urban or settled agrarian society. It was further constituted by a systematic polity, which guided society to preserve its original social condition as settled cultivators. The people of civilization thus constituted an unbroken series of descendants of Adam and Eve. They were everything that the people of hills and forests were not. When Norris uses the term 'degraded' there is naturally no doubt that he is referring to an inferior state of human existence. People living under unsettled conditions were either pastoral tribes, keeping domestic animals—their domesticity proving that they were not completely savage—or hunters and gatherers who were claimed to be incapable of co-operation. In Norris's statement, non-sedentary societies were depicted as the antithesis of civilization.

The close mutual dependence between amateur ethnographers travelling in India and the production of scholarship in Europe is evident in Prichard's work. For Nilgiri ethnography, Prichard relied basically on the eight letters submitted by James Hough to the editor of the *Bengal Hurkaru* in 1826, which were published in a single volume in 1829, and the ethnographic work by Henry Harkness that came into print in 1832 (both discussed in Chapter 2).[18] Prichard's descriptions of mountain tribes state in general that some are 'small, shrivelled, black savages, who have been thought to resemble the Negroes of Africa; others are tall and athletic, handsome, with features resembling the European type.' To the latter category he assigned the Toda, and he explained that these 'handsome tribes' lived at high altitudes 'where a tolerably cool and salubrious climate exists; the blackest and most diminutive tribes are found in the jungle near the rivers, and in low and unhealthy districts.'[19]

As noted earlier, the Nilgiris were specifically recognized for a beneficial climate, and the healthy native inhabitants of the region were held up as evidence. Hough paid much attention to climate and topography, observing that the region was entirely free of 'morasses and vast collections of decayed vegetables that generate miasma'. By this, he was referring to the generally accepted idea that disease, in particular fever, was caused by climate and ecological conditions such as those found in marshlands and jungles. Stagnant water and dirt together with heat and moisture were believed to be veritable pools of miasma. Both the Toda and the Badaga were claimed to be ignorant of endemic disease: 'the stout athletic appearance of the Thodawurs bespeaks the salubrity of their native mountains.' Astonishingly, the Kota, 'a low, filthy race', were also found to be free of disease—a situation which could only be explained by the purity of the mountain air. Harkness, who apparently spent more time walking from settlement to settlement making enquiries among several of the communities, had a slightly different impression. The Badaga may have seemed healthier than people on the plains and claimed to have no sickness, but they omitted to mention both fever and smallpox, the former being attributed to the necromancy of the Kurumba community and the latter to the presence of the goddess Mariamman.[20]

Interestingly, the two sets of reports converge in their organization of nature and people. Neither referred explicitly to medical or botanical works, but both were written within the general themes of contemporary scholarly debate. Hough more explicitly than Harkness provided detailed statistical evidence of temperature and climate. He emphasized natural conditions which influenced the human body, and which were also treated in medical topography. By the turn of the nineteenth century, statistical surveys had become an important empirical method for the systematic gathering of information, the method it self implying statecraft. In form and presentation, though, Hough and Harkness differ significantly. Harkness's texts largely resemble the style of early-nineteenth-century travelogues typical of the far more prominent surgeon and surveyor Frances Hamilton Buchanan.[21] Statistics have a limited place in Harkness's text, being briefly narrated in the first chapter and summed up in two tables and a Toda—English glossary at the end of the volume. His text is characterized, rather, by its many personal narrative representations of travel experiences. Yet it needs to be remembered that his observations were profoundly empirical. Interestingly, in his preface Harkness stated that he had the intention of writing a short dissertation on the origins and languages of the various tribes in the Nilgiris. But lack of confidence about public interest in his opinions on the subject caused him to abstain from pursuing this ambition. His intention, however, shows how works on natural history, such as those of Blumenbach and Prichard, had influenced his conception of important matters of debate.[22]

Ethnology in the Administration of the Nilgiris

Sullivan often referred to Harkness's work as a learned authority that could not be questioned. A long minute of 1835, forming part of an investigation of Toda land claims, relied almost exclusively on Harkness's volume on the Toda. Among the many texts produced by the EIC, those of Sullivan bear perhaps the most eloquent testimony to how the mutual influence of scholarly work and ethnographic reports also made itself felt in colonial administration. His most emphatic statements, for which he found support in ethnographic surveys, were those that had legal implications for Toda proprietary rights. And, as we shall see, the central themes of scholarly work on the origin and evolution of man served as a constant resource for legal arguments as well.[23]

A central question, and one on which most other questions depended, was that of human degeneration. This could be argued both as a fact and as a risk. The use of scientific arguments to prove a fall from a pure or high origin into different, hierarchically ordered varieties or races came to have implications for the rights of 'hill tribes'—pastoralists or shifting cultivators—to claim possession of land by reference to aboriginal entitlement. Hunting and gathering communities such as the Kota and Kurumba were never considered suitable for holding title to land, and legally securing their means of livelihood never appeared on the agenda. Furthermore, determining the racial origin of a certain group of people became important both for the sake of racial hierarchy and for the purpose of interpreting the polity of a particular society. Ultimately, questions of origin and authenticity went hand in hand. Finally, the evolution of a particular race or region, which was in fact a measure of its level of development, could prove whether a people had the capacity to run their own affairs or needed guidance and supervision. Within such an evolutionary scheme the debate about the difference between the Hindu Aryan race and the South Indian or Dravidian race was used to locate and prove the uniqueness of a tribe.

Sullivan left office as district collector of Coimbatore district in 1830 and spent a number of years outside the country before returning to become a board member of the government of Madras in 1835. During his absence, land disputes in the Nilgiris had erupted into open conflict. Formal grants of land were required. These then brought the land occupied by the military cantonment, the government farm and a private individual—William Rumbold—under critical scrutiny. But as a consequence of the government's interference in the region, the district administration had itself become the subject of investigation, and the laxity with which land had been handed out was being closely questioned. The government's pronouncement on Rumbold's land in 1836 is quite significant: 'an assignment of land the very situation and limits of which appear to be now unknown to your officers, and to which the grantor certainly possessed no legal title'.[24] The Court of Directors had also become involved. They objected to the normal procedures and were concerned to secure the trust of native subjects of EIC rule by introducing legal measures. As early as 1832, the court called for an investigation into the rights of the Toda and, in 1836, the report was submitted.[25]

The investigation came at a time when conflicts in the Nilgiris were at a peak and the Toda living near and inside Ootacamund, in particular, were actively confronting the administration. Their strategies and the politics of conflicts will be discussed in Chapter 5; here, we will look more closely at how scientific arguments and amateur ethnography provided fuel for the legal debates. For this purpose, the investigation of 1836 provides a good starting point.

Initially, it was concern for the well being of the Toda that caused the Court of Directors to ask for an investigation: 'It is our wish that their rights in the most ample sense of the term, should be respected; and that they should not be deprived of any portion of their long established privileges without liberal compensation.'[26] The court's strong emphasis on Toda rights appears to have had the effect both of restraining the Madras government from acting more rapidly and forcefully to establish sovereign rule, and of prolonging an administrative process which produced numerous surveys and reports. The government needed substantive arguments to confront the early ethnographic accounts, which were sympathetic to Toda proprietary rights, and was keen to send its own officers to the Nilgiris. At the same time, the district administration churned out its own reports to counter the government's position.

Sullivan began his minute by establishing the hierarchy of expertise, referring to his own long residence in the hills and his particular interest in the Toda, he having been the one who introduced strangers among them. Noting that the government had called on the collectors of Malabar and Coimbatore to submit reports in order to furnish the Court of Directors with information, he added that, as expected, they had little or nothing to add to Harkness's published work. His message was clear: short-term visits by bureaucrats and their subordinates, taking depositions from a few individual Toda or Badaga men, could never replace years of personal experience and information-gathering based on empirical enquiry.

Sullivan's selection of information from Harkness's work indicates his awareness of the arguments needed in support of claims to absolute title in land. He emphasized the uniqueness of the Toda's origin and language, their aboriginality, the singularity of their race and their superior moral character. He described their bodies in gendered terms to distinguish them from the feminized Hindus. Within this evidence, origin came first. Sullivan commended Harkness for his ability to find empirical evidence of Toda society and history in spite of the fact that they themselves had no records or oral traditions of their origin. Harkness's observations of Toda language, features, manners, habits, appearance, and religious customs had led him to deduce that the Toda had an origin distinctly different from that of the 'tribes' of the low country. The ethnological position that 'hill tribes' or 'mountaineers' lived far from civilization, yet in climates and at elevations that were beneficial for a healthy life, invited interpretations in either a positive or negative direction. Sullivan chose to downplay arguments, deriving from civilization theory, which spoke of primitiveness. Instead, he quoted from passages stating that the Toda were definitely not Hindus or a branch of the Brahminical faith.[27]

His emphasis on their uniqueness was further underlined by a reference to their language. Although Sullivan kept close to Harkness's text, he added a certain twist to it. Whereas Harkness wrote: 'With the Sanscrit it has not the least affinity, in roots, construction, or sound; and, if I may venture to say so, as little with any other Asiatic language of the present day', in Sullivan's quote Harkness was made to say that the Toda language was assigned by other natives 'not to the Eastern but to the Western Hemisphere'. Projecting them as singular corresponded with the general race theory of the time and served to distinguish the Toda as a separate people. They had not merged with other 'tribes' in India or changed over time by 'insensible gradation'—to paraphrase Prichard. Sullivan strongly asserted that the Toda remained unique.[28]

The point of projecting the Toda as unique is more clearly explained when Sullivan states that they were 'the oldest beyond comparison of the present races on the Neilgherries'. The Madras government had earlier objected to his claim that the Toda were the first to set foot on the hills, making them aboriginal of the place, by pointing to the archaeological remains of cairns to which the Toda—after proper enquiry—had claimed no affinity. Sullivan swept aside this objection by referring to Harkness's intense but failed efforts to trace their first appearance in the hills. He argued that, since no other people could in any way be traced and connected to this ancient history, the Toda were the only now living race who could claim an ancient past in the hills. The logic of his argument was that, by definition and according to common law, this gave them a birthright to absolute property in the land.[29]

Another line of argument, fuelled by ethnological findings, focused on the bodies and moral character of the Toda. As argued in Chapter 2, gendered descriptions of the Toda's physical appearance and 'manners' were structured to distinguish them from both 'Hindu Indians' and Europeans. Toda men bore all the masculine qualities that were generally associated with European or, more specifically, British men, while in their personal character they were described as children. Likewise, women were associated with the ideal stereotype of the British peasant housewife, though simultaneously identified with lower sexual morals. In Sullivan's minute this provided an image of the Toda as holding an exceptional position, an elevated and capable people as compared with other Indian subjects. Like every European observer, he deplored their customs of infanticide and polyandry, but 'nevertheless [they are] held in great veneration and treated with the utmost respect by the other classes, particularly by the Burghers.' The Badaga, so venerated by the Madras government, were acknowledged by reference to Harkness's observation: 'a timid superstitious race', and contrasted with the Toda, 'hardy, fearless, superior in stature, distinct in boldness and freedom unknown to the other'. Again, Sullivan slightly twisted Harkness's words, seemingly to avoid other possible interpretations. While Harkness expressed himself in more tentative terms about Toda superiority, suggesting that 'their apparent consciousness of superiority alone, would readily command a corresponding acknowledgement of it from the [Burgher]', Sullivan quoted Harkness as having written that they 'assume a superiority which the others have no inclination to dispute'. These may seem to have been observations of purely ethnographic interest, but they served in fact as substantive evidence in a legal argument for the right to property.[30]

Hough was also referred to as a reliable authority on the Toda. In addition to the points drawn from Harkness's work, he was quoted for his statement about Toda lordship and possession of the entire Nilgiris before other people settled in the hills. And finally, quoting his own report of 1828, Sullivan concluded:

> The subdivision of the Neilgherries called 'Malnaud' is entirely pasture, and has been in possession of the Todawars from an antiquity remote beyond the reach of tradition. They are the most ancient inhabitants of the mountains, and are recognized as the proprietors of the soil by the people of more recent origin, the Burghers (the agricultural class) who pay them annually as such fees in kind.
>
> The exclusive proprietary right of the Todawars to the pasture country called Malnaad, is not contested by any other class of Natives. On the contrary by the cultivating classes, who occupy at least three fourths of the Neilgherries they are considered as the most ancient proprietors of the whole range, and as such they derive an annual income from the land which both by the Burgher and the Todawars is called Goodoo.[31]

Here, in the twenty-fifth paragraph, Sullivan let ethnography openly merge with law, and this is where he turned his argument in a more technical direction. A common method of finding evidence of land rights in newly conquered territories was to investigate the revenue assessed from the land. Previous or existing revenue or rent payments revealed land relations. Regarding the Toda, the payment of gudu was therefore a constant matter of dispute between the government and district administrations. As discussed earlier, to Sullivan gudu was a form of rent, equal to jenmi tenure, which proved the Toda's absolute property in land.

Interestingly, owing to the way in which Sullivan went on to explain what constituted the giving of gudu, the notion of rent tended to disappear. In addition to describing the amount of grain given for the right to plough a specified portion of land, he claimed that both Toda and Badaga avowed that the annual contribution of gudu was made for religious purposes. For the Badaga, it was an act of propitiation, to secure friendly treatment by the Toda. To Sullivan, they had asserted that their deference was due by prescription from when the Toda had given their ancestors the privilege of cultivating the land. Toda protection would safeguard them against the sorcery of other tribes, and the fear of losing that protection would prevent the Badaga from failing to pay punctually. The Kota, Kurumba, and Irula also received portions of grain, but Sullivan was quick to assert that this was a different kind of gift, made purely in return for specific services. It had no implications for land rights. Even though the services concerned included averting the exercise of preternatural powers, as in the case of gifts to the Kurumba,

Sullivan maintained that such gifts were to be equated with ordinary payments. In Sullivan's argument, only the payment of gudu to the Toda proved lordship and, hence, absolute property.[32]

Such a strict interpretation of complex social, economic, and ritual relationships in terms of systems of tenure or market relations appears in several documents in the correspondence on revenue and land administration. The terminology of 'rent', 'landlord', 'fee', and 'payment' not only figured prominently in reports from the district but was also the discourse of debate about the social order of the hills. It provided the frame of interpretation in the legal debate. Even in cases where this terminology did not seem to fit, officers tended to adjust their information to suit the debate—not necessarily because they believed, for example, that gudu was or was not a form of rent, but because these were the frames within which legal codification was shaped.

Once the report on the 'State of the Todawars on the Neilgherry Hills' was submitted by the Madras government to the Court of Directors in the summer of 1836, it gave the impression of a consolidated administration, within which all were basically agreed. But a closer reading shows that everyone—including the two collectors, the former district collector, the revenue board, and the Madras government—had their own interests to defend, and that they picked out of the report whatever was useful to them, carefully avoiding disagreements, in particular with the Court of Directors. The chain reaction within the administration leading up to the final report began with the collectors' reports of February and April 1835, which were critically commented on by Sullivan in September, after which the revenue board instructed the military board to respect Toda rights and defer compensation payments, awaiting the collectors' opinions. And finally there was the revenue board meeting of February 1836 to which the collectors submitted comments on Sullivan's minute. Based on these documents, the government made its decision.

Consequently, in spite of Sullivan's accusations of incompetence, the Malabar and Coimbatore collectors basically agreed with his conclusions. They never ventured to enter into a debate about his or any other ethnography referred to; their concern was how to convert Sullivan's minute into a functioning revenue assessment. The Malabar collector argued that a low level of assessment would encourage Europeans to make large enclosures, which would harm the cultivation of potatoes and European vegetables by the industrious Badaga agriculturists. The Coimbatore collector complained that much of the land occupied by Europeans had never been enclosed, and went on to sort out the administrative logic of the eleven classes of land and their varying assessments. In complete agreement with the revenue board, the government decided that Toda rights and interests should be respected (as the Court of Directors had ordered) and also that, as long as the Toda paid taxes, they should not be disturbed in their possession of land. Further, it was agreed that land could only be appropriated with their consent and with suitable compensation. Even when the government took land for public purposes, compensation had to be offered. The basic design of the revenue administration suggested in this report has all that could be required of a liberal government policy; the problems arose from its implementation. The sub-collector of Malabar, Daniel Eliott, was subsequently sent to the Nilgiris to settle the conditions on which the government could come into possession of the land on which the military cantonment in Ootacamund was built. Simultaneously he was to sort out the situation regarding William Rumbold's estate. The conflict that escalated as a result of his work will be examined in Chapter 5.[33]

Ethnicizing Subjects, Contesting Land Rights

The process by which legal codes regulating conquered territories were carved out by colonial governments is at times discussed in terms of mapping landscapes. The terminology indicates a powerful and active state outlining ideas of governance, economy, and bureaucracy for large territories, with the purpose of restructuring relationships between people and nature in line with state interests. Such studies tend to emphasize state policy and regulation, and most of their empirical foundations are derived from mid- to late-nineteenth- and twentieth-century contexts. For Indian historical studies, the British imperial state dominates the discussion.[34] Simultaneously, arguments are developed that combine the growth of modern state institutions and the simultaneously internalized racial perceptions that structured administrative logic. Here, the use of ethnology for the purpose of state formation and resource control comes into focus.[35]

However, as the discussion above shows, the Nilgiri situation points in other directions, away from assumptions of a synthesized policy and towards an analysis sensitive to the specific regional situation. In a search to understand the uneven, heterogeneous establishment of colonial bureaucracy, inspiration comes from studies of the discursive level of policy-making and of the questions pursued in late-nineteenth-century research—but only in so far as these studies do not inform assumptions about policy implementation or cause early colonial rule to be read through the rearview mirror of a high imperial age. If that happens, there is an evident risk both of portraying the use of ethnology in an almost instrumentalist way and of exaggerating the reach and uniformity of the state—a uniformity hardly characteristic even of the late-nineteenth-century colonial state. Sudha Vasan's study of forest policy implementation in the small princely states of Himachal, in which she emphasizes the colonial state's limited capacity to order nature and the diverse property regimes that unmade any attempt to enforce a homogeneous policy, is one of a number of works that make this clear. As has been argued, the ethnological treatment of people in forest and hill tracts emerged from different, historically specific interests—scientific, governmental, land- and resource-related—that converged in the ways in which different settler and EIC claims were justified and enforced.[36]

'Political forests' is the term introduced by Nancy Lee Peluso and Peter Vandergeest to explain the establishment of racially structured colonial law in South East Asian forests during the early twentieth century. Their study also has implications for a broader understanding of the formation and territorialization of colonial rule in South Asia. It is located within a period when colonial empires were celebrating victories around the world, and at the same time as the colonial power centres in Europe were under immense pressure from wars and economic depression. The authors chose to emphasize the crucial importance of sovereign state control in the conquered territories. The term 'political forest' implies lands which the colonial state declared as 'forest', thus bringing these within the scope of specific legislation in a manner reminiscent of administrative processes established following the formation of the Forest Department in British India in 1865. The term thus focuses on the decisive ways in which the state could intervene, forcefully and institutionally, to control and manage forests according to its own interests. The authors argue that the process itself was a critical part of colonial state-making in terms of territorialization and the legal framing of forests, as well as of the institutionalization of forest management as a technology of state power.[37]

As argued in studies on other continents, this racial discourse penetrated most colonial administrations at the time. Melissa Johnson, for example, identifies racial-ecological categories as a dimension of colonial control in the British colony of Belize. Here, it was presumed that people of different racial groups had different relationships to the natural environment. Creoles were assumed to be physiologically suited to be woodcutters, the Maya were seen as indolent farmers, and the Garifuna as excellent fishermen. Such racial identity markers contributed to colonial control of access to natural resources. One of the consequences that Johnson identifies is the way it became impossible for the Creole to own any part of the most productive land. At the same time, colonial subjects appropriated this discourse both in creating relationships to land and, simultaneously, challenging the construction of the discourse itself.[38]

The question is, however, how racial discourses were mediated through colonial administrations in different places and at specific points in time. Significantly, in Peluso and Vandergeest's argument, the link between the legal code and its implementation is a close one. Laws are seen as representing a repertoire of colonial forest practices constituting new forms of discipline as well as views of land and resources, the racial component being one of the key elements. Racialized access to forests is said to have been manifest in three major ways: as exclusion through ethnic categories, when ethnically defined groups were denied access; as inclusion, when ownership and use rights were based on ethnicity or race, such as being native to a place; and again as exclusion through administrative categories, for example when conservation regimes restricted access to a certain forest. In the last case, racial exclusion may have been an unintended consequence of administrative regulation, but, according to the authors, it was racial in character all the same.[39]

Peluso and Vandergeest's framing of the problem, with its focus on a strong and aggressive colonial state, explains well why Foucault's and James C. Scott's works on the exercise of power by the state were particularly relevant to their analysis. Foucault's major work on the institutionalization of prisons, in which he developed ideas about techniques of power and discipline, was especially useful, and the authors see their study of state management of forests as a unique opportunity to gain a better understanding of governmentality. They argue that forest management gave rise to specific types of government institutions and legal means of achieving security and discipline. People's actions towards the forest were thus controlled by the way in which 'forest' was defined, and hence socially constructed. The techniques used included territorial zoning and mapping, enacting laws that defined legal and illegal forest uses, and creating forestry institutions. In particular, the distinction between 'customary practices', implying local practices by which people themselves organized access to land and resources, and 'Customary Rights', referring to practices that were recognized and redefined under colonial rule, shows how the state forcibly interfered in local society (the authors use capital letters to distinguish practice formed by local custom from that by formal law). Scott projects the high-modern state as one that seeks simplification and control through large-scale schemes. He uses scientific forestry as a key metaphor of forms of knowledge and manipulation associated with powerful institutions with strong interests, his point being that such schemes tend to fail when they do not recognize local customs and knowledge. Although Peluso and Vandergeest acknowledge different regional patterns of the 'relative hegemonic power' of forestry departments in India, which are also discussed in Sivaramakrishnan's work, they prefer to emphasize that 'the strength of the idea of the differentiated, territorial political forest in the discourses of rule played a major role in its institutionalization.'[40]

The methodology employed also points to the explanatory preference given to the role of the state. Using Foucault's notion of historical 'genealogies', the authors seek to construct a 'history of the present' by tracking events and ideas that led to the creation of political forests, forest law, and customary rights. They argue that during late colonialism, specific systems of governmentality made possible the creation of political forests. In this way, they choose beforehand the historical trajectory they intend to search for, and their historical study helps them fill in the empirical gaps. However relevant the emphasis on the powerful state may be in the South East Asian case, the method of tracking historical trajectories may make it more difficult to find complex and contradictory situations in which state administration may not have been entirely singular or systematic. Hypothetically, we may assume that such situations provided space for protests and resistance that never developed into revolts and were never discussed in such terms in administrative communications—and hence will never be detected in the analysis.[41]

This way of approaching the problematic of human—nature—power relations is reminiscent of several better-known works of Indian environmental history. While their major focus on the crucial role of the state has provided important insights into state logics and aims, their frame of analysis has a limited capacity to grasp the complex processes involved in forming and maintaining the bureaucracy of colonial rule. The growing role of an interventionist state emerges particularly clearly in studies looking at the late nineteenth century, such as Ramachandra Guha's examination of popular resistance to state intervention in the Uttarakhand forests, and Mahesh Rangarajan's work on imperial intervention and ecological change in the Central Provinces. This is not only a result of the dichotomous outline of Guha's research problem and Rangarajan's aim of specifically detecting imperial forest policy (which in Rangarajan's case justifies well his emphasis on the state's large-scale interventionist intentions); it can also be traced to the fact that this was a period when the colonial state was more consolidated than half a century earlier. However, as several studies have pointed out, assumptions about the colonial state's capacity for implementation should be made with some caution.[42]

Sivaramakrishnan, in his study of colonial Bengal, bridges the divide between company and crown rule by distinguishing between the two as different phases of colonial state-making. While the state during the early period is described as more concerned with security, developing regimes of control and striving to sedenterize mobile populations, the later period stands out as characterized by administrative measures to secure control over forest resources through reservation and by attempts to establish specific property regimes in forests for the generation of profit. Centralization of authority and management is thus seen as an effect of policy and policy implementation. However, introduced as a heavy criticism of Saidian followers who give colonial representation primacy over historical experience, and in contrast to studies that take colonial state capacity for granted, Sivaramakrishnan's account acknowledges the incoherences and inconsistencies in colonial administration which reveal the gap between intentions and implementation. At the level of principle, and in spite of the differences between woodland Bengal and the Western Ghats of South India, his elaboration of the creation of 'tribal places' resulting from ambiguous or exceptional administration under colonial rule is of particular interest here.[43]

Sivaramakrishnan argues that preconditions for the exceptional administration of tribal territories grew out of British attempts to incorporate people in south-west woodland Bengal and Bihar into a British-controlled economy and administration during early colonial rule. In a profound way, these regions were defined differently from the caste society of Hindu India and from the agrarian economy of the plains.[44] By constructing an administration based on principles distinct from those adhered to in the plains, the government acknowledged that the areas in question were different, allowing them to remain so for reasons of governance. In the process, restrictions on shifting cultivation became a key strategy that served to pacify a region and control use of the landscape. A comparison between administrators' descriptions of the Paharia shifting cultivators of the hills and the Santhal settled cultivators of the foothills and plains reveals their preference for sedentary production. The Paharia, who cleared fields in the forests to grow minor forest products for sale, were seen as using the forest in a wasteful way, while the Santhal, who cleared forests for the sake of settled cultivation, were commended for their industrious enterprise. However, the administrative strategies that resulted in tribal places were put into effect in a more systematic way only after the administrative reforms that followed the introduction of crown rule. Only then did the tribal heartland emerge, amidst a far-reaching transformation of the landscape, with new villages and ordered fields and groves, supported by efforts to protect tribal control of land and preserve 'tribal republics' in their 'natural habitat'. However, much earlier, during the time of early colonial expansion in the region, Sivaramakrishnan observes a series of episodes of unrest among communities who experienced a loss of economic and political authority when British expansion set both economic and political changes in motion, provoking further renegotiation of local authority and governance.[45]

Interestingly, such descriptions of the state's partiality towards a settled agrarian economy and its negative portrayal of the mobile production forms of most forest and tribal societies almost replicate, even if unintentionally, David Ludden's critical description of the way in which agrarian history and society tend to be depicted in modern scholarly works. Read the following passage, replacing the word 'agrarian' with 'forest': 'Agrarian folk appear as a negative mirror image of all that is urban, industrial and modern; not as makers of history, but rather as inhabitants of history, endowed with mentalities and memories which can be recovered but not with creative powers to transform their world.'[46]

In Ludden's reading, not until around 1870 was agrarian life included as part of the modern Indian state and of modernity. He defines this significant moment in the modern history of India from the point at which institutions of imperial bureaucracy, ideologies of development, and analytical sciences of management combined to domesticate the agrarian economy within the standardized objects of administration, policy, and politics. Ludden observes how the modern scholarly canon has colluded with modern official archives to make it difficult to imagine any real autonomy of agrarian history from the state or elites. His argument thus touches on the logic of the early Subaltern Studies critique. Similarly, a common line of argument in environmental history that seeks to relate forest and tribal societies to larger political-economic entities is to contrast forest (gathering, swidden, and pastoral) economies with agrarian (settled) economies—the one diminishing as the other expands, settled agriculture being the epitome of the expanding modern state. The contrast is obvious. While Ludden criticizes modern historiography for placing agrarian societies in the archaic fold, environmental history focusing on forests and hills projects the same societies as signs of the modern state project. In this connection, it is worth noting that Ludden, when discussing the place of swidden in relation to permanent field cultivation in Indian history, characterizes the two phenomena in terms of the contrast between caste and tribal societies, or between hills and plains: 'the two systems maintained their social distance and otherness, even as they interacted and overlapped.' Yet both these narratives of agrarian and forest production seek to come to grips with a problematic notion of the advancing evolutionary frontier of modernity.[47]

Empirically, the dividing line between mobile and settled production from the land has usefully begun to be questioned. Physically exact boundaries between fields and forests are difficult to determine over longer periods of time, as shrubs and forests tend to grow back on fields and other productive activities take over when economic or other conditions put pressure on the agrarian economy. Moreover, the two were not separate economies but interrelated and connected through economic activities. Kathleen Morrison's study of upland—lowland exchange in the Malabar spice trade (discussed in Chapter 2) provides one example of the extent to which gathering made way for cultivation in the hills in close connection with lowland economies in early modern South India. In similar ways, the Nilgiris also demonstrate the lack of secluded and pristine localities that remained untouched by neighbouring, transforming societies until the advance of the modern agrarian frontier. There is an evident need for integrated analyses in which the interplay of different economic activities is treated apart from notions of linear and evolutionary history that may obscure an understanding of how modernity came to be manifested through interconnected transformations of both mobile and settled, forest, and agrarian societies.[48]

In contrast with the way in which the Bengal government dealt with societies in the vast forests on its southern and western borders, a 'tribal heartland' in South India was never a product of the Madras regime. Although the hills were often described as exceptional, and were at particular points in time administered under regulations specifically drawn up to find a solution to a practical and urgent problem, the government's aim was not to preserve them as an exceptional enclave within the presidency administration. Through the eyes of what we generally discuss as civilization theory, the hills were to be brought into the fold of the modern economy and state administration. It is important to observe the interplay between particular interests and the use of ethnological science in the formation of the EIC bureaucracy in the early-nineteenth-century Nilgiris, in particular during its first two formative decades when the administration was ridden with conflict. Here such theories worked in anomalous ways, as the Badaga community's place in the government's plans for the region shows. Though forced to flee from their status as settled agriculturists on the Mysore plains, they still retained dormant skills that would enable them to again establish settled production in the hills. The attempt to incorporate this 'hill tribe' into the British administration did not involve assigning them exceptional status, but rather assuming their similarity to lowland and Hindu society. In contrast, Toda society remained a battlefield, for which ethnology proved a useful resource by means of which specific claims could be made. Pursuing different causes, the district administration portrayed the Toda as having a noble civilization of great ancestry, while the Madras government described them in derogatory terms. Such notions of tribal difference were not merely a result of attempts to demonize the enemy or the 'other', but also ordered the worldview of administrators. They either valued people as original holders of the land or saw them as migrant barbarians. In the Nilgiris, the exceptional were not tribals at large, but the Toda 'hill tribe'.[49]

The Madras government's general view of people in hills and forests emerged in a more concentrated form in the reply to Sullivan's last report to the government before he left office in 1830, in which the board completely abandoned its usual courteous tone in response to Sullivan's more emotional outbursts. The main thrust of the reply was to prove the Toda's lack of civilization. The framework in which that proof was presented was constructed around the idea of British civilization and its systematic polity built on law. In the document it remained undisputed that the Nilgiri landscape was constituted by 'woods' and 'waste', that any right in the soil depended on it being cultivated, and that the accepted proof of pre-existing land relations was the existence of taxation within the polity of a state. It was further laid down that only a sovereign state held an absolute right in land.[50]

The government remarked that the collector had no ground for claiming Toda land rights, since he had not been able to present any reliable evidence; no written documents were available and no proof of earlier taxation had been accepted by the government. Basically, Toda society lacked written law, fixed habitation, and settled rules of life. The Toda were said to be migrant herders, unfamiliar with the cultivation of the soil, ignorant, naked, and lacking the comforts of a developed society. Accordingly, they lacked the systematic polity that would have granted them a position from which to negotiate with the colonial government. They were thus legally defined to be in a dependent position in relation to British civilization and unable to make legal claims on land in the Nilgiris.[51]

Towards a Public Nilgiri Historiography

By the mid nineteenth century, ethnology had ceased to be an arena for the contest over legal rights in the Nilgiris, but it remained a resource in arguments to prove the capacity or suitability of a certain community to earn legal rights. Prichard's model had lost prominence in scholarly debate and gradually been superseded by physical anthropology and the rigid hierarchies of the human races perceived in social evolutionism. Cultural characteristics, too, were deduced from biological determinants.[52]

Most significantly, from the mid to the late nineteenth century, a singular narrative of the Nilgiris developed. This spoke of the Nilgiris as a transforming landscape, a tribal place, a place of successful improvement promoted by an enlightened and benevolent British government. It was thus a linear historical narrative outlining a trajectory from dark wildness to enlightened development. Interestingly, it has to some extent continued to proliferate in twentieth-century scholarly works, mostly among anthropologists.[53] A brief detour through the ethnological writings of this period shows how the idea of the Toda and the Nilgiris became more stereotyped over time, finally to be confirmed in the imperial gazetteers. These gazetteers were reference books for colonial administrators, a kind of encyclopaedic source of knowledge about a certain region. H.B. Grigg's *Manual of Nilagiri District* was published in 1880 and has since been widely used as a highly reliable historical account, even among academic writers, who have rarely found reason to question its imperial bias.

Blumenbach had initiated the comparative study of human crania as a basis for dividing humanity into different varieties. So when physical descriptions of the Nilgiri 'hill tribes' became more prominent in the 1860s, they represented the continuation of a scholarly interest in the human body and the development of the human species, although now the meticulous attention to detail and measurements bordered on the obsessive. John Shortt's study for the Ethnological Society of London in 1868 is a good example.[54] A Toda's forehead was described as rather narrow and receding (measuring 2¼ inches from the root of the nose to the growth of hair and scalp), eyebrows thick and approaching each other, eyes moderately large, well formed, expressive, and often intelligent. His aquiline nose was measured to the nearest quarter-inch. And after descriptions of male and female upper and lower lips, teeth, ears, skulls, weights, and other measurements, Shortt concluded that men were generally attractive and their carriage graceful, while he had never met a handsome, pretty female face that was anywhere near in 'perfection or beauty to a classical model'. His conclusion that the male Toda were well proportioned, of the Caucasian type, is a mix of Blumenbach's Caucasian and Ethiopian varieties.[55]

The gendered descriptions of men and women followed the ambiguous observations of the 1820s, with good qualities marking a distance from Hindu Indians and a resemblance with Europeans—or, as the discussion went four decades later, Caucasians—and bad qualities distinguishing them from the same. From within Victorian ideals, Shortt remarked that, unlike most of the 'Indian races and Natives', Toda women were treated respectfully by their husbands and not like slaves, as were Hindu women. They observed their responsibilities for household tasks, while attending to needlework and singing in their spare time.[56]

These gendered descriptions were not of a physical but of a moral character. When comparing Toda bodies with those of other Indian communities, Shortt found no differences. This observation stands in contrast to the situation in the 1820s and 1830s, when arguments in favour of Toda property were substantiated by references to their history as aboriginals and as a distinctly different people. Shortt, on the other hand, asserted: 'The notion also that the Todawar tribe present any special peculiarities in their habits and customs, language and religion, costume, or ethnological features, is, I apprehend ... more imaginary than real.'[57] Nor does he show much appreciation of their habits. They were 'dirty and filthy', and the 'odour' that came from the habit of rubbing their bodies with ghee (fat being a poor person's protection against a cold climate, even in Britain) did not agree with Shortt's ideas of proper hygiene.[58] His personal aversion to the community surfaces occasionally in his text, as in his comments on the 'unnatural' system of polyandry—'they all live under one roof, and cohabit promiscuously, just as fancy and taste inclines'—or in his surprise to note that Toda mothers, on hearing their children cry when being vaccinated, 'exhibit marked maternal feeling and distress'.[59]

Prichard, who assumed that all non-Aryans were aboriginals, had asserted that 'the wild races in the Dekhan' were allied to the Tamulian tribe who had fled from 'the approach of civilization and preserved in the remote and least accessible part of the country their pristine barbarism'. Shortt took this idea to account also for the 'hill tribes' whom he believed to share a common origin with the Dravidian races. He therefore concluded: '[The Toda are not] indigenous aborigines of the Hills they now occupy. They are like other half-savage races ... the remnants of a population who once occupied the plains of India, overrun by successive invasions of superior races, before whom they were driven forward for shelter to their present respective mountainous habitats.'[60] His ethnography focused on human physical appearance, and he dismissed all claims to Toda superiority via the precision of physical anthropology. What looked like physical superiority in stature vanished when bodies were properly measured, he argued. It was 'a deceptive impression, produced by the combined effect of their graceful costume, self-possessed deportment, unturbaned heads, and peculiar mode of wearing the hair'. If these outer ornaments were replaced with those of the low-country natives, 'the Todawar, male or female, is not a whit better-looking'. The Toda's easy deportment before strangers, self-possession, and fearlessness were qualities that Shortt assumed had been 'enhanced greatly by the kind, and almost favouring, treatment this tribe has ever received at the hands of Europeans.'[61] Hence, qualities which in the 1820s had been considered admirable and attributed to an ancient history, only to be destroyed by European intrusion, were now either disregarded or else acknowledged as good qualities, but assumed to be due to the civilizing presence of Europeans.

However, derogatory descriptions of people in India and the claims of scientific proof of the difference between them and Europeans show no dramatic differences between early and late ethnologists and natural scientists. In Blumenbach's Caucasian variety, 'the intellectual faculties of its individuals are susceptible of the highest cultivation ... Philosophy and the fine arts flourish in it as in their proper soil: to it revelation was directly granted.' His physical description of Caucasians ends: 'in short, the countenance of that style which we consider the most beautiful'. In contrast, at the other end of the scale, the Ethiopian variety was considered inferior: 'This mental inferiority is attended of course by a corresponding inferiority of the brains.'[62] Thus, physical anthropology had roots going back well before the middle of the nineteenth century. However, the great variation which Blumenbach and Prichard observed within their human varieties, and which Blumenbach found to be so substantial that conclusions about different races were hard to draw, tended to disappear in late-nineteenth-century ethnology.[63]

Shortt's statements about the Toda concur with the general themes of ethnological debate at this time. During the mid and late nineteenth century, articles and reports from the Nilgiris tended to be ethnographic in content.[64] Phrenologists, such as William Marshall, constituted a minor group who measured skulls in order to make inferences about mental capacities. Marshall declared in 1873 that he had long 'been curious to understand the mysterious process by which, as appears inevitable, savage tribes melt away when forced into prolonged contact with a superior civilization.'[65] And—'The Toda is merely a simple, thriftless, and idle man, who will never, so long as his blood remains unmixed with that of superior tribes, or by selection, is improved almost beyond recognition, work one iota more than circumstances compel him to: but without taint of the ferocity of savagery.'[66]

As many studies have acknowledged, the classification of groups of people into castes and tribes on racial grounds structured colonial administrations during the late nineteenth century. Contributions to the creation of such structured difference and responses to bureaucratic classification have been discussed in different terms, from an emphasis on the mutual benefits for British rule and socially and economically advancing groups, and on caste strategies to maintain political control over subordinate groups—as in Susan Bayly's major study on caste—to a more instrumentalist understanding of administrative transformations, as in Sanjay Nigam's work on criminal castes and tribes. Working in a Saidian tradition, Nigam argues that colonial power made colonial stereotypes of peoples in order to pacify and control them: 'the need to police, suppress and control these groups *à la* thugs, had the effect of making thugs of them'. In Meena Radhakrishna's study of colonial South India, the degradation of communities into criminal tribes is attributed to modernization and expanding infrastructure, particularly improved communications, which replaced their itinerant trading operations with transport by road and railway. Rigid forest acts restricted access to traditional livelihoods, forcing them onto the roads, and severe famine robbed them of their draught cattle. In that situation, British administrators began associating their migrant way of life with criminality.[67]

At the time when Grigg's *Manual* appeared, the Nilgiris had become a district in their own right. A comprehensive revenue survey and successive changes in revenue administration had made the Nilgiri landscape more accessible and more easily controlled by the colonial government. The transformations that occurred involved a substantial rewriting of legislative history, among other things for the purpose of legitimizing the refusal to enter individual Toda names into patta documents. An advertisement for a firm of photographers in the *Madras Mail* in 1869 offers a good illustration of how Toda munds inside and in the vicinity of urban centres had been made to represent the stereotype of a Toda tribal life that was to be 'consumed' by European visitors to the hills.[68] 'We would especially mention a view of the Toda Mund near Sylk's, Kandalmund, which is essentially characteristic of the Neilgherries, and a large vignette of a Toda, which would give a very perfect idea to the "old folks at home" of the original inhabitants of the land we live in.'[69]

In his compilation of an officially sanctioned history of the Nilgiris for the government of Madras, Grigg found no reason to be stringent in his use of ethnological terminology. He believed that this 'tribe of barbarous herdsmen' had been treated far too indulgently by the government, and that land settlement acts had by and by rectified this situation.[70] 'The fact that they, relatively to the Badagas at least, the principal cultivating tribe, were the earliest occupants of the plateau, gave rise to pretensions on their part to lordship over the Hills, pretensions which received for many years the enthusiastic support of Mr John Sullivan, of Mr Hough, and of Captain Harkness, but which were as strenuously opposed by some distinguished members of the Civil Service, especially Mr S.R. Lushington, Mr C.M. Lushington, and Mr Bird.'[71] Grigg was clear about whom he sided with. The authors of the early reports from the Nilgiris—a district collector, a chaplain, and a captain—were described as 'enthusiastic supporters' of Toda 'pretensions', while three 'distinguished members of the Civil Service'—a governor, a commander-in-chief, and a chief judge cum member of council—were said to 'strenuously oppose' such loosely based claims. It was the voice of the Madras government that kept recurring in his manual. This is particularly clear in its treatment of issues concerning property and sovereignty in land. The two institutions on which the debates in the early nineteenth century centred were discussed in some detail. One is the exchange of gudu, the other the question of earlier polities in the Nilgiris, i.e. whether the Toda had submitted to Mysore state by paying land revenue. In short, Grigg sought to establish whether or not the Toda had received gudu as a sign of superior socio-political status or as a mere land rent, and whether the payment of taxes to Mysore was a sign of submission of all rights to a sovereign ruler prior to British conquest.

His answer was clear. Deriving his interpretation of gudu from the reports of the Malabar and Coimbatore collectors in the 1836 investigation, he concluded that gudu was nothing but land rent, and that tax payments proved that the Toda had always ceded their land rights to a sovereign ruler. The early British administrators in the Nilgiris had simply misunderstood the situation:

> The 'gudu' or basket of grain ... was regarded as rent paid by the tenants to the landlords for the lands occupied by them. The high position claimed for this tribe of barbarous herdsmen was in great measure due to the ignorance that existed in regard to the nature of this custom. But when it was ascertained that other tribes received from the timid Badagas *benevolence* of a similar nature, the argument grounded thereon lost much of its force ... the payment was not universal, but was mainly confined to Badaga villages neighbouring the Toda grazing grounds of the uplands.... The fond advocates of Toda rights also lost sight of the fact that they had from time immemorial paid to the Circar a tax.[72]

We may remind ourselves of how few the Toda were. The slightly unreliable census in 1826 counted 326 individuals in total, while Harkness put their number at approximately 600, of whom 300 were adult men who attended an important funeral in 1832.[73] The modest size of the population immediately raises questions as to why the colonial rulers, with all their power, did not simply move in and establish firm rules. When Grigg's *Manual* was published, the struggle over the correct classification of the Toda had continued for close on seven decades. The importance of classification is evident in the context of legal history. Sullivan's aim and that of other key players in the administrative disputes was to firmly establish, i.e. to fix, the idea of an authentic Toda identity. Colonial law established, above all, hierarchies and power relations.

Scientific methods—especially ethnology—in combination with race and climate theories were key tools in the settlement of land rights. Sullivan's minute in the 1836 investigation demonstrated most visibly the close connection between scientific methods, theoretical constructions, and law, as he moved from establishing Toda ethnography to local hierarchies of Toda lordship and, finally, to land relations in which the Toda were claimed to be landlords. It remained in his interest to read positive connotations into a clearly defined 'Toda landscape', or to romanticize the past in contrast with the present. From within such a perspective, European intrusion implied a threat to a well-functioning Nilgiri society.

As has become evident, these classifications changed dramatically over time, being adjusted according to political and economic interests and adapted to renegotiated relations of power. However, in spite of their continuous transformation, they were defined as, and claimed to be fixed at, each and every point in time. It was absolutely crucial for the Madras government to rely on civilization theory and establish that the Toda were uncivilized barbarians in need of improvements provided by a progressive British administration. When Grigg, unchallenged, made a priori statements about the Toda and other communities, he was backed by imperial rule in a situation where the contestation of racial categories had basically ceased in the Nilgiris.

In view of the continuously changing descriptions of the Toda community, Ingold's words stand out with a different tenor. Slightly paraphrased, we may conclude that to represent people as existing forever within the ethnographic encounter is to consign their lives to a time that has already been left far behind.

Notes

1. Field notes, Kengodumund, 9 February 2005.
2. Hough, 1829, *Letters on the Climate, Inhabitants, Productions, &C., &C., of the Neilgherries, or, Blue Mountains of Coimbatoor, South India*, 79–80.
3. Harkness, 1832, *A Description of a Singular Aboriginal Race Inhabiting the Summit of the Neilgherry Hills or the Blue Mountains of Coimbatoor, in the Southern Peninsula of India*, 19.
4. Ingold, 1996, *Key Debates in Anthropology*, 201.
5. Hockings, 1980, *Ancient Hindu Refugees. Badaga Social History 1550–1975*; Walker, 1986, *The Toda of South India. A New Look*; Mandelbaum, 1989, 'The Kotas in Their Social Setting'; Walker, 1998, *Between Tradition*

and Modernity and Other Essays on the Toda of South India, 137–42; Hockings, 1999, *Kindreds of the Earth. Badaga Household Structure and Demography*. The linguist Murray Barnson Emeneau made several significant contributions to the study of Toda and Kota languages. See, for example, Emeneau, 1944, *Kota Texts*; Ibid., 1971, *Toda Songs*; Ibid., 1984, *Toda Grammar and Texts*.

6. Blumenbach, 1779, *Handbuch der Naturgeschichte*; Ibid., 1787, *Institutiones Physiologicae*; Ibid., 1820, *The Institutions of Physiology*; Ibid., 1825, *A Manual of the Elements of Natural History*; Reill, 2005, *Vitalizing Nature in the Enlightenment*.
7. That is, West Asians, North Africans, and Europeans except Laplanders. Blumenbach, 1825, *A Manual of the Elements of Natural History*, 36.
8. '… the remaining Asiatics, excepting the Malays; in Europe, the Laplanders; and, in North America, the Esquimaux, extending from Behring's Strait to Labrador.' Ibid.
9. The translator being John Elliotson. Ibid., 15, 36–7.
10. Ibid., 37.
11. Stocking, 1987, *Victorian Anthropology*, 26, 44, 48–51; Ibid., 1988, *Bones, Bodies, Behavior. Essays on Biological Anthropology*, 4–7.
12. Prichard, 1843, *The Natural History of Man*, 132–3; Stocking, 1988, *Bones, Bodies, Behavior. Essays on Biological Anthropology*, 4.
13. Prichard, 1855, *The Natural History of Man*, 122–4, 644.
14. Ibid., 1843, *The Natural History of Man*, 162–6.
15. Ibid., 248–9. In the 1855 edition, Prichard had refined his conclusions. Under the heading 'Of the Aboriginal Races of India' we find the Singhalese, the Tamulian race, the Mountain tribes in Dekhan, and the Petty Barbarous tribes in what is today north-east India. The Toda had now been specifically enlisted as a Mountain tribe. Ibid., 1855, *The Natural History of Man*, 251f.
16. Ibid., xv.
17. Ibid.
18. Hough, 1829, *Letters on the Climate, Inhabitants, Productions, &C, &C., of the Neilgherries, or, Blue Mountains of Coimbatoor, South India*; Harkness, 1832, *A Description of a Singular Aboriginal Race Inhabiting the Summit of the Neilgherry Hills or the Blue Mountains of Coimbatoor, in the Southern Peninsula of India*.
19. Prichard, 1855, *The Natural History of Man*, 252.
20. Hough, 1829, *Letters on the Climate, Inhabitants, Productions, &C., &C., of the Neilgherries, or, Blue Mountains of Coimbatoor, South India*, 28–31; Harkness, 1832, *A Description of a Singular Aboriginal Race Inhabiting the Summit of the Neilgherry Hills or the Blue Mountains of Coimbatoor, in the*

Southern Peninsula of India, 117–18; Arnold, 2000, *Science, Technology, and Medicine in Colonial India*, 78–9.

21. See, for example, Buchanan, 1807, *A Journey from Madras through the Countries of Mysore, Canara, and Malabar.*
22. Prichard's earliest publication being Researches into the Physical History of Mankind (London 1813). For a discussion of the role of empirical knowledge in colonial expansion, see for example Grove, 1993, 'Conserving Eden. The (European) East India Companies and Their Environmental Policies on St. Helena, Mauritius and in Western India, 1660 to 1854'; Pels and Salemink, 1999, *Colonial Subjects. Essays on the Practical History of Anthropology*, 85–6, 88–90; Arnold, 2005, *The Tropics and the Traveling Gaze. India, Landscape, and Science 1800–1856*, chs 5, 6.
23. OIOC, BC, 16 February (no. 3), 1836, Mr Sullivan's Minute, 20 August 1835: 12–57.
24. OIOC, MD, Revenue Department, 27 January (no. 1) 1836: 102–3.
25. Ibid., 5 February (no. 1), 1834. OIOC, BC, 16 February (no. 3), 1836, State of the Todawars on the Neilgherry Hills.
26. OIOC, MD, Revenue Department, 27 January (no. 1) 1836: 102–3.
27. OIOC, BC, 16 February (no. 3), 1836, Mr Sullivan's Minute, paras 4–6.
28. Ibid., para 7. Harkness, 1832, *A Description of a Singular Aboriginal Race Inhabiting the Summit of the Neilgherry Hills or the Blue Mountains of Coimbatoor, in the Southern Peninsula of India*, 25.
29. OIOC, BC, 16 February (no. 3), 1836, Mr Sullivan's Minute, paras 8–10.
30. Ibid.
31. Ibid., paras 25–6, referring to his own reports to the Board of Revenue in January and October 1828.
32. Ibid., paras 30–5.
33. OIOC, MD, Revenue Department, 5 February (no. 1), 1834. OIOC, BC, 16 February (no. 3), 1836, State of the Todawars on the Neilgherry Hills. OIOC, BC, 14 July 1836, Extract from the Proceedings of the Board of Revenue.
34. See, for example, Guha, 1989, *The Unquiet Woods. Ecological Change and Peasant Resistance in the Himalaya*; Rangarajan, 1996, *Fencing the Forest. Conservation and Ecological Change in India's Central Provinces, 1860–1914*; Saberwal, 1999, *Pastoral Politics. Shepherds, Bureaucrats, and Conservation in the Western Himalaya*; D'Souza, 2004, 'Rigidity and the Affliction of Capitalist Property. Colonial Land Revenue and the Recasting of Nature'.
35. See, for example, Sivaramakrishnan, 1999, *Modern Forests. Statemaking and Environmental Change in Colonial Eastern India*; Peluso and Vandergeest, 2001, 'Genealogies of the Political Forest and Customary Rights in Indonesia, Malaysia, and Thailand'.

36. Vasan, 2006, *Living with Diversity. Forestry Institutions in the Western Himalaya*, 4–6, 137–42. Sudha Vasan also outlined her argument in an oral presentation entitled Vasan, 2006, 'Forest Settlements in the Raj. Persistent Diversity in Forest Property Regimes in Himachal Pradesh'.
37. Peluso and Vandergeest, 2001, 'Genealogies of the Political Forest and Customary Rights in Indonesia, Malaysia, and Thailand', 766–8, 801–2.
38. Johnson, 2003, 'The Making of Race and Place in Nineteenth-Century British Honduras', 608–9.
39. Peluso and Vandergeest, 2001, 'Genealogies of the Political Forest and Customary Rights in Indonesia, Malaysia, and Thailand', 791–2, 801–2.
40. Foucault, 1977, *Discipline and Punish: The Birth of the Prison*; Sivaramakrishnan, 1999, *Modern Forests. Statemaking and Environmental Change in Colonial Eastern India*; Peluso and Vandergeest, 2001, 'Genealogies of the Political Forest and Customary Rights in Indonesia, Malaysia, and Thailand', 764–5, 801.
41. Ibid., 762–3.
42. Guha, 1989, *The Unquiet Woods. Ecological Change and Peasant Resistance in the Himalaya*; Rangarajan, 1996, *Fencing the Forest. Conservation and Ecological Change in India's Central Provinces, 1860–1914*.
43. Sivaramakrishnan, 1999, *Modern Forests. Statemaking and Environmental Change in Colonial Eastern India*, 78, 83–90, 277–9.
44. See also Agrawal and Sivaramakrishnan, Eds, 2001, *Social Nature. Resources, Representations, and Rule in India*, 2.
45. Sivaramakrishnan, 1999, *Modern Forests. Statemaking and Environmental Change in Colonial Eastern India*, 54–5, 84–7.
46. Ludden, 1999, *An Agrarian History of South Asia*, 7.
47. Ibid., 7, 114–15.
48. Morrison, 2002, 'Pepper in the Hills. Upland-Lowland Exchange and the Intensification of the Spice Trade'.
49. See further Cederlöf and Sutton, 2005, 'The Aboriginal Toda. On Indigeneity, Exclusivism and Privileged Access to Land in the Nilgiri Hills, South India'.
50. OIOC, MRP, 19 February 1830, Resolution no. 5. Part of the document is quoted in ch. 2.
51. Ibid.
52. Stocking, 1987, *Victorian Anthropology*, 53, 64.
53. Cederlöf, 2002, 'Narratives of Rights. Codifying People and Land in Early Nineteenth-Century Nilgiris', 344–52.
54. One of England's leading scientific societies, founded in 1843.

55. Blumenbach, 1820, *The Institutions of Physiology*, 433, 440; Shortt, 1868, *An Account of the Tribes on the Neilgherries*, 4–6.
56. Ibid., 10.
57. Ibid., 26.
58. Ibid., 7.
59. Shortt was himself the Superintendent-General of Vaccine in the Madras Presidency. Ibid., 9; Walker, 1998, *Between Tradition and Modernity and Other Essays on the Toda of South India*, 171.
60. Prichard, 1855, *The Natural History of Man*, 251; Shortt, 1868, *An Account of the Tribes on the Neilgherries*, 27.
61. Ibid., 30–1.
62. Blumenbach, 1820, *The Institutions of Physiology*, 433, 439–40.
63. Ibid., 442.
64. See also Walker, 1998, *Between Tradition and Modernity and Other Essays on the Toda of South India*, ch. 9, see specifically 168–78.
65. Marshall, 1873, *A Phrenologist Amongst the Todas or the Study of a Primitive Tribe in South India. History, Character, Customs, Religion, Infanticide, Polyandry, Language*, 88.
66. Ibid.
67. Nigam, 1990, 'Disciplining and Policing the "Criminals by Birth". Part 1, the Making of a Colonial Stereotype—the Criminal Tribes and Castes of North India', 134–5; Metcalf, 1994, *Ideologies of the Raj*, ch. 4; Bayly, 1999, *Caste, Society and Politics in Indiafrom the Eighteenth Century to the Modern Age*, ch. 5; Radhakrishna, 2001, *Dishonoured by History. "Criminal Tribes" and British Colonial Policy*.
68. Cederlöf and Sutton, 2005, 'The Aboriginal Toda. On Indigeneity, Exclusivism and Privileged Access to Land in the Nilgiri Hills, South India', 176–7. Deborah Sutton has investigated the transformation of the Nilgiri landscape resulting from conservation and the introduction of plantations in more detail from the mid-nineteenth century onwards. See Sutton, 2001, publicly available 2006, *Other Landscapes. Hill Communities, Settlers and State on the Colonial Nilgiris, c.1820–1900*, ch. 4.
69. *Madras Mail*, 22 February 1869: 3, col. 3, also commented on in Cederlöf and Sutton, 2005, 'The Aboriginal Toda. On Indigeneity, Exclusivism and Privileged Access to Land in the Nilgiri Hills, South India'. Sylk's Hotel was formerly the hotel built by William Rumbold.
70. Grigg, 1880, *The Manual of Nilagiri District*, 302, 325, 328.
71. Ibid., 327.
72. *Circar* means 'government'. Grigg, 1880, *The Manual of Nilagiri District*, 328.
73. OIOC, BC, 16 February (no. 3), 1836, Mr Sullivan's Minute, para 12.

5 *Local Politics and Regional Confrontations*

The petition for land sent to the tahsildar this year was only one in a series of pleas to regain the land which Nanicane believes rightly belongs to the mund. Seventy-one acres is the number that keeps recurring in our conversations, from the first field visit to the last. At our very first meeting, Nanicane explains that this land was registered in his father's name. Since the death of his father over twenty years ago he has repeatedly petitioned to have the land transferred into his own name, to be shared by his brothers and sons.

Remembering his childhood, when the shola forest was larger and some twenty sacred buffaloes were brought into the pen next to the temples each night, he explains that all their buffaloes have now been taken to a mund further west, as there is no grazing ground left in their own mund. The Forest Department has planted eucalyptus trees in the uppermost section of the mund, and low-level officials have explained that this particular portion of land is now 'protected'. It turns out to be one of numerous instances in which land specifically designated as

'Toda patta', to be under the exclusive control of Toda munds, has been encroached on. In 1888 it was decided that forty-six acres of land should be reserved per mund,[1] a decision that still resonates in land administration in the region, while the land has been continuously violated by encroachments from the very outset. The fact that some patriclans encompass many munds and others only a few has resulted in an unequal distribution of wealth among the Toda. A recent investigation has found that almost a third of this land is now occupied by either 'non-tribals' or the Forest Department.

It is with some difficulty that the figure of seventy-one acres is traced. A handwritten and signed document of the deputy registrar of cooperative societies in Ootacamund surfaces on a visit two years later. It lists four pattas for Kandelmund and, miscalculating the total by six acres, wrongly adds them up to 71.30 acres. But there is no survey map or number, and no original patta for this land is kept in the mund, so the claims remain weak. The only documented patta available is for less than four acres, resulting from a bifurcation of the main road three decades ago. Yet the Forest Department has refused to allow people to grow vegetables in their mund, arguing that cultivation was never written into the patta. The seventh paragraph of the rules for Toda pattas has obviously escaped the Forest Department. It states that the collector may issue permits for cultivation exclusively to Todas. Once we get onto the subject of land, the complaints go on, echoing earlier experiences. One of many instances of government abuse, they say, is a forest bungalow constructed on land in Kandel in the 1970s. Signatures were taken from thirty-six men while Nanicane and his son were away. The land document turned out to be a *danam*, a donation. 'They are using the ignorance of the Toda', complains the son.

Recently, the Tamil Nadu Unit of the National Commission for Scheduled Castes and Scheduled Tribes received a representation describing the entire situation from Kandelmund's point of view. In his reply, the district forest officer states that Kandelmund possesses only about thirty acres of land (twelve hectares), not seventy-one. According to a land survey, all the other land belongs to the Forest Department. While the confused land situation prevails, the good news in Kandelmund is that this is a valid document. The bad is that they still lack the patta document.[2]

Ill. 6 The Toda temple of Kandelmund
(Photo by the author.)

A Hotel in the Hills Encroaching on Sacred Lands

> [I]n a country where there is an extensive and wealthy population, and the revenue to Government of consequence I simply ask is this the case at Ootacamund, where there is not a native village within 3 miles of the station with the exception of two small Todah munds situated in the centre of two large woods with perhaps eight or ten people in each. Occasionally during the year, where the population consists entirely of gentlemen's servants, followers, and a few natives belonging to the Collector's Cutcherry, where by Mr Sullivan's own acknowledgement to me there is nothing to be had but buffalo milk.[3]

In the legal disputes over land which arose in 1828 when the Madras government was seeking to assert its legal status as a holder of property in land in the Nilgiris, officers like Major Kelso, above, could hardly believe their eyes on realizing that the 'landlords' they were to negotiate a deal with were cattle herders scattered over the hills.

The complexity of the legal situation within which different notions of rights and of law competed and a legal codification of land rights emerged out of the anomalous context, needs to be borne in mind as we explore the specific confrontations resulting from competing claims for access to and control over land. The sometimes confused disputes over legal principles in a given region could be attributed to an unclear situation of conquest before a firm administrative structure was established. However, such a conclusion would be misleading if it builds on the assumption that the norm guiding British administrators was the rapid establishment of singular and supreme law. As noted earlier, in the late eighteenth century the English courts simultaneously handled statute law and precedential law, as for example in the case of forest or manorial law. In his study of early-eighteenth-century southern England, E.P. Thompson describes the role of forest law in establishing equilibrium in the forest economy via reconciling competing interests when legal subtleties varied from one forest to another. Although nineteenth-century utilitarian legislators may have argued that forest law was an unnecessary relic, their position was disputed and the particular jurisdictions were by no means rooted out.[4]

In the administration of British territories in India, the ambition may often have been to find singular principles for administration with the aim of facilitating revenue assessment and control. Ideas about the Indian past supporting such principles were nurtured. Many administrators were influenced by the idea of restoring a Hindu Golden Age—in itself a notion of dubious singularity—and, in the process, they reinforced the rights of an assumed 'ancient aristocracy', simultaneously arguing that Indian states had possessed sovereign rights in land that were to be passed on to a sovereign EIC.[5] Laws which transformed agrarian and land relations in ways that were insensitive to regional variation could be pushed more forcefully in India, whereas in the British Isles strong resistance among influential groups in Parliament would have prevented their implementation.

In this context, it is useful to distinguish between principles of administration and principles of law, while at the same time acknowledging their interdependence, in particular in the administration of revenue. Although in the colonial administration of territories in India there was, for the sake of efficiency, good cause to strive to achieve singularity over vast areas, the diversity of British legal institutions reflected competing interests which were also represented in the EIC. It is no less important to observe that, in India as in Britain, there existed a multiplicity of legal traditions. As Margot Finn observes, the more simplistic arguments in the study of Orientalist discourses tend to play down not only the internal diversity but also the internal dissent that marked English legal culture in the eighteenth and early nineteenth centuries. This explains why, in legal disputes over land, the mere existence and experience of competing judicial principles meant that the government of the Madras Presidency, too, had to argue at length for the justification of sovereignty over local custom and rights. They could not simply proclaim overlordship over the region. Moreover, this situation provided a sphere of justified negotiation, not only for particular rights in land but also for particular legal principles.[6]

The 1830s were marked by land conflicts in the Nilgiri Hills. The initial sign of dispute was the first rules on land grants, introduced in 1828, which represented the Madras government's attempt to take control of events in the region. However, these rules were hardly the origin of the conflicts, but rather a response to emerging land settlement agreements that assumed freehold rights which risked setting a precedent. This zone of unclear legal status within the territories claimed by the EIC may be characterized as anomalous, to borrow Sivaramakrishnan's term—but, we may ask, anomalous in relation to what? Conceptually, his term may be understood to assume the existence of a regularity and consistency of governance, in relation to which territorial zones in the margins were characterized by resistance in various forms. Such zones withstood incorporation and their existence meant that rules could not be as universally applied as intended. A major contribution of Sivaramakrishnan's work is its emphasis on the local history of the Bengal forest tracts, in which empirical enquiry breaks open phenomena such as scientific forestry, colonial discourse, and other 'such lumped categories ... to find the distortions, transformations, and hybridizations that they undergo in the very processes of their construction and implementation in specific historical locations'. Yet when it comes to the Nilgiris in the early nineteenth century, a question remains. In Bengal Sivaramakrishnan finds that the regional variations of forest management in the late nineteenth century built on prior forms of 'administrative exceptionalism'. In the process of incorporating forests into regimes of production, which basically meant settled and taxable cultivation, the administration permitted the continuation of tribal food production strategies when the enforcement of policy would have resulted in threats to colonial rule—hence the exception.[7]

In the Nilgiris, too, the government was slow to enforce the implementation of a land settlement which would force pastoralists to abandon the rearing of cattle for settled cultivation. Even after five decades of administration it allowed for certain rights that were specific to the Toda, arguing that the community was so 'perfectly exceptional'.[8] However, thinking in terms of exceptionalism from the perspective of governance and administration is not entirely helpful for analysing the codification and working of law. The discrepancy between principles laid down in law and the modifications and adjustments in their application points to a paradox of colonial administration—a paradox not unique to British rule in India. On the one hand law is timeless; it is established 'forever' and will not accept change. On the other hand it is time-bound, defined by the present of the time and place in which it is formed to make a difference. While regularities are found in principles, anomalies are inherent in processes of legal codification. It is therefore misleading to assume any immediate implementation of principles, be they those of a revenue settlement, a certain school of forestry, or economic policies. Taking such assumptions as our point of departure may lead to conclusions that claim local histories as characterized by numerous 'exceptions'. Rather than suggesting that the Madras government time and again made exceptions for the specific rights of Toda pastoralists and others, it may be argued that making exceptions was a characteristic part of the process of forming an administration in a particular place.

The attempts made to attract Europeans to the Nilgiris had apparently been successful, because as early as 1827 Sullivan asked for rules to be immediately adopted for the appropriation of land in the region. His letter does not reveal why he found it necessary to ask for 'express sanction' by the government, but the suggestions he put forward were clear enough. Malnad, the area in which European settlement was rapidly increasing, was described as consisting entirely of pasture and as having been in the possession of the Toda since time immemorial, the Toda being acknowledged as proprietors by the Badaga. The very light tax on pasture and buffaloes had remained at the levels at which it had been fixed twenty years earlier. Now, as earlier noted, the rights of the Toda had to be protected from the adverse impact of European settlement. Sullivan described a situation in which houses were being built on grazing grounds, woods cut down, and large herds of untaxed cattle grazing on land for which the Toda paid taxes. To rectify the situation he suggested far-reaching legislation to establish the Toda as holders of absolute property. This, the first document to refer to proprietary land rights for the Toda, seems almost naive, given the response it elicited from the revenue board and the Madras government. It contrasts starkly with the description of the situation by the commandant of the Nilgiris, Major Kelso. Where Sullivan saw a destruction of woods and ownership rights under the onslaught of European intrusion, Kelso asked: Where are the people making these claims?[9]

After Sullivan had left office in 1830, the settlement of Europeans in the region took a decisive leap forward. Acting on government orders, Sullivan's successor in the Nilgiris, Andrew Fleming Hudleston,[10] passed on instructions from the governor, S.R. Lushington, to Ootacamund to ensure the collaboration of his subordinate officers with the commandant in facilitating the settlement of Indo-British agriculturists on wastelands. Cultivators, both European and native, were to be provided with spare implements (later to be repaid by instalments) to encourage the cultivation of European crops in the hills. The instructions landed on the desk of the peishkar Venkata Soobayen.[11]

The correspondence between Soobayen and Hudleston reveals the forceful way in which this policy was applied, as well as the rather unscrupulous means by which the Toda of Kandelmund and Manjakalmund were made to relinquish their lands. However, the inhabitants of these munds turned the tools of bureaucracy against the district administration. In 1832 Soobayen was discharged from office for corruption and, a year later, ordered to repay double what he had exacted from the Toda.[12] The disputes over land did not end with the removal of a low-level Indian administrator, however, but escalated over the following years. Confrontations between the inhabitants of the two munds and advocates of various interests took many different forms, including petitions, depositions, refusal to appear for questioning, delaying investigations by absence, refusal to accept payment (or 'compensation') for loss of land, denying the validity of earlier agreements, filing court cases and so on. In the process, cross-cutting alliances were established and different levels of colonial administration played out against each other. Phrased differently, resistance was articulated in the discourse of the dominant and, in spite of the uneven power relations, the outcome was by no means a foregone conclusion.

Since the disputes in which Soobayen became the mediator between the government and a private investor on the one hand, and the Toda of the two munds on the other, involved several core elements of local politics during conflicts, we shall look at them in some detail. They came to span five years, from the first attempts to persuade the Toda to sign a deed of sale, to a decision in 1836 about the level of compensation to be paid for the loss of land occupancy. However, in broader terms, the duration of the conflict may be defined as beginning with the 1828 rules on land grants and the first account with legal implications in which Toda land rights were defined as usufruct and not as ownership. Its end came in 1843, when the regulations mentioned earlier were introduced, namely 'Rights of the Todawars, and Rules for grants of land on the Neilgherries.'[13]

Moreover, as we enter into questions of confrontation and negotiation between the parties to land disputes in which members of the Toda community were active participants, the importance of Toda social organization comes to the fore. Correspondence and reports in the colonial files never go into such details. To the officers investigating land claims, they were Toda 'pattadars' of a certain place. However, on the basis of the place, the mund, probable kinship groups or patriclans can be assumed, particularly as the patriclan commonly takes its name from its chief settlement. Toda society was—and still is—divided into two subgroups: Tartharsh and Teiveli. Tartharsh comprises the larger number of patriclans. Kandelmund and Majakalmund were two important munds, as Kandelmund (Kashmudr or Ishkiti in the Toda language) was the head hamlet of the Kash patriclan, while Manjakalmund (or Melgashmudr) was the head hamlet of the Melgash patriclan. Both these clans belonged to the Tartharsh subgroup.[14]

The land dispute that lost Soobayen his position arose out of an extensive claim made by Sir William Rumbold, a baronet married into the highest circles in search of profit. Rumbold had realized the good returns that a hotel in Ootacamund would yield, given the lack of accommodation for Europeans and the high rent which could therefore be charged. Having run into financial difficulties as a result of failed investments elsewhere, he put up an extravagant building that reflected his ambition to cling to his noble status while making a fortune that would repair his losses. In 1833, however, shortly after the hotel had opened, he died.[15] Hudleston's instructions to Soobayen in 1831 were to take active steps to put as much land as possible into circulation. If people whose land was required objected to parting with it, Hudleston wanted to know the particulars of their objections and the terms on which they would consent to its occupation. The land under consideration was Toda grazing land.[16]

Shortly after the first letter, Soobayen received instructions to pay special attention to a particular 'purchase' and convince the Toda living in Kandelmund to give up not only their grazing grounds and shola, but also the site of their mund. This was the land that Rumbold had chosen for his hotel. Major Crewe, the commandant, had spoken to Soobayen about the purchase even before Hudleston gave his first instructions, and Hudleston had learnt from him that there were three or four Toda houses on the site.[17] The mund itself, including its buffalo pen, was estimated to comprise six cawnies or almost eight acres. It was fertile with water, but had to be cleared of its 'jungle', according to Soobayen. Acting on Crewe's orders the latter sent for Addy and Nary, described as the 'owners' of Kandelmund, together with seven or eight other Toda men, and Koondan Kallan, the monigar. Reporting on this meeting to Hudleston, Soobayen explained how he had offered them Rs 350 for the land, but even after two days of negotiations they refused to part with it: 'they objected, on the plea that as the place was the habitation of their Kooladeyvom or tutelar God, they would be ruined if they were to sell the land.'[18] On hearing their objection Crewe ordered Soobayen to find out the particulars of the deity to which the place was consecrated, and Soobayen reported: 'I went to Candulmund and seeing no image anywhere, I inquired further, and learnt that they consider the house in which they make offerings of milk, butter, &cet as the habitation of their God, and that they would part with the spot on no account whatever.'[19] Hudleston then ordered Soobayen to again send for the 'owners' and 'in a conciliatory manner' persuade them to yield and, if necessary, offer them another spot: 'Should you find there any image, you should send for a Brahmin and consult him to carry the same to such other spot the people may wish to have it removed to, affording every assistance to perform any ceremony that may be required to that end.'[20] But Brahmins played no part in Toda cults. As the Toda explained, their divinity lived on the land. The temples and all that was connected with them were divine and could not be carried off to some other spot. The Toda therefore could not accept the suggestion, since they 'dreaded the malediction of their deity'.[21]

In a more desperate tone, Soobayen reported back that he had spent fifteen days persuading the Toda of Kandelmund and, finally, they had agreed both to part with the land and to accept the new land offered. Crewe had immediately arranged for them to sign a 'Deed of sale' on stamp paper in the name of Sir William Rumbold. Having encouraged Rumbold to be prepared to increase his offer to Rs 500, Crewe had settled on Rs 400 with the Toda. As Soobayen subsequently went on to strike new deals, Hudleston found reason to strictly instruct him 'to understand that unless the present occupant freely consents to the transfer, he is not on any account to be deprived of the land either by force or any other means.'[22]

These words of caution seem appropriate, considering the increased interest in securing government-acknowledged rights in land in the Nilgiris. After Sullivan's resignation and the 1828 resolution determining the prerequisites for land grants, applications had been arriving in the Revenue Department. At the same time, it had been established that the Toda had continued to pay grazing tax on the land that Sullivan claimed to have purchased from them, while he himself had never paid any assessment. Among the first new applicants for land grants were R. Crewe, commandant of the Nilgiris, J. Lushington, son and private secretary of the governor (purchasing land for his father), and C.M. Lushington, judge and brother of the same.[23]

At this point it may appear as if the legal procedures employed rather conveniently served officers of the colonial government, securing land for Europeans. However, only months after Soobayen had successfully closed the deal with the Toda of Kandelmund, he had to appear before a court set up by the sub-collector, having been discharged from office just two months after the deed had been signed. In the case of Tothawar Kandil Nary and others *versus* Venkata Soobayen, the latter was convicted of corruption—he had been found guilty of taking Rs 80 for himself from the Rs 400 paid as compensation.

The witness statements all supported Kandil Nary's claim that, after Rs 400 had been received for the Kandelmund lands, two *kolkars*,[24] Syed Kasmi and Syed Neef, arrived in the mund to collect Rs 80, which was to be given to Soobayen. The latter had detained the monigar Koondan Kallan in the administration office, the cutcherry, telling him that the additional money had to be paid directly at his home. Consequently, the following day, Nary sent two men from the mund, Kevi and Tarayalum, with the money. The witness Syed Kasmi explained that he had taken the message from Soobayen to Kandelmund, and the monigar witnessed that he had seen the money being tied up and sent to Soobayen. Finally, Kevi and Tarayalum said they had delivered the money at his door. As might be expected, Soobayen was of a different opinion. But the sub-collector ruled against him.

Soobayen then appealed to the collector, and his main objection can be summed up in one of his concluding statements: 'It was in consequence of my having in pursuance of the Principal Collector's order, purchased the spot of ground whereon their houses stood, that the

Tothawars entered into this conspiracy against me and made a false accusation.' In his eyes, he was made a scapegoat. The detailed petition he filed opens a window on local politics in the Nilgiris.[25]

Up to the point at which the Toda finally conceded their land for Rs 400, his petition corresponded to the letters exchanged between him and Hudleston during the negotiations. But having reached the signing of the deed of sale, Soobayen now claimed that the Toda had been blackmailed:

> As the Tothawars complained very much that the sum of 400 Rupees was not enough, the Deputy Cutwall Baala Krishnayan and some other persons observed to them that in consequence of Nunjah Cawnden having refused to receive the price offered him for a tract of land which was required for the Government Garden at Kartee, the price was not paid him, but that the land was taken and added to the garden. Upon which the Tothawars consented to the Deed of sale being executed for 400 Rupees, and it was accordingly written in the name of Sir William Rumbold, and they received the sum of 400 Rupees in the presence of the witnesses who affixed their signatures to the Deed.[26]

The Toda had been told that, in Ketti, the site of the government farm, the Badaga cultivator Nunjah Goundan had similarly refused the compensation offered and had, in spite of this, lost his land.[27] Faced with such a threat, the Toda of Kandelmund had signed the deed. When they subsequently complained, however, Crewe acted to have Soobayen immediately replaced as peishkar.

At the time, the petition reads, the raja of Nelliyalam came 'on his usual tour' to Ootacamund. According to Soobayen, the Toda of Kandelmund then turned to him to restore their land and the two parties 'entered into a conspiracy'. Acting as a patron, the raja filed a petition to the Malabar collectorate on behalf of the Toda, requesting either the restoration of the land or the payment of Rs 700—an amount the Toda claimed first to have been promised. The subsequent court proceedings were said to have been a complete fraud orchestrated by the peishkar who succeeded Soobayen, and supported by the kolkar, who himself made a small profit from the process.

Thus far, the petition may seem like the plea of one of the parties to the internal disputes over petty corruption in which subordinate civil servants took their chance to gain promotion, much like the earlier infighting at Sullivan's head office in Coimbatore.[28] This was not the first time that accusations and counter-accusations were hurled in all directions and low-level officers discharged. But Soobayen's petition also provides us with information about how local politics were tied into the cutcherry and common popular strategies of resistance thwarted. As Rangarajan and others have observed, absence was a common way of avoiding colonial authority and, in the Nilgiris, Soobayen now maintained that he had hindered the Toda from resorting to that strategy, causing them to take revenge on him. The Kandelmund Toda claimed that the monigar Koondan Kallan had been detained, while Soobayen stated that he had prevented the Toda from disappearing. Thus, constraining the physical movement of the monigar was not a punishment but a kind of safe custody. To make himself clear, Soobayen referred to an earlier incident.[29]

> When Mr Stevenson the Sub Collector of the Zillah of Darwar proposed to purchase the land called Kotahkaad mund for the purpose of building a bungalow there, the late Tahsildar of the said Talook agreeably to an order from the Huzzoor, sent for the abovementioned Maniagar Koonda Kallen, but he absconded and was not to be found for the space of three months. In consequence of my having caused the attendance of the owners of Kandala mund without allowing them to run away and having purchased from them the land in question they, out of spite, got up the complaint against me.[30]

We need not pass judgement on whether or not Soobayen was corrupt to reflect on how the Toda of Kandelmund acted to regain control over their land in this situation. Having been practically coerced into signing the deed of sale, they turned to the Nilambur raja of Nelliyalam in neighbouring Wynad. Although the Wynad rajas had been 'pacified' through the death of the Pazhassi raja in 1805, they had influence in the region and, as discussed in Chapter 2, the Toda living near the Pykara river were tied to Nelliyalam through bonds of grazing rights. As the raja represented a centre of authority and influence, the Toda of Kandelmund turned to him for help. Soobayen claimed that the raja had received a donation from the Toda in return for his assistance. The petition written by the raja served to initiate legal proceedings against the peishkar. The Toda thus responded by acting in the arena established by the British authorities. But if we are to believe Soobayen, the petition appeared only after the Toda had been deprived of the opportunity of absconding from the scene.

Another aspect of the petition and the earlier correspondence well worth noting is the terminology used. Soobayen called Addy and Nary 'owners' of land, and they were asked to sell it. Commandant Crewe wanted a deed of sale to be signed on payment of Rs 400. The government's elaboration of the legal terminology in 1828, in which 'purchase payment' was replaced with 'compensation payment' and ownership never granted to the Toda, had obviously not filtered down through the administrative echelons.

From the perspective of the EIC the legal procedure provided them with a medium of communication. The hearing in the cutcherry was not a formal court hearing, but a form of arbitration such as occurred in lower courts, based on case law and presided over by the sub-collector. From a larger perspective the dispute under consideration was only a hurdle in the process of settling land. However, dismissing the peishkar did not solve the problem. The following year, the Madras revenue board sent a letter to the government with a view to restoring the land to the Toda. From the district's reports they concluded: 'it appeared to the Board that the primary object of the Todawers in preferring their complaint was not so much to accuse the Peishcar of extortion as to obtain the assistance of the higher authorities in recovering the possession of land which had been wrested from them against their will.'[31]

The board noted, moreover, that the Toda had '"represented the antiquity of their residence", [and] they urged their religious veneration for the spot where they "had the effigies of their gods and the monuments of their ancestors"'. The board thereby noted the primacy of aboriginal right and the right to remain undisturbed in places of religious significance. Taking such land was not what was implied by the government when they had urged the collector to settle Indo-Britons on wasteland. The board observed in particular that Rumbold had neither enclosed nor built on his land, and that he had never obtained a grant for its possession. Concluding that 'the Todawers had been constrained by illegal means to consent to the sale of the land and that it was very far from being a voluntary act on their parts', the board considered it its duty to ask the government to grant the Toda repossession of the land. Thus, when the petition and reports reached the presidency level and the agenda of the Board of Revenue, the legal procedure turned to the Toda's advantage.[32]

It has sometimes been argued that in disputes such as this, people in forest and hill tracts sought primarily to secure large payments. This would occasionally cause them to delay and renegotiate agreements. The argument echoes colonial reports. A passage in an investigation of 1833 has been much quoted in late-nineteenth-century imperial historiographies and likewise by present-day scholars who, in turn, often quote the imperial historiographies, incompletely. The investigation suggested that 'The Todawars are a simple race and till our arrival on the Hills were unacquainted with the use of money of any description, but they have now become fully aware of its value, have learnt to assert and protect their own rights on all occasions and never fail to make a good bargain in disposing of their lands.' This is a partial quote, excluding the statement that the Toda never wanted to part with their land at all. The transaction of money appears rather to have had a symbolic value, while land itself did not represent a commodity. In this particular case, not even when they were offered Rs 700 did they agree to yield control of their land. If any sacred mund resembles the one today remembered as Oshthaars, it was once on the land claimed by Rumbold.[33]

Colliding Norms for Rights in Land: Conflicts in the 1830s

The many enthusiastic reports about the Toda circulated widely and served to draw attention to the specific circumstances of this community. It appears that the further from the Nilgiris these reports were discussed, the greater was the concern for Toda well being at the level of principles, rather than on the basis of the actual situation in the territory they occupied. When the Court of Directors asked for a report on the past and present state of the Toda, it also ordered the Madras government to respect Toda rights and liberally compensate them for any loss of land.[34] The survey officers were less enthusiastic. The preliminary report in 1835, which included Sullivan's seventy-nine paragraph minute complained about the difficulty of ascertaining existing rights when such rights were founded on prescription and on information derived from oral statements by Badaga cultivators. At the same time, it was reported that the Toda of Kandelmund or, most likely, their kin of the Kash clan, had extended their claims to include the land of the Ketti farm. Complicating the situation still further, Sullivan claimed that no payment had ever been made to the Toda in compensation for the cantonment land. By the time this report reached the Court of Directors, Rumbold's claim had lost all validity: it was observed that 'the grantor certainly possessed no legal title'. A full survey followed of the two lands in Ketti and Ootacamund.[35]

The contrast is striking between the way in which land had been forcibly taken from Kandelmund in line with the revenue board's instructions to extend cultivable land in the Nilgiris, and the submissive attitude of the board and the government *vis-à-vis* the Court of Directors:

> we concurred in the views taken by the Board for respecting the rights of this people, and resolved that so long as the taxes payable by them were duly paid, they should not on any account be disturbed in the possession of the lands heretofore held by them, which they may desire to retain for pasturage; that private persons should not be permitted to appropriate any of those lands without the consent of the Todawars interested in them; that no part of those lands should be taken for public purposes without compensation to the Todawars who had previously occupied them; and that compensation should be given to the Todawars for land already occupied by the Government and private persons at Ootacamund and Coonoor ...[36]

It now remained to carry out these orders, and the two sub-collectors of Malabar, first Daniel Eliott and then E. Smith, were sent to Ootacamund for the purpose. Securing land grants for the cantonment came highest on the agenda. The site comprised almost 2,900 acres, of which 22 per cent was occupied by private individuals for buildings and agriculture and 78 per cent by the government in the form of bazaars, huts, public buildings, and waste. Eliott sent his first report after having called all the 'pattadars' (landholders) of Kandelmund and Manjakalmund, together with the Toda and Badaga monigars, to the cutcherry to obtain first-hand information about their rules for possession of land. From their explanations he understood that in Malnad the land, which had always been in the exclusive possession of the Toda for pasturage, was the common property of all Toda within the nad. No inhabitant outside the mund and no individual Toda within it could dispose of any land without the consent of all the Toda in the nad. The lands in Malnad were thus completely free from any claim that the Wynad rajas could make on land or revenue. Here, land rights were defined exclusively by the social organisation of Toda society.[37]

From this information Eliott arrived at the conclusion that the only way in which the government could obtain absolute property over the land within the limits of the cantonment would be to first pay the prescribed compensation to the Toda for all the land. Thereafter, they could go on to grant leases to individuals who wanted to use the land. Through this purchase, it was assumed that the Toda would dispose of their 'common rights' over the land in question, and that the government would obtain absolute property as well as the right to levy revenue. It was suggested that the money be paid to the monigar of Malnad and the pattadars of the munds having land within the cantonment. Eliott's confusion about the terminology—claiming that the Toda were simultaneously landholders and in possession of common rights— was not unique, but rather significant of the legal procedures involved. However, the revenue board objected that Eliott's suggestion would neither destroy nor even disturb the Toda's proprietary right in the land. The difficulty was paying for the land without acknowledging ownership by the other party.[38]

Manjakalmund's claims were easy to deal with, relating to only a portion of C.M. Lushington's garden, which happened to be a site of Toda worship. It was agreed with the inhabitants of the mund that the land could remain in Manjakalmund's possession, while Lushington's occupation of it could continue undisturbed. However, the Kandelmund claims were of a different nature, since both Rumbold's estate and most of the cantonment had been established on Kandelmund lands.

Attempting to narrow the dispute to a core area, Eliott argued that since most of the land taken by Rumbold and the government had not been used, it was merely a nominal issue and could simply be reassigned to the Toda. Land on which no houses were built, no fences put up, and no cultivation carried out could be left in its present state, and there was no reason to expect objections from the Toda. But land that had been built on was more of a problem. According to Eliott, the Toda had recently made new claims: 'they have loudly and perseveringly complained of the intended occupation of the grounds about the Mund, and as the occupation has continued many years without question on their part, they may be considered as having tacitly consented to or acquiesced in it.' This was reason enough to deny them reallocation of the land.[39]

Prior to the second report, the sub-collector E. Smith had summoned Toda men from Malnad for questioning. The copy of their deposition does not reveal the names of these men or their number, but from other correspondence we may assume that they were the 'pattadars', the men considered by the administration to be in control of land in Kandelmund and Manjakalmund. At the meeting they were asked to sign the document that would seal the agreement and fix the level of compensation. The Toda refused to sign. The level of compensation was not an issue; they argued that the ground which they and the sub-collector had mutually agreed belonged to the two munds was not included in the document. It only included land in the immediate vicinity of the munds. Smith then argued that they would certainly have all the land returned that Rumbold had taken, '[b]ut why do you now claim in addition lands which have been included in the Cantonment, and have been occupied, without, as appears, any objection on your part?'

> All the ground which we have now pointed out has always belonged to Caundalmund, we did not sell it to Sir W. Rumbold by our own consent, we were taken to the Cutcherry and they wrote whatever they liked as the boundaries. We are ignorant whether the ground which we wished to reserve and which is not within the limits of Sir W. Rumbold's property, is included in the Cantonment or not. We believed up to this time that it was our own. We now only understand it after Your Honour has explained to us. We must have the ground which we showed, because if we sell it we shall undergo great inconvenience, if our Buffaloes enter into it, and this, the reason of our wishing to keep the ground.[40]

In addition, they refused to accept any compensation for lands such as those used for Lushington's garden. These were places of worship, and they argued that receiving compensation would mean they had given up the land. Appended to the deposition were the exact land claims made by the two munds. Their limits were defined entirely with reference to European properties—in the case of Manjakalmund to the north-west, the land bordered on J. Lushington's property; to the south-east, including part of C.M. Lushington's garden, it reached up to a hill just behind Kelso Cottage; and its southern boundary was defined by C.M. Lushington's house.[41]

In the government's response to Smith's report, the main objection related to any acknowledgement of proprietary rights to either native or European individuals. Within months, letters arrived at the collectorate office from Europeans who had been convinced that the land they had built on and cultivated was freehold property, to be inherited by coming generations forever. Mr W. Davis was just one of several who pleaded with the administration. His letter gives us a good idea of the situation of common Europeans who settled in the Nilgiris—people of a lower social order than the governor's kith and kin.

Davis explained that, in 1832, he and Mr McNair had applied to Commandant Crewe for a plot of land lying waste and covered by jungle. As the land was outside the cantonment, Crewe had informed them that he would make an application in their name to the collector, Sullivan, and ask the peishkar, Soobayen, to inspect the land. If it was found to be claimed by Badagas, they would have to make the best bargain they could with them. When the land was inspected, Badaga cultivators from Davany village came forward and claimed it. The price was set at Rs 20, which was subsequently paid into the Ootacamund cutcherry for the benefit of the Badagas. (The receipt was enclosed with the letter for the collector's information.) Davis had since invested over Rs 1000 in clearing and fencing the land, and all the wealth that his family had managed to save up over more than a century had been spent on its improvement. The land had become their only source of subsistence. Davis now found the entire procedure unfair. Had he known that this was not freehold property but only leasehold, they would never have invested all their money in the land. Now he had been further informed that the government favoured the Badagas. Being the original proprietors—'and from whom by order of the officer commanding and the Principal Collector we purchased the land'—they did not have to give up their land at the expiry of a given period. Davis felt trapped. Trying to dispose of the land as leasehold would only give him half its value compared with his investments.[42]

Europeans' letters to the colonial administration, pleading to have their freehold property guaranteed in perpetuity, and the government's response, denying this for the sake of establishing government sovereignty, are perhaps the clearest examples of colliding interests resting on conflicting legal principles. The government had no intention of establishing private and absolute property in land for individuals. Only a few days after the revenue board had dealt with Davis's and similar letters, it received further instructions from the Court of Directors confirming its view of the situation. In summary, and going against the general attitude of the Madras government, the court stated that, although the Toda were most likely not the aboriginal inhabitants of the hills, their occupation was far anterior to that of the Badaga, Kota, Kurumba and other tribes. The argument was underpinned by the fact that all these other communities respected the immemorial rights of the Toda, acknowledged their supremacy and punctually paid tributes for the land they were permitted to use. The court noted further that the settlement of Europeans had resulted in both the material improvement of the Toda's circumstances and the deterioration of their general character. To rectify the latter, they supported Sullivan's proposal to establish schools for their instruction in civilization and a knowledge of useful arts. All in all, unknowingly, the Toda had strong supporters in the Court of Directors.[43]

In the meantime, Smith had been negotiating with the Toda of Kandelmund and Manjakalmund for the purpose of securing the crucial signatures, but without success. Initially, everything seemed to be going according to the government's plans. After being given 'every possible explanation ... which they seemed perfectly to understand', twenty-six Toda pattadars signed the document by which they gave up the cantonment land, excepting land of religious significance. The two monigars, of whom Koondan Kallan was one, and witnesses from the cutcherry were present at the meeting. Afterwards, however, on considering the system among the Toda for authority over land, Smith thought it wise to call in some other 'influential Todas', even though they were not pattadars in the eyes of the government. Since the interest in the land included in the cantonment was common to all the Toda of the mund, Smith argued that their signatures would prevent the occurrence of disputes as to the right of the monigar to receive the compensation money. This was why other men, who were most likely elder brothers, cousins, uncles, and grandfathers, were called in.[44]

When these men arrived they refused to sign the document, and made it clear to the sub-collector that they would never give up their land. In addition, seven individuals present who had earlier signed the document, including Koondan Kallan, now retracted their consent. After a full day of reasoning, Smith gave up and took a deposition in which the Toda stated their reasons for refusing to part with the land.

Koondan Kallan's position is worth noting. He was monigar of the Toda in Malnad and an influential person. Not only was he an intermediary between the cutcherry and the Toda, but on the basis of the earlier document he would become the person through whom the government channelled the compensation payment to the Toda. At the same time, his name indicates that he was a Badaga, even if he noted his settlement to be in a Toda mund, in Madeneemund. In the deposition the Toda men blamed him for causing the original twenty-six signatures to be given. They claimed that the men had signed 'at the instigation of Goondoocul, who being a Circar [government] servant was interested in doing so.'[45]

In the deposition, the Toda stated clearly that they had no objection to Europeans settling on their land, but they absolutely refused to lose authority over it. Again, they explained their reasons: 'within this last fortnight after the signing of the Kararnamah, eight of our people have departed this life and some of us have been seriously warned by our Deity in their dreams, that those who sell the Ground shall be deprived by him of all their prosperity, that they and their Buffaloes shall be brought to the brink of destruction. In consequence of this we are now subject to the loss of plenty of our Buffaloes, and those surviving amongst them are dry and do not give milk as before.'[46] Smith tried reasoning with them—the document had been signed a fortnight earlier, but some of the eight deceased persons had died twenty days previously: where was the logic in that?—but to no avail. He then resorted to bargaining with the Rs 3,564 waiting for the Toda in the cutcherry, the sum agreed as compensation during Eliott's visit: 'This will be the last time it will be offered to you and it will be to your advantage to accept of it, what do you say?' The Toda were reported to have replied: 'We did not only mean this Kararnamah, but also that which was taken from the Todas by you at the time Mr Eliott was here. We have heard of the arrival of the money, we are unwilling to accept it for the above mentioned reasons, and we will never agree to accept it hereafter.'[47]

The Toda's refusal to accept monetary compensation for the land was met with a decision by the revenue board to keep the sum in deposit for one year and, if the Toda did not change their minds, both the money and the land would be lost. This was the same tactic as had been used to put pressure on unwilling Badaga landholders in Ketti only a month earlier.[48] At this point the Court of Directors intervened. Communication between Madras and London took a long time, but two years later the Madras government received orders regarding the step of depositing the compensation money. Considering the procedure to be 'a mere arbitrary exercise of power' on the government's part, the court feared that it would 'shake the confidence which the simple fact of their obstinate refusal to transfer their rights, shows that the Todas now place in the justice and moderation of our Government.' These were two arguments in one. The Munro doctrine, which emphasized the importance of establishing a government that rested on trust among the native population, was still strong. Trust would minimize the risk of disturbances and revolts and, in this situation too, the court encouraged the government to find ways to reconcile the parties (implying the government to be one of them) and secure consent for the legal settlement of land. Simultaneously, the Court of Directors went against the decision made by the sub-collector and confirmed at all higher instances up to the Madras government, arguing that it was an arbitrary exercise of power. It thus entered into the legal process.[49]

When the sub-collector negotiated with the Toda in the Nilgiris to establish legal rights in land, he was seeking to settle both a simple land transfer and, at the same time, the code by which such transfers could be made. As emphasized earlier, the meetings in the cutcherry did not represent a formal court where a judge acted on the basis of statutes, but a legal institution in which the sub-collector was vested with authority to act in the light of case law. This meant that Smith had authority to make precedential decisions, which would stand unless higher authority intervened. In the process, he had to act equitably, and on the question of equity the Court of Directors disagreed. It argued that to inform the Toda that the amount adjudged as compensation would be held in deposit and, if not claimed within a year, considered forfeited was unreasonable, and refused to sanction the proceeding.[50]

This situation mirrored legal procedures in Britain. The common law courts were superior courts and expensive systems of justice, while the lower courts were staffed with magistrates without formal legal training, whose decisions were based on case law and on the assumption of equity. Arbitration and negotiation, as in the case of the Nilgiris, was therefore part of the legal process. However, this was not arbitration between two parties with equal power, and what was equitable was in the last instance decided by one of the parties. And yet both benefited from avoiding open confrontation. It is significant that the subcollector hesitated before concluding the case, in order to ascertain that the settlement was logical also according to Toda norms for authority over land. Learning the hard way that it definitely was not, he was forced to continue the negotiations. While the sub-collector threw in arguments concerning conduct (the principle of upholding earlier agreements) and bargained for the land as a commodity, the Toda men pointed to a threatened lifeworld of meaning and livelihood. In this social contact zone, which materialized in disputed lands, the 'grand narrative' of the establishment of sovereign EIC rule should not overshadow the local histories in which human interaction made a difference and contradicted the broader historical transformations. At the level of principle, the district administration was acting out the orders of the Court of Directors. But their interests differed, and the consequences they drew from the general orders could be contradictory. While a district collector could advise a subordinate officer to carry any religious effigy to another spot so that the land could be purchased, he effected the order not to disturb religious sentiments by separating religious cult from attachment to place. In contrast, the Court of Directors may have disagreed on the importance of the Toda divinity in a transfer of land, referring to it as 'superstitious motives', but acknowledged the Toda's right to defend the land on such principles.[51]

Turning the perspectives around, the meetings in the cutcherry reflect some of the conditions in which the Toda responded to the government's decisive step to take over the control of land. From Eliott's investigation Smith learnt that the Toda in Malnad decided jointly about transfers of land, while land use was more likely to be decided at the level of the mund. Malnad was the only part of the Nilgiris where Toda remained in effective control of land, using most of it as grazing land (wasteland in the eyes of the government). It included both the lands surrounding the European settlement of Ootacamund and the Ketti valley. This means that the notion of pattadars or holders of a land title was a misconception, hence the fierce response from the 'influential Todas' when they were asked to add their signatures to the document that had been signed by twenty-six men, obviously without the consent of the other Toda men.

The deposition by which the Toda ultimately refused to part with their land was signed by twenty-one men, representing nineteen munds in Malnad. Their names and munds reveal that they were members of at least four patriclans: Kash, Melgash, Nosh, and Kyodr, and hence also members of both subgroups among the Toda. This shows, further, that decisions to give up authority over specific lands were a matter of importance for all the Toda of the nad. Only seven of the men who had signed the first document returned to strike out their names and add them to the deposition of protest. A reasonable assumption is that the other nineteen lacked authority to negotiate on land issues for the Toda.[52]

Some confusion can be observed in the colonial correspondence about the nature of Toda land relations. In 1835 George Dominico Drury, collector of Coimbatore, reported on the community's system of land management. As he had trouble explaining its details, he translated the information he had been given on a visit to Kodanad into a familiar terminology. Customary and oral agreements were described in terms associated with written contracts. Land under the control of family or kin was said to have been entered in an individual patta. Toda settlements were termed either *mund, moort,* or *baste*. The collector wrote:

> Each Mund or Moort has its separate grounds, including woodlands and pasturage and I understood from the Todawars of the Khodanaud Munds that they do not consider themselves as proprietors in common with other Todawars, that their rights in their own Munds are independent of other Munds and each family held its own right in the Mund which was invariably respected. The Todawars drive their herds backwards and forwards from one of their own Munds to another, to seek better pasturage without interruption, the Mund vacated by one family of Todawars is never occupied by another, nor do the cultivating classes attempt to take possession of the lands of the Mund while it is vacant. Lands are sometimes exchanged by one family of Todawars with another but no land belonging to one baste is transferred to the people of another. In Ootacamund and Munds in its immediate vicinity, it is understood that any Todawar may sell the portion of the Mund entered in his own

> Puttah, without reference to the Todawars of the same Mund, he is however obliged to obtain the consent of his own family and relatives.[53]

Most importantly, Drury was describing the situation from information he had gathered in Kodanad, a region in which Badaga cultivators had, relatively speaking, more influence than in Malnad. Most of the information he received related to the right to use the land, not dispose of it, and this use was decided at the level of the mund. However, in contradiction to the information given by the Toda of Malnad a couple of years later, the Toda of Kodanad had explained that the Toda in Ootacamund, at the heart of Malnad, could decide on the sale of land at the level of the mund. Whether this was incorrect or not, at the peak of the conflict the Toda in Malnad explained that no man could dispose of Toda land in Malnad without the consent of all the Toda in the nad. In this situation, fragmented land control would definitely have weakened the Toda's hold on the land.

During this period Toda society was clearly under stress, not only from British encroachments but also, on a longer time scale, from the increasingly settled and advancing agrarian economy of the Badaga. As noted earlier, a pastoral economy in which Toda clans had complete authority over land probably remained only within the centremost part of the Nilgiri plateau. Seen in the context of an ongoing process of changing production of value from land, shifting cultivation and pastoralism may not have coexisted quite as harmoniously as is often assumed when the system of socio-economic, political, and ritual relations between the hill communities is described. The British administration's immediate claims to the lands remaining under Toda authority also need to be seen in the light of these larger political-economic processes in which two extensive production systems, one cultivation-based and the other based on cattle, competed for access to land. Being a slow process, that competition may have been indirect and nontransparent, yet with the additional stress of British claims it was experienced more intensely by the Toda munds. Taking a longer-term historical view also puts the establishment of European farms and plantations such as those of Davis and McNair in a different light. Competition for land was obviously not initiated by European intrusion, though it was significantly speeded up by it. Defending rights in land was thus not an unfamiliar concept for hill communities. This is shown not least by their clear pronouncements about the boundary beyond which the Nilambur raja's right to claim jenmi from land ceased. But the rules by which rights could be claimed were changing as a result of British encroachments.

This observation may cause us to rethink and refine the notion of a 'contact zone' in which colonizer and colonized interacted in mutually formative ways, and introduce the aspect of time. Historicizing this sphere of interaction means that we also acknowledge the importance of transformative processes of social conflict, originating before the arrival of the colonizer, for the interaction that emerged. In the space of interaction that was created by the meeting between colonizer and colonized, the parties not only formed their understanding and practices in interlocked ways, but the sphere of communication was simultaneously brought into—or perhaps we could say appropriated by—past legacies of local and regional historical processes. In this particular case, the contact zone came to be affected by ongoing competition for land control, which means that an analysis in these terms needs to take account of attachment to time and place.

The Sovereign Government Sets the Rules: The 1843 Regulations

As the reports on the land disputes make amply clear, the Toda community were far from the stereotype of the ignorant tribe, locked into pristine landscapes and relating only to other tribes in their remote forest and hill setting. Their actions during the conflict with the EIC government prove beyond doubt that they were accustomed to dealing with bureaucracy and hierarchical state authority from a time before British administration.

In 1840, three years after the deposition in which the Toda of nineteen munds refused to accept any weakening of their authority over land in Malnad, the collector of Malabar, H.V. Conolly, concluded an agreement whereby the 'principal men' of ten munds agreed to let go of 97 per cent of the cantonment land. Of a total of 2,896 acres, the Toda of Kandelmund and Manjakalmund were permitted to re-reserve 87 acres. On paying a quit rent of Rs 150 per year, the government 'continued in possession' of the land they had occupied on Toda grazing grounds.

The shifting interpretation over time of the government's hold on the land is important. If any correspondence preceded the agreement that would explain why the Toda were now prepared to sign, it has not been preserved in the files. Most likely, though, the collector's correspondence on the issue was meagre, since he did not need to report such details to his superiors.[54]

The agreement carefully stipulated that it was the signatories' hereditary property on which the government and private gentlemen had built houses and cultivated gardens. The undersigned now agreed to let the government retain the land in their possession for as long as they pleased and do whatever they liked with it. However, the form of payment reveals the contradictory nature of the deal. The sum of money was to be paid annually 'in the same manner as the Berger Ryots of these hills pay us "Goodoo" from our lands which they cultivate.' At the same time, the government was said to have 'retained possession' of the land by paying a quit rent that was modelled on a form of tenure. The transfer of land without acknowledging former ownership gave the advocate general, G. Norton, quite a headache as he was requested to ascertain the legality of the deed.[55]

Once again, it was Sullivan who set the wheels of bureaucracy spinning. On finding that his 'grant' had been turned into a 'lease', and this only after he had already sold the land, he suggested that all leases should be converted back into grants, so that the government gained the right to give land titles. The Toda, he suggested, should be paid a quit rent as an acknowledgement of their superiority. The advocate general, who was asked to give his opinion on the legality of such documents, responded by giving the Board of Revenue and collector of land customs in Madras a lesson in law: 'The object of a *certificate* is not in itself to *create* any new right and, least of all, on behalf of the party issuing such certificate, but to specify some matter of fact, or act done, or custom prevailing or claim made, and it should be confined to matters within the accurate knowledge of the party certifying.' It should be noted, though, that Norton was not neutral on the question of land settlements in the Nilgiri Hills. In 1834 he had been one of sixteen applicants who sought government grants for their holdings in the hills. Three years later he had been among the most active petitioners seeking (unsuccessfully) to prevent their grants being turned into leases.[56]

Meanwhile, the settlement of Europeans on wasteland continued unabated. An application by a Mr Grove to cultivate 2,644 acres of land near the Katy (i.e. Kattery) waterfalls received strong support from Conolly. He had no sympathy for the Toda of Katterymund, who refused to yield their land. The tahsildar had found that three-quarters of the land was 'immemorial waste' and that the remainder had not been cultivated for the last thirty years. All was more or less jungle or coarse grass, according to the tahsildar. Conolly noted that 661 acres had, from time to time, been used by two Toda men for grazing, 'but this fact will not, I presume, be any impediment to the acceptance of Mr Grove's offer.' Arguing that land could hardly be allowed to remain waste if there were opportunities to bring it into profitable cultivation, he concluded that when the Toda declined to pay tax—as these men did—'the Government has clearly the power to insist on their making way for those who will.' However, the deposition attached to his letter gives a slightly different picture. The two men, Kedal Venoo and Akashee, explained that while they were prepared to give up three-quarters of their land, they wanted to keep the remaining portion. It had been in the mund's possession from time immemorial and they used it for grazing buffaloes, but neither they nor the other Toda had the means to pay any assessment to the government.[57]

Depending on the recipient and purpose of his correspondence, Conolly adjusted his description of the landscape at the Katy waterfalls. To the revenue board he emphasized the jungly character of the land, to impress on them the importance of letting Grove put it under the plough. For the government's decision, he pointed to its beauty. Having first described the land as overgrown with jungle or coarse grass, he now wrote that it was covered with long grass and, in some places, with low jungle wood. There were also some fine forests or sholas, and he stressed that he had explained to Grove the need to preserve the woods and that nothing should be done which would injure their beauty. It was later agreed that Grove would not take water from above the waterfall so as not to spoil the scenery.[58]

Following the protests in 1831–6, the growing number of applications for grants and of letters to the revenue board, objecting to the reclassification of land rights for Europeans and immigrant Indians, indicates the slow but persistent establishment of EIC rule in its bureaucratic form in the Nilgiris. The bureaucracy itself became both a tool of power and an arena for contesting principles relating to rights, not only in land in its material sense, but in nature for both the material and non-material values attached to it. As late as 1841, however, the government still lacked a code for rights in land in the Nilgiri Hills. In the process described, Grove's application for land became one of the more important cases on which such a code could be based.

To Conolly the complaint of the Toda of Katterymund was one of the obstacles that had to be overcome. Their claim was 'untenable' since they would not use the land for cultivation, which produced much higher revenue returns. But 'in order to avoid the shadow of injustice' Conolly constructed an agreement with the Toda that both declared government sovereignty in the land, which gave the government the right to issue a land title to Grove and deny property rights to the Toda. He also instituted the payment of 'a fee' on the same principles as the gudu given by native cultivators to the Toda in the Nilgiris. In consequence, Grove was to pay both land revenue to the government and gudu to the Toda. In addition, the Toda were allowed to use Grove's land for pasture as long as it was not taken up for cultivation. Formally, this had been a 'privilege', not a right. To the Toda of Katterymund the legal change must have been deceptive. After the agreement had been signed, things went on as before. It took a long time for Grove to bring any appreciable area of land under cultivation, and meanwhile the buffaloes continued to graze and the Toda received gudu (at least in theory, as there are no records of whether Grove ever paid any fee to them). The way revenue was organized also signalled a new centre of power. Different qualities of land were assessed at different rates and, moreover, those rates were defined by the distance from Ootacamund—the rising centre of colonial power in the hills. Grove's land was again made a case on which new regulations could be based.[59]

Having been ordered by the government to establish rules for the administration of the hills, Conolly sometimes went a bit far. In a detailed instruction (a *hookumnamah*), he suggested rules which would in fact make shifting cultivation illegal. Aiming to rectify the wasteful habit among hill cultivators of allowing land to lie fallow while taking up cultivation on an equal area of land elsewhere, and paying revenue only on the land cultivated, he suggested a form of land ceiling. Any given cultivator was only to be permitted to hold as much land as he had the means to pay the full assessment for. Revenue would thus curb the practice of shifting cultivation. However, the revenue board objected that such rules were unsuitable in the hills. They saw no intention of fraud in the cultivators' practices, and, derived as they were from low-country practices, these rules were not appropriate for conditions in the Nilgiris.[60]

Conolly went on to explain that hill cultivation caused problems when it came to establishing principles of administration. One cultivator, who had been allowed to take up unoccupied land, claimed that this land belonged to him even though he had not cultivated it for eight years. Another man, a Badaga cultivator, objected to Grove's land near the Katy waterfalls, claiming that it belonged to him and that he might cultivate it in future. 'He thought, as do the Ryots generally, he had a right to the land he had once cultivated, however long it might be left fallow, without paying any assessment.' While Conolly did not associate the Badaga's claim with earlier land arrangements between Toda and Badaga, clearly the argument followed the logic of gudu. On hearing of Conolly's problems, the revenue board decided that a period of five years' fallow would suffice to meet the cultivator's needs. Unless cultivation had begun at the expiry of that period, he would lose his right in the land entirely. Conolly again responded by suggesting that a period of two years, or alternatively the consent of the first holder, would be enough. As in many earlier instances, singular principles of administration and agrarian change were confronted with local practices.[61]

Nonetheless, the process of drawing up rules for administration and codes for land rights in the Nilgiris continued and, as one of the main promoters was the governor, S.R. Lushington, securing sovereign rule became the foremost principle. In a draft by John Bird, a member of council and chief judge, the main narrative of the settlement of land rights crystallized into what came to remain a historiography of the colonial bureaucracy. The draft solidly affirmed the just and benevolent treatment of the Toda and their land, and its narrative remained the dominant mode of British history in the hills, clearly reflected in Grigg's *Manual of Nilagiri District* (1880). First, Bird declared that the government's intention was not on any account to dispute Toda possession of the land they desired to keep for pasturage. It would remain theirs as long as they paid the leases, and no land was to be taken for public purposes without compensation. The Court of Directors was said to have approved of the government's determination in this regard—there is no mention of the court first having ordered the government to act liberally. However, this endeavour was thwarted by the Toda, who refused to accept the compensation offered for land taken for public purposes. At that point, the collector of Malabar was directed to negotiate with the Toda for the purpose of immediately making over the land to the government on condition that an annual quit rent be paid, and a year later he was successful. The agreement was claimed to have followed the government's instructions on reservations to the letter.[62]

In every detail, Bird presented the Madras government as the prime mover of order and justice, and we can see how the agreement followed the logic of precedential law. Toda notions of land rights were respected, while being brought into the domain of EIC rule. The amount of compensation was based on the sum Sullivan claimed to have paid to the Toda in 1822 (a sum which the Toda were thus assumed to consider just). Conolly's deal with the Toda basically confirmed details that had been accepted in earlier negotiations. All in all, the draft conveyed an image of a bureaucracy with clean hands that went to considerable lengths to meet the demands of the native population. This image was further emphasized as Bird went on to explain the impossibility of admitting claims of Toda property in the soil. The one argument that would make all others superfluous was the fact that they had always paid tax to the government for pasture lands. In the voluminous documentation available to the government, Bird claimed that there was nothing that gave it cause to make an exception for the Toda from the sovereign rights of the government on all matters.[63]

During 1842 the principles for a regulation of land rights were moulded and discussed in ever more detail. For every minute and report produced, the actual claims of the Toda faded further into the background, while the determination 'not to disturb the Toda in their possession' was turned into a stepping stone to a legal elaboration of how to disallow them any right similar to freehold property. It was now certified that, until that point, the exact nature and value of Toda rights had never been fixed and their land claims remained undetermined. The increasing immigration into the Nilgiris and the grants of wide tracts of waste for coffee plantations required 'a precise and legal understanding' of the rights and interests concerned. In this process, gudu was disqualified as a reliable indicator of rights and, to avoid confusion, 'compensation' was the only term to be used to denote the annual sum disbursed in return for the land taken by government, while 'quit rent' and 'gudu' were to be carefully avoided. The Toda were allowed to continue grazing cattle, but only as long as such rights did not 'bar the progress of improvement or hinder the application of the land to more useful and valuable purposes.' Soon after, Conolly reported that he had obtained the consent of the Toda to substitute 'compensation' for the term 'Goodoo'.[64]

In June 1843 the Court of Directors sanctioned a set of rules governing the nature and extent of the Toda's rights over land in the Nilgiris and the terms and conditions on which lands in the hills were to be granted to parties who wanted to bring them under cultivation. By this decision it was legally stipulated that the Toda had no other right in land than that of 'immemorial occupation'. They were understood to have 'been in the habit' of pasturing herds across undefined areas of land, and had allowed Burghers, 'an agricultural tribe', to cultivate the land, for which the Toda had received 'annual donations'. Neither the extent of the land nor the meaning of gudu had been 'satisfactorily ascertained'. The choice of legal terminology was decisive in making the reassignment of rights from the Toda to the EIC appear unquestionable. The Toda had occupied the land—simply lived there—not possessed it. The nature of gudu was still unknown, but since it was described as a matter of annual donations, future compensation payments could be modelled on the same system.[65]

From a comparison with rules on wasteland in Malabar and mirasi tenure elsewhere, a legal norm was deduced. This stated that where a person wanted to take up cultivation of wasteland, he should either be allowed to do so under full assessment of the land or else the holder should pay the full assessment to be allowed to keep the land, even if it remained fallow. The Nilgiri regulations stipulated: 'From a consideration of the universally acknowledged rights of the Government in respect to uncultivated lands, as well as of the peculiar circumstances of the case under discussion, we cannot admit the existence of any such proprietary right in the soil on the part of the Todas, as can in any way interfere with the right of Government to permit parties willing to pay the full assessment to bring it under the plough.'[66]

All that remained then was to determine the Toda's right to be compensated for the 'abridgement of the grazing privileges' they had exercised in the hills. The answer came in a truly utilitarian form: 'the only advantage which they have derived from their occupancy (with the exception of the annual payments received from the Burghers) has been that of pasturing their herds. The injury which they will sustain from the settlement of strangers on the hills, will consequently arise from the diminution of their pasture grounds, as the lands are gradually brought into cultivation.'[67]

So, after gudu had been invalidated as anything but a mere name for a payment for land use, Toda authority in the Nilgiris was reduced to the need for grass for their buffaloes. However, pasture was acknowledged to be a 'privilege' they had enjoyed from 'time immemorial' and was therefore a fair subject of compensation. In the margin of the document, a civil servant with the initials 'AG' has scribbled numerous notes which indicate that he disagreed with this liberal treatment of the Toda. The paragraph on the Toda's loss of privilege was marked with the comment: 'and without paying anything for that privilege'. Further comparisons with the jenmi landlords of Malabar, for the sake of establishing a payment equivalent to gudu, also prompted angry remarks: 'This is all very right if indeed it were ascertained that the Todawars have a property in these lands—but until this shall be ascertained surely we cannot assign to them any payment for that would be to admit a *title* the existence of which is not ascertained. AG.'[68]

The form of compensation payment laid down was elaborate in its design. The payment for land taken for public purposes, which in fact included both the government and private individuals who wanted land for cultivation, was to be added to the assessment of the land, so that the Toda would receive compensation directly from the collector's treasury. In order for the money not to be dissipated by 'the simple race', it was to be invested to yield an annual income which could be distributed as and when the Toda wanted to undertake agricultural operations. Munds and religious sites were secured from all interference by granting the Toda absolute rights to these lands, and it was advised that lands in the immediate vicinity of the munds should be spared. The idea was that, in due course, the Toda would be encouraged to take up cultivation and no longer depend on the herding of buffaloes. In this way, the legal code for rights in land was, simultaneously, a policy to transform the hill economy into an agrarian one.

When the sequence of events in the Nilgiris is compared to colonial intervention in neighbouring hill regions in the Eastern Ghats, east of the Nilgiri Hills, we may see similar legislation being passed, but with different consequences, depending on the particular colonial interest in the regions. A pattern of regional difference stands out even more clearly as the Eastern Ghats are made up of a number of smaller hill tracts. In spite of the fact that most of them were administered within one district, Salem, a singular policy was not adopted specifically for these hills or for tribals. For example, while timber extraction was intensive in hills rich in sandalwood from the time they came under EIC control in the 1790s, the Kalrayan Hills were left under the existing administration of *jagirdars* and were not surveyed and brought under colonial administration until 1868. At that time, revenue from the land had begun to increase, while previously these hill tracts had not been considered to possess any valuable resources.[69]

In the Kolli Hills, one of the regions where sandalwood was cut on a large scale by private contractors, the Madras government attempted to curb excessive extraction, which was causing denudation of the hills. Ajit Menon notes that, in 1835, contractors were prohibited from cutting sandalwood in the Kolli Hills and merchants were similarly forbidden to purchase the timber. Nevertheless, the government remained dependent on private entrepreneurs for timber supplies and, until 1835, they maintained a laissez faire administrative policy in these hills which allowed the Malayali inhabitants to lease out portions of land. From the mid 1830s onwards, however, people were increasingly seen as poachers and tighter restrictions were imposed.[70]

In contrast, in the case of the Shevaroy Hills, Velayutham Saravanan notes how the growing coffee plantations triggered a number of legal regulations which were introduced to establish government control over European entrepreneurs and the land market. The Shevaroy Hills thus make an interesting parallel to the administration of the Nilgiri Hills. In the former, coffee planters began establishing estates primarily by means of land grabbing in the 1820s. In 1833 the Government of Madras consequently restricted land transfers by legislating that land could only be obtained on lease from the government. The intention was not to hamper the expanding coffee industry: the land was rent free for the first five years and, after that, rents were kept at low levels. Owing to considerable expansion of European coffee plantations on land under the Malayali community, the government issued regulations in 1842 for the purpose of restricting planters from settling on land when it caused inconvenience to the local population. In the light of the legislation simultaneously passed for the Nilgiris, it may be observed in particular how the Madras government sought to achieve sovereign control over land in the Shevaroy Hills, too, while demonstrating its ambition, however toothless, of acting as a benevolent ruler.[71]

We may also include the administration of the hills of Coorg, located in the Western Ghats north-west of the Nilgiris, in a discussion of the administrative principles of the Madras Presidency and of popular responses to legal regulations. These forest tracts were rich in teak and were an important source of timber, not least for the Bombay docks, from the early nineteenth century onwards. As discussed in Chapter 2, when shifting or kumri cultivators were targeted as causing large-scale damage to forests, the administrative measures taken in the 1840s to curb the felling and burning of trees brought into sharp focus the different consequences of kumri under the control of large landowners and kumri directly controlled by the government. While the latter arrangement was easier to control, the former increased in scale in spite of the Madras and Bombay governments' concerns, this being the result of a situation in which kumri cultivation itself increased the landowners' influence and their control of additional labour, bringing even more land into cultivation. Not until 1855, when the basis for the assessment system for kumri changed from the number of billhooks to the acreage under cultivation, did shifting cultivation decline in this region.[72]

The problem of ownership was similarly acute in the Nilgiris. One of the concluding paragraphs in the 1843 regulations on Toda rights and rules for land grants in the Nilgiris also placed restrictions on EIC officers, as it prohibited civil and military officers from holding land while exercising civil authority in the district. The government could in addition refuse or withdraw at its discretion permission to hold land when it deemed this to be detrimental to the public interest. The civil servant AG again disapproved strongly: 'By Law all British subjects are entitled to hold land. Therefore I take it all we can do is to "withdraw at our discretion their employment in our Service in case of their holding lands objectionably." AG.'[73]

Concluding Remarks

What stands out as a major difference between the situation in the Nilgiri Hills and many earlier studies of popular resistance to colonial aggression in hill and forest tracts is how integrated people appear to have been into a state's or a large bureaucracy's way of functioning. In the central Nilgiris, people's perceptions of what constituted a right in nature certainly differed from those of British officers, but a situation in which notions of rights could be different and, moreover, could be negotiated does not seem to have been alien to them. The increasing influence of Badaga cultivators in the fringe areas of the plateau, weakening Toda authority over land, and the deed tying Toda pastoralists into a language of jenmi rights are signs of the simultaneous working of different rights systems in the late eighteenth and early nineteenth centuries. This was not a situation created by the British presence in the hills, but rather the situation into which the British entered. The idea of the diku, the non-tribal outsider, therefore does not help us to understand either Toda or Badaga responses to European and immigrant-Indian claims to land. Here, the divisions do not seem to have been so clear cut.

Popular responses in the Nilgiris can be observed if we broadly divide the transformation of land settlement under EIC influence into three phases: the first characterized by strong individuals at the district and regional levels extending European settlement by crude means, the second by legal negotiations in the administrative offices as the presidency administrators took over the initiative on the question of land settlement, and the third by the final establishment of a legal code for rights backed by a more powerful state bureaucracy. As the first European settlements appeared in Malnad, the Toda of those munds were also the first to respond to the intrusion. Later, when Europeans claimed lands that were under the rotations of shifting cultivators, the Badaga, too, objected to the incoming settlers, while the British immediately mistook the Badaga for landholders.

The first confrontations in the early 1830s resulted in the removal of the peishkar. This step was taken after the Toda had involved the Nilambur raja, a patron with influence which extended to the right to collect taxes within his domain, and subordinate government servants had supported the Toda's charges against the peishkar. In the mid 1830s, when the sub-collectors negotiated but failed to strike a deal with the Toda in central Malnad, the courtroom itself, or the cutcherry, became a means of protecting authority over land. In that context, one of the sub-collectors took the view that the Toda used the legal process tactically rather than justly. The Toda, for their part, realized the importance of refusing to accept payment, as well as refusing to sign documents laid before them. They also used the vehicle of a deposition to annul an earlier agreement. These were by no means the actions of people who were encountering state authority for the first time, but those of a community who knew how to fight the EIC on the terms set by its administration. The absence of reports of protests from 1840 onwards is striking, as absences and silences are important but difficult to interpret. However, the businesslike tone in the correspondence between the collector and the revenue board and the collector's brief visit when a deal was signed at that time demonstrate that the revenue board was allowing no further space for legal negotiations: sovereignty was now to be established unquestioned.

When the Toda of Kandelmund first refused to part with their land, Europeans and immigrant Indians had lived in the region for about a decade, Sullivan's house at Ootacamund being recorded as the first, built in 1821 or 1822.[74] It would be a simplification to assume that the reason they did not object to the appropriation of land for houses was that, to begin with, houses were few and land plenty, as if the Toda did not care what happened to the land over which they held authority. Such an argument would rather reflect the logic of *terra nullius*, which assumed that people whose livelihood was secured within extensive lands did not need all that land and would hardly notice if European cultivators used portions of it. But South Indian hills do not easily compare with the deceptively empty lands of regions such as the North American or Australian plains, either in extent or in terms of past histories of state authority. While the plains of Australia, for example, were by no means empty of people controlling and using the land, the influence of ruling elites and state bureaucracies does not seem to have been as apparent there as it was in South India. Moreover, arguments in support of *terra nullius* mostly seem to have been applied after land had been appropriated, not before, as a way of legitimizing and rationalizing settlement with reference to a legal principle. Very clearly, the peishkar's request to the Toda to sign a deed of sale in 1831 provoked strong reactions. No one objected to houses being built on grazing grounds, just as the Toda of Manjakalmund fully accepted that Lushington's garden could remain, even though it was established on sacred ground. But they were not prepared to yield control of the land to the British. As within the logic of gudu, granting rights for others to use a piece of land did not threaten Toda authority. On the contrary, relations of power and exchange were reinforced as the Toda allowed outsiders to settle. This was not only a matter of economic control of the land, but also a reconfirmation of political and ritual relations. Consequently, the Toda of both Kandelmund and Manjakalmund and, later, of many munds in Malnad refused to enter into agreements that limited their authority.

The work of the sub-collectors, who were entrusted with all the groundwork for a deal by which the EIC could secure absolute rights over those parts of the Kandelmund land that comprised the cantonment, was simultaneously a confirmation of benevolent and just British rule. We may therefore ask what kind of justice they were trying to deliver. It is important to note that both sub-collectors were careful to establish and relate to norms of land control among the Toda. Whether they got those norms right or not, they did not bypass them. The most pragmatic reason for respecting native rights was connected with the success of legal settlements; as sub-collector Smith noted when he asked another group of Toda men to sign an agreement already concluded, no one was to have any cause to disregard an agreement on account of the deal having been signed by men without the proper authority.

On four occasions Toda men from munds in Malnad were recorded as having negotiated with the British authorities at the administrative office. Most likely, there were other similar occasions, such as when the petition was handed over and, subsequently, witness statements were taken and the peishkar discharged. But in the EIC accounts these four occasions stand out because they involved the signing and revoking of documented agreements. Other accounts relate how disputed lands were debated and measured on site, and how government servants took notes of Toda men and women crying and pleading for the integrity of their temple grounds. Most of these interactions, whether they occurred in the cutcherry or in munds, shola forests, or grazing grounds, were recorded and incorporated as part of the negotiations and legal disputes over land.

In the early phase of the conflicts it still remained an open question whether or not native claims to land should be respected, but as the conflicts progressed the aim of establishing the sovereignty of the EIC in the Madras Presidency was undisputed in all quarters. The only question was how to achieve and formalize that goal. Most importantly, in the process, means and aims were confused, since the system of justice the EIC's officers represented was, in fact, the institution used both to sort out the legality of claims and to establish a basis for codes through precedent. The subcollectors' experiences in the Nilgiris seem to have been problematic and, in the end, not achieved much. But they were the vehicles by which the collector, a few years later, could lay down the conditions for land transfers and the rights of the Toda, ultimately to be formalized in the 1843 regulations. The negotiations, in which the parties interacted through the other party's domain of authority as each was understood by the individuals and institutions involved, formed a zone of contact and interaction. As we have seen, there was a high level of interdependence, albeit based on a fundamentally uneven balance of power and resources.

This chapter has provided a close encounter with the trajectories of certain specific land disputes. Each step in these conflicts was part of the everyday experience of emerging colonial rule. They were not necessarily significant enough to have an impact outside the most local of realms, but larger issues of principle were at stake, beyond the loss of land experienced by a few individual Toda munds. The contrast between the low stakes of conquest and the intense attention to detail even within the Board of Directors reveals both the importance, at the level of principle, of land settlement in the Nilgiris for similar situations in the British territories in India, and the consequences of such a slow pace of subjugation. In marked contrast to the rapidly formed oppositions described in many historical works influenced by early Subaltern Studies, the interaction between colonizer and colonized resulting from conflicting land claims in this part of the Western Ghats appears variegated and rich in complexity. Resulting from two decades of a slowly expanding EIC conquest—more rapid in theory than in practice, and with a variety of incoherent interests among the immigrating Europeans and Indians—contest, compromise, and overlapping perceptions of how claims in land were formed and articulated marked the legal discourse. Until, that is, the Madras government decided to put its foot down.

References

1. The Toda's Agriculture Co-operative Bank, copy of document: In the G.O. No.: 240, 11 March 1893 (1888), Toda Patta land rules, para 7. Copy obtained in Kandelmund. Udhagamandalam District Records, Proceedings of the Madras Revenue Department (LR), 27 March 1888, no. 309 in Sutton, 2001, publicly available 2006, *Other Landscapes. Hill Communities, Settlers and State on the Colonial Nilgiris, c. 1820–1900*, 198–9.
2. Field notes, Kandelmund, November 2001, September 2003. Field notes, C.R. Sathyanarayanan, 2004.
3. TNA, NDR 1827–35, 4184, Military, Commandant's Letter Book, Letters sent, 15 February 1827–16 June 1829, To J.C. Morris, Act. Sub Coll., from Major W. Kelso, n.d. [judging from letters copied immediately before and after this letter, most likely February 1828], 44–9.
4. Thompson, 1975, *Whigs and Hunters. The Origin of the Black Act*, 36–9.
5. Washbrook, 2004, 'Sovereignty, Property, Land and Labour in Colonial South India', 86–8.
6. Finn, 2000, *Law, Debt, and Empire in Calcutta*, 7.
7. Sivaramakrishnan, 1999, *Modern Forests. Statemaking and Environmental Change in Colonial Eastern India*, 276–7.
8. TNA, MBRP, 12 May 1863, no. 2831: 2779–80, P. Grant, Collector of Coimbatore to the Madras Board of Revenue, 27 April 1863. See also Cederlöf and Sutton, 2005, 'The Aboriginal Toda. On Indigeneity, Exclusivism and Privileged Access to Land in the Nilgiri Hills, South India', 173.
9. Kelso having been appointed less than two years earlier, the subsequent disagreements between him and Sullivan may have resulted in the latter's request for immediate rules limiting European access to land. OIOC, MBRP, 3 January 1828, To the President and Members of the Board of Revenue from J. Sullivan, Principal Collector, 2 October 1827.
10. Andrew Fleming Hudleston held office as the Principal Collector of Malabar 1830–2.
11. A peishkar was in charge of the taluk office, the cutcherry, and Venkata Soobayen was head of the Ootacamund Peishkar Cutcherry. OIOC, MBRP, 5 August 1833, no. 6: 9589–90, To Major Crewe, Commanding on the Neilgherries, from J. Lushington, Private Secr., 6 August 1831.
12. Ibid., 21 January 1833, no. 2: 802–5, Decision, Tothawar Kandil Nair and others versus Vekat Soobayen late Peishcar of the Neilgherry Talook, and 5 August, no. 1: 9582–3, To Vencutoobien, Acting Peishcar of the Neiligherries from A.Fr. Hudleston, Principal Collector, 16 August 1831.

13. Ibid., 27 November 1828, no. 516: 12229, From the Secretary to the Board of Revenue ... the rights of the Todawars and the enclosures on the Neilgherry Hills, and 5 August 1833, no. 1: 9582–3, To Vencutoobien, Acting Peishcar of the Neiligherries from A.Fr. Hudleston, Principal Collector, 16 August 1831, OIOC, MD, Revenue Department, 27 January 1836, no. 45: 7086–96, Minutes, and 21 June 1843, no.13: 51–92, Rights of the Todawars and Rules for grants of land on the Neilgherries.
14. Men and women were allowed to marry within the subgroup, but always outside the patriclan. The number of patriclans has not remained unchanged over the last two hundred years, as some have died out. *Pattadar*, holder of a title to land. Walker, 1986, *The Toda of South India. A New Look*, 65–7.
15. William Rumbold was the grandson of Thomas Rumbold, Governor of Madras 1778–80. Lady Rumbold was the daughter and co-heiress of Lord Rancliffe and a ward of the first Marquis of Hastings, Governor-General of India 1813–23. Price, 2000 (1908), *Ootacamund, a History*, 134–5.
16. OIOC, MBRP, 5 August 1833, no. 1: 9582–3, To Vencutoobien, Acting Peishcar of the Neiligherries from A. Fr. Hudleston, Principal Collector, 16 August 1831.
17. Ibid., 5 August 1833, no. 2: 9583, To Venkata Soobayen, Acting Peishcar at Ootacamund, from A. Fr. Hudleston, Pl. Coll., 26 August 1831.
18. Koondan or Goundan. The name Koondan Kallan is in several documents also spelt Goondoocul, Goondoculla or Goondogul. OIOC, MBRP, 5 August 1833, no. 3: 9583–5, To A. Fr. Hudleston Esq., Pl. Coll. of Malabar, from Venkat Soobayen, A. Peishkar, 28 August 1831.
19. Ibid., 5 August 1833, no. 3: 9583–5, To A. Fr. Hudleston Esq., Pl. Coll. of Malabar, from Venkat Soobayen, A. Peishkar, 28 August 1831.
20. Ibid., 5 August 1833, no. 4: 9585–7, To the Acting Peishkar of Neilgherry, from A. Fr. Hudleston, Pl. Coll., 8 September 1831.
21. Ibid.; OIOC, MBRP, 20 November 1834: 12791, no. 1, Collector's letter 8 July 1833.
22. Ibid., 5 August 1833, no. 5: 9587–8, To A. Fr. Hudleston Esq., Pl. Coll. of Malabar, from Venkat Soobayen, Acting Peishkar, n.d., no. 7: 9590–1, Extract of Demi-official letter from Major Crewe to Mr Hudleston, 21 August 1831, and no. 10: 9592–3, To Venkatkoopayen, Acting Peishkar at Ootacamund, from Fr. Hudleston, Pl. Coll., 10 October 1831.
23. OIOC, MD, 26 October 1831, Revenue Department, 1159–62, OIOC, MBRP, 14 November 1831, To the President and Members of the Board of Revenue.
24. Duffadar or Indian Army cavalry officer, equal to sergeant.

25. OIOC, MBRP, 21 January 1833, no. 1: 791–801, To the Board of Revenue, the Petition of Venkata Soobyen, late Peishcar of Ootacamund in the Neilgherry Talook in the Zillah of Malabar, 22 May 1832, and no. 2: 802–5, Decision. Tothawar Kandil Nari and others versus Venkat Sobayen late Peishcar of the Neilgherry Talook, 8 May 1832.
26. Ibid., 21 January 1833, no. 1: 791–801, To the Board of Revenue, the Petition of Venkata Soobyen, late Peishcar of Ootacamund in the Neilgherry Talook in the Zillah of Malabar, 22 May 1832.
27. In 1837, Nunjah Goundan was the monigar of the Badaga in Malnad. Ibid., 13 April 1837: 4226–7, Translation of a Deposition given before E. Smith Esq. Sub Collector of Malabar by the undersigned Burghers Inhabitants of Kaitee Village in the Nielgherry Talook.
28. OIOC, MRC, 3 June 1829: 2655–6, To the President and Members of the Board of Revenue from John Sullivan.
29. Rangarajan, 1996, *Fencing the Forest. Conservation and Ecological Change in India's Central Provinces, 1860–1914*, 118–26.
30. OIOC, MBRP, 21 January 1833, no. 1: 791–801, To the Board of Revenue, the Petition of Venkata Soobyen, late Peishcar of Ootacamund in the Neilgherry Talook in the Zillah of Malabar, 22 May 1832.
31. Ibid., 20 November 1834, To the Chief Secretary to Government, signed J.A.R. Stevenson, Secr., para 2.
32. Ibid., paras 2–3, 5.
33. In the same document, Clementson explained that the Toda in Kandelmund never wanted to part with their sacred grounds and that 'Repeated entreaties and the offer of a large sum of money (From four hundred Rupees) at length induced them to yield though reluctantly as acknowledged by the Peshkar himself'. OIOC, MBRP, 5 August 1833, paras 2, 3, 6. Quoted, for example, in Grigg, 1880, *The Manual of Nilagiri District*, 332. Grigg, in turn, is quoted by the anthropologist Anthony Walker. Walker, 1986, *The Toda of South India. A New Look*, 243, 246.
34. OIOC, MD, Revenue Department, 5 February 1834, Letter dated 17 September 1832, no. 8, para 36.
35. OIOC, MRP, 26 February 1835, To the Board of Revenue from F. Clementson, 9 February 1835, OIOC, MD, Revenue Department, 27 January 1836, no. 1: 102–3. OIOC, BC, State of the Todawars on the Neilgherry Hills, Mr Sullivan's Minute, 20 August 1835: 12–57.
36. Ibid., State of the Todawars on the Neilgherry Hills, Extract Revenue General letter from Madras, 16 February 1836, no. 3, para 38.
37. OIOC, MRP, 27 December 1836, no. 43, Memorandum for the consideration of the Board of Revenue, D. Eliott, 30 November 1836: 7055–69.

38. Ibid., 27 December 1836, no. 43, Regarding Memorandum from Mr Eliott, from the Revenue Board, A.P. Onslow, 8 December 1836: 7051–5, para 4, and Memorandum for the consideration of the Board of Revenue, D. Eliott, 30 November 1836: 7055–69.
39. Ibid., 27 December 1836, no. 43, To the Chief Secretary to Government, from A.P. Onslow, 19 December 1836, Memorandum, D. Eliott, 10 December 1836: 7071–9.
40. Ibid., 27 December 1836, no. 43, To the Chief Secretary to Government, from A.P. Onslow, 19 December 1836, Translation of Deposition given before E. Smith Esquire Sub Collector of Malabar by the undersigned Malnaud Todavars, 7 December 1836: 7079–84.
41. Ibid., 27 December 1836, no. 43, To the Chief Secretary to Government, from A.P. Onslow, 19 December 1836, signed E. Smith, 15 December 1836: 7084–6.
42. OIOC, MBRP, 13 April 1837, Investigation of European land claims, Enclosure no. 1, To Edmund Smith, Sub Collector of Malabar, from W. Davis, 22 March 1837: 4214–19.
43. OIOC, MD, Revenue, 19 April 1837, para 38, 'State of the Todawar in Neilgherry Hills.'
44. OIOC, BC, Revenue Consultation, 9 May 1837, Letter from the Sub Collector E. Smith, 27 March 1837.
45. Ibid., and field notes, C.R. Sathyanarayanan, October 2004.
46. OIOC, BC, Revenue Consultation, 9 May 1837, Letter from the Sub Collector E. Smith, 27 March 1837.
47. Ibid.
48. OIOC, MBRP, 13 April 1837, Investigation of Kaity lands, Resolution thereon: 4727–8, OIOC, Board's Consultations, 9 May 1837, Board's resolution, signed A.P. Onslow, Secretary.
49. It is doubtful whether the Court's silence on the same procedure used in the Ketti case was a result of its less indulgent treatment of the Badaga community, on account of their being agriculturists and therefore not fitted, as the Toda were, for the role of indolent savage, as Deborah Sutton has assumed. The court's remarks were primarily concerned with principles of governance, and ultimately the Badaga claimants in Ketti were paid compensation. OIOC, MD, 10 April 1839, no. 3, para 49: 524–8. Sutton, 2001, publicly available 2006, *Other Landscapes. Hill Communities, Settlers and State on the Colonial Nilgiris, c. 1820–1900*, 29.
50. OIOC, MD, 10 April 1839, no. 3, para 49: 524–8. For a comparison, see Finn, 2000, *Law, Debt, and Empire in Calcutta*, 8–9; Karsten, 2002, *Between Law and Custom. High and Low Legal Cultures in the Lands of the*

British Diaspora—the United States, Canada, Australia, and New Zealand, 1600–1900, 124–8.

51. OIOC, MD, 10 April 1839, no. 3, para 49: 524–8.
52. The deposition bears the signatures of Goondoogul Monigar of Madeneemund, Naradodee of Caundulmund (head hamlet, Kash patriclan), Jhorthauum of Caundulmund (head hamlet, Melkash patriclan), Narecote of Munjacalmund, Pelnaroo of Manjecalmund, Kairuun of Gagaramund, Aluum of Cundymund, Boochavain of Peunabamund, Cadvouum of Manjanacoramund, Cain of Pellathoocaramund, Caudur of Cuckodoomund, Cavee of Pennarmund, Curthamathee of Iabud Kundmund, Curthan of Malekantmund, Jheloosoorum, Mootanaudmund (head hamlet, Nosh patriclan, Taarthaarsh subgroup), Jhollavun of Malecoodoomund (Kyodr patriclan, Teivali subgroup), Machath of Cuthcudamund, Mencate of Puckodoomund, Nadee of Munjathoal, Ponnanvun of Coondagoodoomund and Puttavail of Camboothookeemund (Nosh patriclan, Taarthaarsh subgroup). OIOC, BC, Revenue Consultation, 9 May 1837, Letter from the Sub Collector E. Smith, 27 March 1837, and field notes, C.R. Sathyanarayanan, October 2004.
53. George Dominico Drury, Collector of the Coimbatore district 1833–41. *Bustee*, a hamlet, small village, in this case a mund. OIOC, BC 63.953, State of the Todawars on the Neilgherry Hills, Extract of Revenue Consultation, 6 October 1835.
54. OIOC, MBRP, 3 August 1840, From H.V. Conolly, Acting Principal Collector, 13 July 1840, App. To the Honourable Company, Kararnamah.
55. Ibid.
56. OIOC, BRP, To the President and Members of the Board of Revenue, from Fr. Clementson, Pl. Coll., App. A, para 2, 16 June 1834. BRC, From the Chief Secretary, 1 May 1837: 4819–20, From the Principal Collector of Malabar, 11 January 1838: 715, 718, From the Chief Secretary, 12 January 1838: 1937, Proceedings, 29 March 1838: 3966. OIOC, MBRP, 30 July, App. A, To the Honourable Principal Collector of Malabar, from J. Sullivan, 15 January 1840: 9235–6. Ibid., 25 February 1841, About Mr Sullivan's tenure on the Nilgiris, App. A, To the Collector of Land Customs, Fort St George, from Geo. Norton, Advocate General, 3 February 1841, para 5: 2808–19, emphasis in the original.
57. Kattery waterfalls are located eight miles south of Ootacamund and four miles south-west of Coonoor. Ibid., 13 May 1841, To the Secretary to the Board of Revenue, from H.V. Conolly, Collector, 24 April 1841, no. 2, Translation of the Kyfiet…, signed H.V. Conolly, 1 April 1841: 6926–8.

58. Ibid., 13 May 1841, To the Secretary to the Board of Revenue, from H.V. Conolly, Collector, 24 April 1841, para 1: 6922–4, Ibid., 9 December 1841, About Grove's land, para 3: 18629–31. Ibid., 30 June 1842, on Mr Grove's application for land, signed H.V. Conolly, 10 June 1842: 7743.
59. Ibid., 30 June 1842, on Mr Grove's application for land, signed H.V. Conolly, 10 June 1842: 7743. Ibid., 13 January 1842, from the Collector of Malabar to the Secr. To the Board of Revenue, para 2: 696–7.
60. Ibid., 10 November 1842: 14618, To the Board of Revenue, from the Collector of Malabar, no. 1, and Proceedings thereon, para 1.
61. Ibid., 2 December 1842: 16832, To the Board of Revenue, from the Collector of Malabar, and Letter to be sent in reply to the Collector of Malabar, 15 December 1842: 16835–6, para 2. Ibid., 13 February 1843, To J.D. Bourdillon, from H.V. Conolly, 2 February 1843: 2456–7.
62. TNA, BRC, vol. 550, no. 6: 5208–14, signed John Bird, 10 April 1841.
63. Ibid.
64. OIOC, MBRP, 17 October 1842, Extract from the Minutes of Consultation, 17 September 1842, paras 2, 3, 5, 6. Ibid., 9 January 1843, on Toda compensation, para 1: 721–4.
65. OIOC, MD, 21 June 1843, no. 13: 51–92, Rights of the Todawars, and Rules for grants of land on the Neilgherries, para 3.
66. Ibid., para 7.
67. Ibid., para 8.
68. Ibid., marginal note at para 9. Emphasis in the original.
69. Saravanan, 2003, 'Colonial Commercial Forest Policy and Tribal Private Forests in Madras Presidency, 1792–1881', 415–18; Ibid., 2006, 'Economic Exploitation of Forest Resources in South India During the Early 19 th Century', 7.
70. Menon, 2004, 'Colonial Constructions of "Agrarian Fields" and "Forests" in the Kolli Hills', 323–4.
71. Saravanan, 2004, 'Colonialism and Coffee Plantations. Decline of Environment and Tribals in Madras Presidency During the Nineteenth Century', 475–6.
72. Pouchepadass, 1995, 'British Attitudes Towards Shifting Cultivation in Colonial South India. A Case Study of South Canara District 1800–1920', 132–3, 137–42.
73. OIOC, MD, 21 June 1843, no. 13: 51–92, Rights of the Todawars, and Rules for grants of land on the Neilgherries, paras 10, 11,16.
74. Price, 2000 (1908), *Ootacamund, a History*, 18.

6 *Towards an Environmental History of Law*

We were on our way back from a seasonal mund near Upper Bhavani. The three women were singing in the back of the jeep. We had left Ootacamund in the morning in the company of a couple from one of the Ootacamund settlements. On the way, a family from Tapkodumund, further to the south, had joined us. As on many earlier occasions, the further away we got from towns and tourists, the better off the settlements. Fields were cultivated, tea bushes grew on hillsides, and portions of the land were leased to tenants. In Tapkodumund, side by side with the Toda temple, we found another, recently inaugurated temple dedicated to Ayyappan. Both were carefully tended.

The day had been filled with laughter, memories, and stories. Now, the singing brought together the day's experiences and we could hear how we too, the two visitors, were woven into its texture. As we passed through the mountainous region which for some of the Toda clans formed the boundary to the afterworld, a large number of barking deer on the hillside made us stop the jeep. As we got out, one of the men took

Ill. 7 The sacred peak Godmenthitt, also visible in Illustration 5
(Photo by the author.)

the opportunity to explain the importance of the place. From personal experience he knew of the power that rested in these hills, power which on one particular day had given him supernatural strength. This was a place where the old gods crossed the valley and assembled to dispute with one another behind the nearest hill. No wonder, he said, he became so strong when he walked through the valley.

He pointed in the distance to a particular hilltop, naming it Godmenthitt, and explained that this was the most important point. Beyond it no man should pass if he wanted to remain in this world. In the evening sun, shining from behind the mountain, its dark silhouette rose sharp against the sky. However, at its very peak was a small protuberance, like a large rock. We could clearly see that it was not an extension of the mountain but a man-made addition, and we looked enquiringly at our host. His good mood immediately evaporated. It turned out that this was a small shrine, erected by Badaga; a shrine to a Hindu god. 'It does not belong there', he said. 'It was built against our will.' For our Toda companions, the hilltop beyond which only the non-living passed had been invaded.

A little later, though, we stopped by another small shrine, dedicated to Bhavani Amman. Built next to a stream, at the top of a cleft and overlooking the hills, it was guarded by Nandi, the bull and vehicle of Shiva. The men and women stopped to worship at the shrine. 'Can you see the connection?' our host now asked, drawing a line with his finger between the shrine and the same sacred peak, this time seen from the northwest. To him there was no contradiction between the sacred world of the Toda and Bhavani Amman. Clearly, the peak with its Badaga shrine had been the subject not of an invasion on religious grounds, but of one representing the social power of the Badaga community.[1]

Four Key Arguments

In a broader perspective, the present book is about the role of law in the process of consolidating colonial sovereign rule in South India. As such, it is part of a larger effort to understand the social transformations of territorial conquest during the years of radical change in India resulting from warfare—from the Anglo-Mysore wars of the 1780s to 1818 and the defeat of the Marathas, and beyond, through an interregnum of peace, to the intense conflicts between British troops and Sikhs and Afghans in the mid nineteenth century. In the ongoing debates within the EIC on whether to continue to expand or to consolidate control of already conquered territories, the Nilgiris stand out as an example of the closing of inner frontiers by the exercise of British 'benevolent justice'. This was the EIC acting as the state institution it sought to establish.

More specifically, this book focuses on human—nature relations from the perspective of the appropriation and control of nature for both its material and non-material value. For a long time, various regions of the Western Ghats had been considered for their resources of high-quality timber. As late as the 1820s, however, there remained a patchwork of approaches to gaining access to these resources, while the Company endeavoured to secure control of the land itself. Once the Madras administration turned its attention more seriously to the Western Ghats in the late 1820s, the move to bring the Nilgiri Hills, too, within the reach of the general principles of administration applied elsewhere was backed by strong forces. As has been shown, these forces were not unitary in character but were divided by their different and often contradictory interests. One of the major challenges for the EIC was to curb private initiatives among Europeans—both EIC officers and private entrepreneurs—who were seeking to make a profit for themselves. Resistance from the native population was to be expected, but in the Nilgiris native interests and responses became entangled with colliding European interests.

In the disputes that followed, conflicts at the level of legal principles were particularly important for the regulations and acts subsequently passed. The legal principles that were adhered to in rhetorical statements could not be bypassed or ignored, and their relevance to the Indian situation was constantly debated. In complex ways, land settlement turned into a process of negotiations at various levels. We have repeatedly observed how forcefully pursued political visions and deeply rooted perceptions of land and people influenced arguments in support of different legal positions on the question of rights in nature. Natural science in general, and the new empirical scientific methods of ethnology in particular, promoted an approach that tied people native to the Nilgiris to its landscape and history, thus ordering them into categories that structured ideas about transforming the region. Throughout the conflicts that erupted in the 1830s, the enforcement of interests was achieved in a legal sphere in which the rules were continuously changing as a result of competing interests utilizing varying resources of power.

We will now, finally, address four key arguments that derive from the study as a whole. This work is located within what can tentatively be termed an environmental history of law. It brings together the aspects necessary for an analysis of the relationship between human action and nature in the process of codifying rights in nature. It examines the many transformative visions for a particular landscape, the battle between interests pursuing different legal principles which underpinned the formation of codes, the influence of scholarly thought on legal debates, and finally, in a close empirical study, the trajectory of land conflicts during their most intense period up to the adoption of the first more comprehensive code of rights in nature for the Nilgiris in 1843.

First, located as it is in the late eighteenth and early nineteenth centuries, the study focuses on an era of liberal thought in which calls for freedom of property legitimized claims on 'empty lands'. It was at the same time an era when trading companies were consolidating colonial rule over conquered territories in the face of fierce competition between different commercial interests. In South India, land conflicts also manifested themselves in disputes that were played out within a politicized bureaucracy. The EIC's Madras government, the Court of Directors, and the British Parliament through the intermediary of the Board of Control were major actors. Claims to individual property thus collided with an enforced establishment of sovereign rule by which private interests could be controlled.

Secondly, the study revolves around the role of law and, in particular, the contested domains in which legal codes were established. The commanding capacity of law is broadly taken for granted in many studies, but, in addition to seeing law as a tool of power, it is necessary to acknowledge the ongoing process of making law. This means seeing law as a process by which competing interests of varying strength sought to set the agenda, in this case for the settlement of rights in land.

Thirdly, important contributions to the study of popular response or resistance to colonial encroachment have emerged from intense debates of the past three decades. Although conflict between state (or global capital) and people affected by state policies remains the dominant focus, research has now largely moved away from notions of the two as separate domains—as in early Saidian-inspired works—to their joint impact on conflict. The present study points to the need to recognize major existing contradictions, and yet to break up dichotomously structured oppositions in analyses of particular conflicts. Specifically, it brings out the role of multiple layers of authority and internal divisions during conflicts over land.

Finally, the process of land settlement in the Western Ghats of South India prompts us to reconsider our definitions of regions in relation to local and general histories. Hill tracts tend to be viewed as boundary regions, frontiers, or territories that divide large political entities, marginal or anomalous from the point of view of grand histories. Such perceptions of regions tend to map not only geographies but also preconceptions which structure histories of hill and forest tracts. This book suggests the strong interconnectedness of hills and plains and the fluidity of geographically demarcated regions. It calls into question the conventional division of regions assumed in regional histories of South India.

Private Interests in Conflict with Sovereign Claims

The issues under study were not unique to South India. In the more intense migrations from Europe to other continents, a strong driving force was the sense of and search for freedoms available outside European nation states. The EIC was not alone in trying to gain control of land transfers and land settlements, and in the mid 1840s investigations resulting in resolutions and treaties, similar to those undertaken in the Nilgiris, were conducted by colonial officers in other parts of the world as well. The Treaty of Waitingi in 1840 is an example of wider importance by which, simultaneously, New Zealand was constituted as a British colony in its own right and native Maori rights were acknowledged. Or, as the British officer argued at the time, the Maori had to cede their sovereignty in order to save their patrimony. In effect, the New Zealand Company wanted to curb the private purchase of Maori land by Europeans. In exchange for giving up sovereignty to the British crown, the Maori chiefs who signed the treaty were guaranteed 'Lands and Estates, Forests, Fisheries and other properties which they may collectively or individually possess so long as it is their wish and desire to retain the same', and so long as the crown had the right of pre-emption over land transfers.[2]

In recent decades the Treaty of Waitingi has reappeared on public agendas, and laws like the New Zealand Fisheries Act have been amended to secure Maori rights that were granted in the treaty but have since been violated on many occasions. At the same time, it has been brought to the fore in the assertion of Maori self-determination, and the words used in the Maori translation in 1840 are being re-examined in order to prove the legal sovereign status of the Maori through this document. Once again, colonial documents are being invoked to prove indigenous people's rights. More important for the present study is that Waitingi, too, demonstrates the colonial authorities' concern to stay on top of events when private initiatives to purchase land from the native population were threatening to take their own chaotic course. This was also a concern for an 'ordered' settlement in the new territories, secured by law. It was assumed that, unrestrained, the New Zealand Company would eventually dispossess the Maori of their heritage, and the Colonial Office decided that Maori land should only be transferred via the crown.[3]

A similar logic in the relationship between the settlement of Europeans on other continents and the application of law appeared in late-eighteenth-century North America, in part of the European settlement on the lands of native communities. While squatters who had independently grabbed land were removed, on some occasions by the federal Congress and on others by the United States army, after Congress had purchased the land rights from the Indian communities the squatters were allowed to return. Thus, private initiatives came under the control of a ruling authority. In the end, though, preventing settlers from encroaching on reserves was as difficult as trying to stem a flood. Moreover, as on other continents, the emerging state authorities were in fact interested in an increased settlement of cultivators and entrepreneurs, as long as it took place under the auspices of government.[4]

When migrants from the British Isles settled on other continents within the realms of British rule, they generally searched for ways of establishing strong, autonomous rights in land. As discussed in Chapter 3, common law was seen as granting such rights. Although it was rarely cited as such, the logic of common law can be clearly perceived in the arguments of many early-nineteenth-century disputes. Embracing the legal integrity of local custom as well as protecting the right to land, common law was invoked by Europeans to legitimize the purchase of absolute rights in a particular piece of land from an 'aboriginal' population. As aboriginals, holding their rights 'from time immemorial', people were ascribed absolute proprietary rights in land and hence also the power to dispose of the land, including the rights invested in it. In contrast to such an application of common law, in the Indian situation the integrity of native custom became a hurdle that had to be overcome in order to set the rules for EIC sovereign rights in land. Since the Madras government was informed that, according to native custom, ultimate authority over land was vested in cattle herders, the government had to come to an agreement about the rights of this particular group of people. Supporters of the government's standpoint argued that these were people of a kind who were not in a position to appeal to the logic of common law. Exactly what kind of people they were was determined through ethnographic surveys and defined according to more general interpretations in the scholarly debates of the time.

Having to deal with native claims to rights intended for British subjects was commonly perceived as a problem in the settlement of Europeans on other continents, irrespective of whether those claims were made by the people concerned or by settlers who wanted to strike a land deal with them and therefore claimed that they were as much subject to British rule as any European in the Indian territories claimed by the EIC. In the process, common law's concern to protect the liberties of subjects against arbitrary or absolute rule could be projected onto the EIC, which was then seen as invading those liberties. As has been argued in other studies, common law, being constantly negotiated and adapted to particular local circumstances, had a capacity to adjust to new requirements created by changing socio-economic or political conditions. Its principles therefore became a constant field of dispute in colonial land settlement.[5]

The ryotwari revenue system, which both removed middlemen and granted individual or joint titled rights to land, was progressively elaborated to secure EIC sovereignty while denying freehold rights to individuals. As David Washbrook observes, the system was premised on the notion that all land belonged to the sovereign. According to

Washbrook, this appealed to the EIC as it promised far higher levels of revenue extraction than any system that observed the landed rights of communities or individuals, such as the lordly *kaniachi* and *inam* rights. Robert Frykenberg argued in his study of inam land rights (1977) for the existence of a combined land settlement policy, in which EIC sovereignty was accomplished through a combination of ryotwari and private agreements with inamdars. His contribution was one of a number of studies that aimed to show that ryotwari was not the only or even, as Frykenberg hinted, the dominant form of landholding in early colonial South India. In Burton Stein's words in the same debate, the policy of favouring landlord interests by granting privileges such as inam rights 'has been less clearly seen by scholars owing to the rhetoric of the ryotwari revenue system'. According to Frykenberg, Munro's settlement of inam land was the 'dark side of the Ryotwari Settlement'. The inam settlements were most likely 'political pacts' that guaranteed landlord support for the EIC in return for the preservation of hereditary rights in perpetuity, and their existence under British rule proved the reality of private property in India.[6]

In contrast, Washbrook emphasizes a shift away from inam grants and towards ryotwari settlements from as early as the 1810s; in 1824 the Board of Control ordered the Madras government to stop granting inams and to investigate the legal validity of existing inam claims for the purpose of invalidating them. For the EIC, ryotwari both met the need for revenue and provided the ultimate control of land that had earlier remained in the hands of heavily criticized 'Oriental despots' such as the Mysore rulers. In line with David Ludden's argument, however, we need to acknowledge the opportunities that the ryotwari system gave native government officers to enter a rural elite. Quoting a collector in the Tinnevelly district, who saw the purchase of land as 'the first object of every public officer', Ludden concludes that it was in the interests of individual native officers to stabilize the powers of the new regime. In effect, for such interests the difference between holding land as absolute property and obtaining a title by paying an annual cash rent was almost negligible. But it was a difference of crucial importance to people native to the hill tracts such as the Toda, and to European private entrepreneurs.[7]

However, this constantly revised system was never intended for the particular conditions of forest or hill tracts. It rested on the presumption of an existing agricultural economy. The Nilgiris in fact constituted a poor source of revenue income. As can be seen from the way land grants and pattas were introduced into the Nilgiris, they were primarily established in order to bring the hill economy into line with the agrarian economies of the plains, and to ensure that all land first came under government control before being granted or auctioned out as titles to landholders, European and native alike.

In much the same way as common law principles were referred to in arguments for land rights, the aim of making policies to promote the 'public good' was also rhetorically argued by parties who disagreed on its meaning. From different positions, officers within the EIC sought to define who constituted the public and what was good for it. Perhaps the implications of these disputes emerge most clearly in the legal procedures when the government, either of its own volition or prompted by the reprimands of the Court of Directors, restrained its actions with a view to being just and benevolent. When land was taken by government for public purposes, for example, the native landholders were to be liberally compensated for their loss. But the quality of that loss, which ultimately was assumed to rest on the purpose for which the landholder had taken control of the land, was decided by the government, i.e. the sovereign.

The exercise of law or of the legal authority vested in EIC officers was another area under the keen scrutiny of the highest body of the Company. The misuse of power was ultimately a misuse of popular trust, which would undermine stable governance. As was the case when the idea of depositing compensation payments (until landholders agreed to cede their lands) was confronted as an arbitrary exercise of power, legal procedures reflected the working of equity principles in the exercise of law. The consequences of legal decisions were not to be unreasonable for the individual, and the purpose of well-functioning and just legal institutions was also to instil trust into the new subjects of British rule. Law was thus made the guarantee of a civil conquest and settlement. The process of compensating Badaga cultivators for the lands they had lost access to because of the government farm in Ketti, discussed in Chapter 3, is a case in point. When the Badaga claimants chose to refuse the government's offer of alternative land, and instead claimed the land on which the farmhouses and attached gardens were situated, the government appointed arbitrators, one to be chosen by the government, one by the Badaga, and one by the other two arbitrators. But the settlement of the farmhouse land was not an open question, since the government never intended to give it up. The Board of Revenue was given a free hand to sort out the situation and in order to prevent delay.[8]

The application of legal process as a means of achieving an end was never as simple as the government expected, however. In Ketti, the disputed lands were to be settled by legal procedure, but the Badaga claimants refused to be bound by their arbitrator's opinion, distrusting his knowledge and objectivity in relation to their interests.[9] In this situation the government's arbitrator—an Ootacamund landholder assigned the task by the government—thought that appointing a third arbitrator 'would only embarrass our proceedings' and, for want of further instructions from the revenue board, he resigned. In the process, the most important documents of the Ketti village accounts had accidentally been burnt, and the arbitrator complained that 'owing to the monsoon rains ... I have been unable to procure the attendance of these people or the revenue servants, except for a few hours in the afternoon occasionally'. After these initial complications, the arbitration process was dropped and the Ketti case turned into a simple calculation of the amount of compensation to be paid to the claimants.[10]

There was no obvious way to settle land in the Nilgiris, no unquestioned pattern to follow, which is partly why the process took such a long time. Since rights had to be based on existing land relations and, as a matter of principle, justified property had to be acknowledged, proponents of different interests went in search of other agreements between the EIC and South Indian landholders that could serve as precedents in support of a particular position in the dispute. This comes out most clearly in the disagreement about whether Toda authority over land was equivalent to the jenmi rights existing in Wynad and Malabar, or simply a question of tenure. Comparing Toda rights with jenmi was intended to secure the Toda absolute and inalienable rights in land. However, granting such rights was unthinkable for the Madras government, not only in the Nilgiris but also in relation to the landlords of Wynad. According to the core principles of ryotwari, the powerful landlord-middleman was perceived as a threat to sovereign rule, and new land settlements had to avoid acknowledging such autonomous legal actors. By refusing to grant the Wynad rajas the status of independent lordship, the EIC disregarded the fact that Wynad was claimed as part of the Malabar royal houses and the government further limited the influence of Malabari land relations.

In light of these land disputes, the Nilgiris serve to demonstrate how colonial rule in the early nineteenth century was not primarily or intentionally concerned with introducing autonomous, private property in land in South India. On the contrary, claims to freehold and property became an enormous problem and had to be contested and disallowed. European immigrants and employees of the EIC pursuing private interests were seen as a threat to colonial sovereign rule. They had been quick to establish themselves as holders of absolute and eternal rights to land, having purchased those rights from natives who were claimed to have an aboriginal birthright. As the Madras government caught up with events, it argued vigorously to prove that such rights were exceptional in South India and that the Nilgiri Hills were not part of that exception. However, as a consequence of the claims for freehold rights that were made in land disputes, and of the assumptions about existing native property on which such claims could be based, the notion of individual property became central to the debates.

On empirical grounds, therefore, the findings here contrast with those of other work emphasizing the forcible implementation of private property as a core characteristic of the expansion of capitalism in India—such as Rohan D'Souza's study of the effects of colonial revenue administration in early nineteenth-century deltaic Orissa. Disagreeing with Amiya Bagchi, who emphasizes that for the sake of maximizing revenue the EIC turned land in Bengal into an alienable commodity and not into absolute property, D'Souza claims administrative efficiency and the *longue duree* of pre-capitalist social relations as insufficient to explain colonial revenue strategies. He argues that such strategies depended on the realization of land as capitalist private property, i.e. the recasting of land as a pure economic form: alienable, individuated, monopolized and exclusively held, and as a commodity regulated by market imperative. According to D'Souza, such decisive strategies brought about the simultaneous transformation of socio-economic relations and ecological systems. In effect, an inflexible revenue system turned a flood-dependent agrarian regime into a flood-vulnerable landscape.[11]

D'Souza thus equates capitalism with the introduction of British rule, 'colonial capitalism' as he terms it, for which, in his view, a *longue duree* does not carry much explanatory power. According to D'Souza, colonial capitalism represented a significant departure from indigenous pre-capitalist social relations. In the context of the present study, however, it is more useful to avoid viewing existing social relations merely as disappearing, archaic social forms, to be replaced by capitalist relations introduced by colonial power. Nor was the implementation of private property coerced. While important differences certainly existed between the Bengal and Madras administrations, the Madras government was as hesitant in portioning out absolute rights in land as was the Bengal government in Bagchi's description. We may think rather in terms of Ludden's argument, which suggests a recasting of premodern territory and space, while searching for their modern legacies. Ludden claims that, until well into the 1850s, existing sociopolitical and economic systems ('ethnic territories' in his terminology) were appropriated and encompassed by the British administration. Old polities and forms of leadership were still visible in the new forms of zamindars, native state rulers, and ryotwari landowners. Their vitality disappeared only gradually, as modern political and legal institutions made them increasingly irrelevant, industrial capitalism drained their resources, and modern property law became established in practice and not only in theory. Accordingly, the history of capitalism in South Asia need not be entirely equated with that of European rule through colonial territorial expansion. These various studies taken together suggest, rather, that its establishment may have come about unevenly, incompletely, and contextually.[12]

This study also points to the need to view land settlement in regional contexts during the early nineteenth century from the combined perspective of the EIC's economic and political ambitions. In the South Indian situation it seems unwise to emphasize the introduction of private property at the expense of an analysis of the determined policy of the Madras government to secure and consolidate sovereign rule and, as a consequence, to make all rights ultimately dependent on the sovereign. This meant that although land was bought and sold as a commodity, it was not to be exclusively or autonomously held by the holder; in other words, the property in it was not entirely private. Through regulations that applied to the Nilgiris and Wynad, the land market was thereby to remain under the control of the EIC and not become 'free' in the liberal market-economic sense of the term. In the settlement of these lands, in the aftermath of the conquest of Mysore, only the jenmi rights of Malabar were perceived to equate to absolute rights in land as property—a questionable notion, as discussed in Chapter 2—and the government made determined attempts to limit the prevalence of jenmi land. In all other cases, in order to avoid granting anything similar to freehold to individuals, existing rights—as understood by revenue officers—were investigated, and ultimately denied the status of autonomous property.

The Contested Process of Making Law

It has been fairly common for studies of forest and environmental history in colonial India to adopt an instrumentalist view of the working of law. Rather than being seen as a space for contestation, conflict, and negotiation, law has been described as a simple tool in the hands of the colonial government for the purpose of territorial expansion and the reordering of nature. This may partly be explained by the fact that most studies focus on historical trajectories during crown rule. Consequently, the emphasis tends to be on large-scale interventions by an increasingly strong colonial state—perhaps even instrumentalist in its factions, according to James Scott's model of the high-modern authoritarian state—such as timber extraction for railway construction and regions managed under principles of scientific forestry. It may also be assumed that the late-nineteenth-century state was less likely to consider local claims and customs when rights in land were decided, compared with colonial rule under the EIC in the 1820s.[13]

However, such positions may also result from the lack of studies pursuing the question. Neeladri Bhattacharya's study of Punjab points significantly to the ambiguous nature of attempts to establish colonial administration and law while acknowledging native tradition, even in the late nineteenth century. Similarly, in the case of late-nineteenth-century Himachal, Chetan Singh emphasizes local ecological and historical differences, resulting in locally different patterns of accommodating colonial regulations. In common with a growing number of studies that are forced to qualify earlier general statements about precolonial village communities' control and use of nature as 'common property resources', and about colonial destruction of self-sustaining Indian village communities, Singh goes to some lengths to empirically demonstrate the long-term, though weakening, legacies of precolonial states in terms of the nature of revenue systems, resource use, and rights. The process of incorporating these hill states was far from linear, and the colonial rulers preferred to adopt a line of least resistance, as long as it still resulted in profit. 'While one can hardly overlook the impact of British forest conservation policies in the region, the larger yet highly penetrative influence of a colonial economy in certain areas had a logic of its own.'[14]

Nevertheless, an influential mode of studying the legal process of restructuring nature is—rather than asking how law was negotiated—to project law as an immediate consequence of policy decisions. Discussions about the effects of legal regulations tend to proceed from the all-India acts related to the powers of the Forest Department, such as the Forest Acts of 1865 and 1878. Being the result of years of legal elaboration at lower levels of administration, these acts represented the codified end result and not the conflictual judicial process leading up to their adoption. Mahesh Rangarajan argues that the 1865 Act 'was the first step towards a rule of property for the forests of British India',[15] and in his study of Uttarakhand Ramachandra Guha states: 'Predicated on the ideological setting in which they operate, the techniques of scientific forestry are, as it were, designed to reorder both nature and customary use in its own image.... In the event, both legislation and silvicultural technique were designed to facilitate social control.'[16]

The tools of law may have been ineffective or, as Guha describes, unable to eliminate customary uses of forest resources by simply redefining them as 'illegal'. And social protest may have slowed down colonial expansion or encroachment on forest land. But a significant aspect of many studies is that law per se—or the process of legally codifying various rights—is left unproblematized and is therefore a condition that is taken for granted, i.e. one which the study of confrontation takes as its point of departure. The legal codes and law itself thus tend to be viewed as unquestioned statutes and as far more essentialized than the manner of their establishment justifies. In many analyses, there is not much room for the legal wrestling by different interests over what customary rights to allow and why. In most studies, other equally important questions are given priority, as in Guha's study, where the existence of certain limited rights under colonial authority—'specified in elaborate detail', according to Guha—is first verified, but then put to one side as the study moves on to focus on protests arising from the enormous loss of access to forest brought about by the stringent provisions of the Forest Acts.[17]

By avoiding the assumption that a European presence in the Nilgiris resulted in a dichotomous confrontation—a clash between colonial administration and people native to the hills—it is possible to make visible the broad variety of interests laying claim to land, resources, and authority, and cross-cutting alliances linking current disputes to regional histories. Acknowledging these many contradictory interests does not devalue the force of colonial power, but recognizes its complexity, and emphasizes the multifaceted and integrated ways in which it was established.

The interaction of law-making and strong interests is important to observe. As the present study makes evident, the existence of a legal space was taken for granted from the very first European intervention in the hills. That space does not appear to have been a fixed one, but one that could be battled over and negotiated. The district collector was for example quick to secure a land grant in the early 1820s, but soon after that the grant turned into a stumbling block for the granting authority, the Madras government. A few more such grants were made at the district level before the government decided to bar similar purchases, and yet without questioning the collector's rights on the basis of his earlier grant. The means by which it achieved this end was to use the monetary payment made for the first grant as a model for the level of compensation for appropriated native land. Clearly, private interests collided with those of the EIC as a ruling authority, and officers of the Company who pursued private interests were navigating a legal space that allowed conflicting principles to coexist. When the government assumed a more active role in the region in the late 1830s, private interests had become the weaker party and individuals began to lose substantial investments.[18]

As we observe the process by which legal rights in land were settled, there is reason to ask what kind of court and what kind of justice the collectors and sub-collectors tried to put in place. As a rule, the legal process set in motion by the EIC—marked by investigations, surveys, the taking of depositions, consideration of petitions, arbitration, and so on—was one of negotiation. The process was to some extent a reflection of the small courts of England, which dealt with cases outside the superior courts on the basis of principles of equity. Importantly, as they reached their decisions, the EIC officers also laid the foundations for future laws and regulations, since the decisions taken could subsequently be claimed to be precedents. For many of these decisions, the administrators also sought in a targeted way to establish native custom and thus to legitimize legal regulations by claiming that native custom force as precedent. As has been shown earlier, the meaning and legal implications of native custom were disputed, but not disregarded. At times, equity principles may have worked in favour of native rights and against raw exploitation. Yet, as the Madras government more forcefully advanced its positions in the Nilgiris, it also set the agenda for the direction in which the judicial process was to move.

In this way, the legal space that was available for conflicting interpretations of rights in nature narrowed. The 1843 regulations, granting only grazing rights to the Toda in the Nilgiris on account of their 'immemorial occupancy', were the ultimate result of the government's ability to rule out all claims to property or other landed rights for the pastoral population.[19] But despite such decisive policies, laws were not taken straight from the policy-makers' or lawyers' drawing board for immediate implementation, nor were they decided in formal court. In the space provided by the process of establishing control through the legal codification of rights, conflicting interests were articulated and, ultimately and to different degrees, influenced the way in which sovereign colonial rule was established in the region.

Similar processes also characterized European settlement on other continents where governments and trading companies acted within the jurisdiction of British (particularly English) legal traditions. Peter Karsten describes land conflicts in North America, Australia, and New Zealand from the seventeenth through to the nineteenth century, in which principles of aboriginal rights were set against government sovereignty. When Mohegan Indians complained in the early eighteenth century about mismanagement of the trust fund set up for them in return for allowing a colony to reside on their lands, for example, the commission of New York jurists claimed that the Mohegans were a separate and distinct people with a polity of their own and property of the soil. Only one dissenting judge believed such a position to have dangerous consequences. By the nineteenth century, however, the dominant legal discourse had changed. According to a ruling by the chief justice of the Supreme Court, the British crown and its heir, the United States, held sovereign title to all land and native people were 'tenants at will' on account of their unsettled livelihood.[20]

As can be seen in all these cases, law was a central means of establishing sovereign rule, and in India the EIC bureaucracy formed statelike institutions which served to mediate control. In a broad sense, to paraphrase Radhika Singha, law-making was a cultural enterprise in which the colonial state struggled to draw upon existing normative codes and, in the process, formed a more exclusive definition of sovereign right. Placing her study of the working of criminal law in early colonial India in a post-Saidian perspective, Singha positions herself in contrast to, on the one hand, Bernard Cohn, and on the other Lata Mani and Gyan Prakash. Her work thus shows how the study of law has mirrored the changes in general historical debates. There was an important move from Cohn's understanding of law in terms of confrontations, as a clash of values between indigenous and colonial legal systems, to the Saidian-inspired studies of Lata Mani and Gyan Prakash. The latter emphasize the role of constructed colonial knowledge of indigenous legal traditions, which served to manifest relations of domination and subordination: Mani in the case of European colonial views on widow burning, and Prakash on the changing discourse of bonded labour. For Singha, it is important also to understand how the colonial legislative initiative sprang from 'a constant reworking of the ambitions and perspectives of political authority and the forms in which this was to be communicated'. In her view, the outcome of colonial attempts to construct legal subjects was less easy to control than is often assumed in studies emphasizing the overarching power of the colonial state. When the state negotiated with indigenous normative codes in communication with elites among the colonial subjects, the meanings of particular symbols of authority could not easily be restricted to the objectives of the state. Similarly, the British, too, had to accommodate themselves to the law.[21]

In this context, however, it is important to remind ourselves of the different bodies of law forming the basis for judicial processes, which complicate comparisons between legal studies. Singha and, more broadly, Mani and Prakash deal with criminal law, while the present study is concerned with property law. The former regulates human behaviour in relation to social norms and is based on the idea that social order, which is in the public interest, is established by means of penalties and sanctions for specific crimes. As a consequence, debates about the proper social norms on which to found criminal law were crucial. In principle, the penal codes of the nineteenth century were intended to have general application. In contrast (as discussed in detail in Chapter 3), laws regulating rights in land and natural resources were based on common law, which was fundamentally an extensive, non-statutory body of law based on consensus and custom. Regionally specific phenomena, such as natural preconditions for livelihoods, therefore formed part of the framework for legal codes. Such profound differences limit the sphere of comparison to that of general principles of law under the EIC regime in India at a specific point in time.

From such broad perspectives, the making of law needs to be seen in the light of the EIC's transformation from its mercantilist past into a state-like bureaucracy from the late eighteenth to the mid nineteenth century. In the process, law was one of the more prominent means by which the colonial government protected its own interests against particularist private interests acting within the framework of the Company. Projected as a neutral space, blind to such interests, it was seen as an agency of reform. Yet, as Singha and others have observed, changes in the legal codes paralleled the steps taken to remove the remaining marks of Mughal sovereignty and establish the EIC as the paramount power. These legal systems maintained their own 'particularisms', with regard to issues of race, status, gender, etc., parallel to the universal principles of jurisprudence. However, the criminal law was generally seen as less problematic, since it did not raise questions of property.[22]

Returning to the Nilgiris, we see that law was a strong tool for projecting a vision onto nature in the region. But many different visions existed. We may contrast the grand visions of a small-scale capitalist model society, mirroring liberal visions of rural England as well as the anti-liberal vision of an all-encompassing state, denying its subjects the freedom of individual property, with the petty, individualist interests of an estate in the hills, a profitable hotel for travellers, or a production unit for the local market taking advantage of high prices. Both landscape and people, whether natives or immigrants to the Nilgiris, were fitted into these visions in different ways. All the visions had the aim of exploiting the hills, yet all of them claimed to do it for the betterment of the place and the people living there. Whether they idealized people or nature for their superior capacities, or rejected the quality of their present existence, these visions had transformation as their goal.

Reports in scholarly and public journals on the need to preserve the life and history of the 'unique Toda herders', for example, had a significant impact in terms of moderating decisions on land rights by the Madras government and the Board of Revenue. When the Court of Directors repeatedly sent orders to Madras to respect Toda rights for the sake of building trust among the people, those orders were repeated as a creed in directives emanating from Madras. With reference to the Toda as an exceptional people, the government also restrained its methods of acquiring land from them, mostly by insisting on detailed surveys prior to decisions. Over time, however, the content of decisions changed, while the 'creed' remained the same, echoing an increasingly hollow rhetoric. The government, which never made a secret of its intention to bring the hills, too, under sovereign rule, began to search more openly for the most efficient way of administering the transfer of complete control of the land. In the process, the quality of Toda uniqueness was devalued from aboriginal to barbarian. Eventually, the creed of protecting their rights withered and made way for a conviction that the barbarian Toda had been treated far too indulgently.[23]

Spaces of Negotiation through Multiple Layers of Authority

Something of a keynote throughout the disputes, which in the colonial files was dealt with in terms of land rights, is the constant oscillation between immediate life-world and larger administrative entities of power, defining a space within which people native to the Nilgiris and in particular the

Toda tried to manoeuvre to maintain authority over the place. As discussed in detail in Chapter 5, the head munds of two clans in the central Nilgiris took decisive action to protect their control over land in general and places of worship in particular. They accepted outsiders' occupancy of their lands, but not their claims to ownership. Just as Badaga cultivators used portions of land for cultivation, and even regarded certain lands as theirs in the sense that they knew they could return to them after years of fallow, so too Europeans were allowed to use plots of land for gardens and houses. But the Toda were extremely reluctant to yield control over the land, and when it came to sacred lands they refused.

No objection by the Toda to the incoming Europeans and Indians was recorded before the British administration requested the signing of documents to transfer land rights. Significantly, at the very first attempt to make them sign a deed of sale, they refused. Clearly, documented agreements were part of their relationship to hierarchical authority, and the British administration was by no means the first to appear in the living memory of people in the Nilgiris. As they responded to British requests to take over land control, they did so in communication with the administration, perceived as representing hierarchical power. First, they argued and pleaded with the low-level administrators, the peishkar and his subordinates, who visited the mund. Then, on regretting the sale they had been forced to make, they appealed to higher administrative instances, apparently assisted by other low-level administrators, accusing the peishkar of corruption. Furthermore, they approached the Nilambur raja as a local patron, getting him to assist them to file a petition with the district office. Eventually, the peishkar was removed from office and both the Board of Revenue and the Court of Directors supported the Toda's right to claim land. The entire process speaks of people who were used to dealing with authorities equal or similar to states. Plainly put, the Toda of the head munds of the central Nilgiris were skilled in local politics.

Over long periods of time, these ranges of the Western Ghats were linked to hierarchical authority to the east, north, and west of the hills. Immigration, taxation, and changing land arrangements and social organization followed. Against this background, the different interests that made claims on the hills at the time of European encroachment became entangled with both divisions and alliances among the native population. Pastoralists, shifting cultivators, and regional centres of power responded differently to British claims. Immediate reactions, such as those from the Toda settlements of Kandelmund and Manjakalmund, sprang from a realization that their authority over land was about to be lost. When the Nilambur raja assisted them in their attempt to restore that authority, by doing so he was also confirming his own influence, perhaps even a form of royal status in the regional setting and in conflict with the EIC. Simultaneously, Badaga cultivators were able to strengthen their hold on land in the central Nilgiris at the expense of the Toda when the British administration granted them land as patta. This was land that they had been accustomed to cultivate with the permission of a Toda mund, within a social system of mutual exchange and hierarchy. As discussed earlier, changes in land use and production patterns constituted a long and ongoing process of socioeconomic change in the hills. There is convincing evidence that cultivation had increased over a long period of time, and while formal authority may have remained in the hands of Toda munds, the land was in fact tilled by Badaga ploughs. A further small but significant sign of the changing position of the Badaga community can be seen in the distrust between the Toda of Kandelmund and Manjakalmund and the monigar who carried out government orders at the village level. When conflicts intensified and the legitimacy of his office was questioned, it should be noted in particular that he was not only a government employee, but also a Badaga man. As is evident, different interests were present in the Nilgiris, and the British presence enforced existing or gave rise to new alliances and divides.

Another point that clearly emerges is that, during the early decades of the nineteenth century, people native to the hills related to multiple layers of authority. In the immediate region, socio-economic, political and ritual relations were regulated through mutual and hierarchical relationships which, in different ways, involved the main communities. The exchange of gudu worked as a glue in local society. It may not have had the overarching importance that is sometimes assumed, but since it could be interpreted as a form of tenurial payment, the British tended to emphasize its role as they sought ways of purchasing land rights.

The central part of the Nilgiris was as we saw linked to a larger region. The Toda munds located in the western Nilgiris were on the land of the Nilambur raja. This tied the Nilgiris indirectly into the realms of the Malabar royal houses. Representing an authority of regional importance, the raja's influence was not restricted to the collection of tenurial fees on jenmi land and certain land revenues in the Nilgiris. As a patron his political influence could be called upon, as when he assisted the Toda to file a petition to regain land. Further, it may be recalled that less than two generations prior to the land disputes of the 1830s, and still well within living memory, the Mysore state had collected revenue in parts of the hills. The deed linking the Nilambur raja and some Toda munds in the western Nilgiris testifies to their deep awareness of the impact of the Anglo-Mysore wars on the region (see p. 82).

There were therefore several centres of power in the Nilgiris the impact of which differed significantly. Demands limited to revenue and jenmi fees may have had a long-term influence on forms of production, but most likely their principal impact was as a means of reaffirming and legitimizing power. Over a longer period, during which immigration and general population growth occurred among cultivating communities, the area of land under cultivation appears to have increased, while the regional importance of the Toda pastoral economy was confined to the centremost region of the plateau. In the longer term, changed population and production patterns affected social organization. Neither the Mysore state nor the Malabar or Wynad lords interfered to engineer and reorganize the Nilgiri economy. As long as revenues were paid, local social organization was left undisturbed. In contrast, European and Indian immigration under the aegis of British rule resulted in permanent settlements, roads, plantations employing migrant labour, changed land relations, and legal codes worked out specifically for the Nilgiris. After the first two decades of British administration, the 1840s marked a decisive leap in the presence of external governance under colonial rule.

The role of documents and documented agreements requires further attention. Being the main substance on which historical studies rely, written documents can divert attention from the importance of oral negotiation and agreements. In the societies dealt with in this book, oral settlements came first and the written document mainly served to confirm it. This situation was in no way uniquely 'Indian' or 'tribal'; in Europe, too, legal settlements rested largely on oral contracts. In the

Nilgiri negotiations, even if oral agreements were in principle binding, the written document was intended to rule out misunderstandings between different legal systems and establish a particular bureaucratic presence. At the same time, the process of codifying oral contracts and customary law (based on both native Indian and British/English principles) in written texts implied many compromises and bargains, which ultimately left a good deal of room for interpretation and reinterpretation in the settlement of later cases and conflicts. The constant insistence on written agreements by the EIC needs to be seen in this light. This was an institutionalizing bureaucracy at work, seeking step by step to legitimize its advancement.

The situation further underlines our need also to search for and compare different types of written texts at the level closest to events. We may need to remind ourselves that, as different voices speak to different audiences in different texts, the correspondence and the marginal notes as well as the question-and-answer depositions and the petitions need to be read critically and side by side with resolutions and minutes of the various EIC boards. In contrast to the official documents, the day-to-day documentation, such as demi-official correspondence and notes made during questioning, reflect the oral disputes that preceded decisions or invalidated documents.[24] This situation may also shed light on why documents became a target during conflicts. It was not just any documents that the Toda opposed, but those containing performative statements: the deeds, settlements, and formal agreements. As we saw, at one point the Toda declared their intention never to yield land in one of many signed documents.[25]

The Toda deposition taken in 1837 when the negotiations had completely broken down, is particularly important since it was a statement of joint action by several clans representing both subgroups of the Toda community. The nature of this action, though, is not quite clear. In the last instance, the individual mund had authority over land specifically connected with it, and consequently no other munds had previously interfered when Kandelmund and Manjakalmund had been approached by the district authorities for the purchase of their land. It is therefore difficult to arrive at a likely conclusion as to why the Toda decided to act jointly at this point. It may have been due to a realization that they were all at risk of losing land, but it may just as well have been a consequence of the administration calling in more men. In the latter case, what looks like joint action may have been influenced by the administration's perception of the Toda as a single tribal group. Ethnographic reports rarely included observations of divisions or kinship groups among communities in the Nilgiris. As a rule, social organization was structured in terms of essentialized tribes. This may in turn be the reason why the administrators summoned men from various munds within the local administrative district of Malnad, irrespective of their clan affiliation. The joint action may, in this way, have been mutually constituted. What remains clear, however, is that no one accepted British authority over lands in the hills.

How, then, are we to comprehend popular responses to colonial encroachments? When conflicts over land first arose, people native to the hills and incoming Europeans and Indians had already established a relationship. Although they did not understand this relationship in the same way, they communicated. Surveyors and travellers like Sullivan, Harkness, and Hough were received in villages and munds, and outsiders and natives alike asked questions and observed one another. Houses, gardens, the church, and the cantonment were constructed and the local market developed. When conflicts gathered momentum, people were no longer new to each other. There was a sphere in which they communicated; a sphere in which perceptions of who the others were, what they represented and how their society was constituted had begun to be negotiated. This situation further emphasizes the need to break open the idea of a dichotomous confrontation between two strangers, one a conqueror and the other a resisting or oppressed victim, as if the two represented completely alien worlds.

Recent studies in environmental history elaborating the present trajectories of local livelihoods in forest tracts reflect the unease with which analyses remain within the confines of oppositional pairs. One example is provided by Antje Linkenbach, when she describes how the environmental history of Uttarakhand has been divided by a perspective either from within the state or from within local populations struggling to maintain their livelihoods against state restrictions on forest use. She calls it a twofold history of deprivation and protest, where one strand centres on state appropriation and exploitation of natural resources, curtailing customary rights, the other on a tradition of resistance to forest laws and state policies. And yet in her study she finds that hill residents refer to nature through the pragmatic experience of life. This, I conclude, is not easily summed up as resistance to the recently formed Uttaranchal state. According to Linkenbach, owing to the pressure of state agencies and industry on forest resources, the role and significance of forest for people is being redefined: 'complementary perspectives have emerged', constituting 'a diverse field of perceptions defining the various attitudes and practices of local and translocal actors.'[26]

The frontiers between colonizer and colonized at this time were not sharp. We may look in the rear-view mirror and conclude that, of course, colonial rule would eventually succeed; it was only a matter of time before the superior power of the EIC would crush all opposition. However, this was not apparent in the Nilgiris at the time. It therefore remains problematic to view people's actions in terms of anomaly, since an anomaly assumes a divergence from a general trend or trajectory. Sivaramakrishnan's term 'zone of anomaly' may therefore be of greater use in studies of state policy and state strategy, for example an analysis of the Madras government's attempts to implement sovereign rule in the Nilgiris. If, however, our focus is on the interaction that shaped the ways in which conflicts were played out, how individuals or groups with different interests read and chose to respond to the situation, and how they perceived their own resources of power, we may do better to think in terms of a relational space. In such a space, which was created through everyday experience, pastoralists, shifting cultivators, private entrepreneurs and British and Indian administrators all contributed, actively or passively, to the ways in which communication took shape. When conflicts intensified, it was within this social space that various forms of negotiation took place. Negotiation was then much more than a mere verbal battle over the right to a particular piece of land. In addition to the economic value of land—or, in a broader sense, of nature—its social, political, and ritual meaning and value were also negotiated within and across social boundaries. Thus, negotiation implied acknowledging, influencing, and making use of the other party's domain of authority for the purpose of enforcing a certain interest.

As earlier observed, the rewriting of history for the purpose of legitimizing legal codes needed to secure sovereign rule is significant not only of the longer-term process of land settlement in the Nilgiris, but of the establishment of colonial sovereign rule as such. The further away the authors of the texts were from actual events, the more ideologically coloured their generalizations tended to be. There is always a risk involved in assuming that texts produced far from the situations they claim to describe reflect, to the same extent as those written locally, the perceptions and beliefs of the colonial administrators who negotiated and enforced every step in the settlements throughout the decades of colonial expansion. However, while from the texts of resolutions, large-scale revenue systems, or forest management plans we may assume that the local language and institutions were completely 'unintelligible' to the British, or that officers were 'mystified' and 'baffled' at various Indian customs—as if the notion of custom itself was unfamiliar to Europeans, closer to the centre of events, administrators directly involved, even if often mistaken, tended to be less 'baffled', as a close reading of local history shows.[27]

James Scott notes that 'officials of the modern state are, of necessity, at least one step ... removed from the society they are charged with governing.' Likewise, statecraft relies on the use of simplified typifications, such as maps, censuses, and standard measurements. Officials tend to view reality through the lens of such simplifications, distanced from realities on the ground. Although Scott is referring here to the high-modern state, the point he makes may also be applicable to the higher levels of bureaucracy in South India and to situations in which EIC rule was more consolidated. But we may go on to critically ask to what extent the EIC as a state-like bureaucracy represented a modern state. It then becomes problematic to allow Scott's observation to guide analyses of the establishment of legal codes in specific regions and the negotiation of rights in specific land. The guidelines for drawing maps and the use of ethnological terminology certainly directed local enquiries and interpretations, but were simultaneously confronted and questioned by everyday experiences and practices. It took at least two decades of British administrative presence in the hills, and twice that period of proclaimed conquest, for officials to become removed from events in a sense that made them rationalize notions of land, people, and their own presence to fit a historiography of sublime colonial success. At that point, from the 1840s onwards, the legal process became increasingly bureaucratic and more difficult for non-bureaucrats to influence.

Rewriting Regions in Regional History

This book raises questions about the reach and limits of regions. The Nilgiri Hills are among the many regions whose boundaries are taken for granted, being defined either by nature—a plateau at 2,000 metres above sea level, with a particular ecology and surrounded by steep slopes—or by a particular society: a 'unitary' society, to use Paul Hockings' term. To many researchers who have studied the Nilgiris, its boundaries are self-evident. At the same time, this limited region is mostly framed and discussed in relation to a much larger region—India—and here, too, the regional, continental boundaries tend to be determined without much discussion. As the present study moves within early modern and modern South India, where, in the face of historical transformation, the boundaries were unclear, overlapping, and in flux, assumptions of fixed, yet unproblematized, regional determinants tend to skew the analysis.[28]

As indicated earlier, empirically detailed regional and local histories that search for a local logic, which have become a more common genre in environmental history in recent decades, tend to arrive at numerous 'exceptions'. Where a collapse of indigenous society due to commercialization of forest production, orchestrated by colonial forces, is generally assumed, particular strategies for sustained livelihoods and changes in social organization may be found. Where collective tribal identities are assumed to confront aggressive plains-based states, deep-rooted conflicts between different socio-politically defined and kinship-based societies in hill and forest tracts—some of which might have counted as small states had they appeared on the plains—tend to shake synoptic assumptions of a precolonial 'tribal India'.[29]

When moving in late eighteenth- and early-nineteenth-century South India, it is useful to be aware of how the term 'tribe' was introduced into the lingua franca of colonial jargon and how it was derived from evolutionary assumptions about historical change, or about 'development' towards 'progress'. However, although the processes by which tribe came to be known as an antithesis to state, and tribal societies were situated in a pre-state stage of development, are now part of our conventional knowledge, their consequences for early modern history are not always recognized. While more research needs to be done on the early modern history of forest and hill tracts, together with their fluctuating interlinkages into societies and states in the plains, we may still question some of these positions on the basis of a simple critique of historical assumptions.

Continental India remains a dominant frame of early modern and modern environmental history, and the continental scale of India is rightly emphasized when the nation state and modern politics are discussed. However, in a study of early modern history or even of histories up to the mid nineteenth century, unquestioned notions of a continental India may prove to be an obstacle rather than a means of understanding regional pasts. On the one hand, it can be argued that, for studies focusing on imperial visions of a future, all-encompassing British India, a continental perspective is embedded in the research problematic and therefore relevant. On the other, assumptions of a systematized colonial administrative practice will stumble even at the grand level of the competing presidencies and their different principles of administration, not to mention at the level of local administrative implementation. More importantly though, in research on precolonial polities and states, approaches which take the continent as a point of reference are bound to lead to the conclusion that its impact in the particular region under study was insignificant, since the decisions of kingdoms and societies were rarely informed by such notions. In that sense, histories of early modern India need to be disentangled from the webs of the future colonial or independent states on the Indian subcontinent. Janaki Nair points to the unfortunate dominance in academic work of notions inherited from colonial administration, which distinguish 'South India' as a region of exception and lack, and thus pay disproportionate attention to North in relation to South India, and to Bengali and Tamil history in relation to other regional histories. In an attempt to thematically rephrase South Indian history, she points to the many recent regional historical works that draw on the hitherto neglected fields of literary, gender, identity and cultural studies.[30] The intention of the present study, however, is to focus on the variety of simultaneous regional attachments which people developed, rather than to highlight the neglected, disqualified or hidden histories of regions sidelined in current historiography.

As far as the limited region of the Nilgiri Hills is concerned, David Mandelbaum's view is quite representative. He claims that, in spite of being part of South Indian culture according to both etic and emic criteria, the Nilgiris remain a distinct locale throughout history. He divides the past into three periods, aboriginal, colonial, and national independence, and finds that until the nineteenth century the region was almost isolated. He claims that, apart from the immigrating Badaga, the terrain caused other contacts to be brief and sporadic. In spite of colonial settlement and the incorporation of the Nilgiris into the political and economic life of independent India, it remains a distinct region.[31]

This view of a hill territory as a distinctly separate locality is quite representative of and often emphasized in many historical works dealing with other hill and forest tracts. Linkenbach notes a development discourse that depicts the Uttarakhand mountains as a natural barrier responsible for the remoteness of land and people, causing marginalization and backwardness. Wolfgang Mey observes how a similar image of the Chittagong Hill Tracts has been used to legitimize state acquisition of natural resources in the name of development. As a rule, mountains and forests have tended to mark boundaries between larger, politically defined territorial entities. Whether such boundaries are sharp and demarcated by exact frontiers, or broad in the form of zones, from a plains view mountains have tended to look inaccessible. Such regions have been viewed as marginal, the last to be conquered, mapped and administered. These notions of both boundaries and margins have simultaneously entered into and defined the questions and analytical frames of many historiographies and historical works. Even when the goal has been to highlight events, trajectories or societies in the hills, their histories tend to be portrayed as exceptions from the general histories of the Indian subcontinent. But if we turn the perspective around and observe how people living in these tracts have experienced various encroachments, claims, and demands on the centres of their life-worlds, the need to rethink the regions of regional history becomes apparent.[32]

One set of boundaries with a more enduring legacy, which has structured numerous academic works, is that of colonial administrative divides. Outlined by the EIC, deeply engraved in the administration under imperial rule and still largely reflected in the present-day states of federal India, such administrative boundaries also tend to map research. However, although presidency administrations jealously guarded their 'fiefdoms', organizing policies, investigations, and arguments in support of their particular interests, the people who were the targets of administrative measures rarely had such a bird's-eye view of their own locality. Acknowledging that people's regional attachments were not carbon copies of those recognized by the EIC, we see that regional histories need to be defined by other boundaries. As has often been observed, the colonial archives which researchers consult for voices of the past are organized almost entirely according to the principles of colonial administration, in terms of both collections and physical locations. Studies of issues that were of colonial administrative concern therefore require a conscious cross-boundary reading which is not automatically provided in the files. This is even more essential for studies of situations where administrative boundaries had not yet been fixed and colonial rule was uncertain.

In the early nineteenth century, in rhetorical terms, the core administration emphasized boundaries such as those of the Madras Presidency as evident—not because they *were* evident, but because they were intended to become so. The colonial project shared this characteristic with modern nations and nation-state projects. The boundary dispute between the Malabar and Coimbatore districts in 1829–30 is a case in point, revealing the strong interests involved in upholding or contesting administrative territorial divisions. The administrative division of the Nilgiris lasted thirteen years, but has had no lasting effect on historiography.[33]

Until the mid nineteenth century there is reason to assume that the Madras Presidency's administration of forests and hills was guided more by administrative pragmatism than by coherent, systematically pursued policies. This may at times even be the case at the discursive level. As discussed in Chapter 5, there was no general policy for the administration of the South Indian hill tracts until well into the 1840s, nor was there a comprehensive forest policy or a particular principle for the governance of tribal societies or people. If we are looking for something more general to say about the administration of the Nilgiri Hills, Coorg, and the Eastern Ghats, including the Shevaroy, Kalrayan, Kolli, and Panchmalay Hills, it needs to include a reference to the administration's particularist search for practical solutions to immediate problems. In reports and correspondence, we may find general pronouncements about curbing tribal use of forest resources, at least from the late 1830s onwards. But rhetorical statements and polemical outbursts should not be mistaken for administrative practice.

In South Indian history, many historical studies are further confined within linguistic boundaries. Often they are based on an underlying assumption of a foundational influence of cultural-linguistic coherence. This may be due partly to the influence of twentieth-century discourses, marked by strong cultural movements in which language has been a core issue of cultural and political manifestations, and partly to the creation in 1956 of states based on majority language, in combination with the powerful mental legacies of two hundred years of nation-state histories. However, it is useful to recognize that when, for whatever purpose, linguistic boundaries are used to define geographical space, multilingual pasts are left outside the norm. As Ludden has observed, pre- and early modern Tamilnad did not give priority to linguistic divides; Tamilness is a modern phenomenon. Most of South India was multilingual and multicultural, which means that regions such as the Coimbatore upland—now counted as part of a Tamil history and culture, but a region in which Telugu-speaking communities have formed a substantial part of the population—testify to the need to observe the mobile character of regional affiliations defined by language throughout history.[34]

In his influential volume on the economy of rural South India from 1880 to 1955, Christopher Baker chooses to define the geographical limits of the region with reference to ten Tamil-majority districts of the Madras Presidency, encompassing almost but not quite the whole of today's Tamil Nadu. His choice of area is largely defined by a civilizational argument: the region is claimed to have been held together throughout history by economic and social structures formed by warfare, migrations, and the creation of kingdoms and religious institutions. Shaped as his study is by the debates of the 1970s, he further defends his selection by arguing that this is not a 'micro study', even though it does not include all of India. The region is large enough, he argues—'ancient, complex and fragmented'—to reflect larger socio-economic questions. Deliberately confronting the colonial administrative divisions, which he argues fail to reflect geographically and historically created divisions in Tamilnad (the land of the Tamil population), Baker organizes his study in terms of three sub-regions or ecological zones with distinctly different economies, cutting across the colonial administrative districts.[35]

Published in 1984, Baker's work is still an indispensable contribution to the study of the modern South Indian economy. But just as a definition of norms automatically results in exceptions, so his preference for majority linguistic-cultural boundaries and expanding kingdoms to define the geographical scope of his work means that regions such as the Western Ghats remain exceptional and, significantly, are left outside the study.

No geographical space or limits should be taken for granted in studies of regional history; that is to say, while research questions may proceed from a perceived region, its boundaries should not remain unproblematized. In the disputes over contested natures in the Nilgiris, from the smallest spot to the largest realm which ultimately claimed that spot, the spatial difference could be that between an acre and the British empire. The difference in the perceived space in which the claims rested defined the centre and the margin, or the life-worlds of the parties—the actors, interests, and sources of power. When people native to the Nilgiris related to multiple layers of authority (as discussed earlier), they also related to multiple geographically defined regions. At certain times and in specific situations, one particular regional realm was more relevant than others. Often, the boundaries overlapped. The reach of different regions may therefore be defined from within the interests, livelihoods and life-worlds of different segments of the population. These contextually defined regions may then be contrasted with the boundaries established by political authority.

As noted in earlier studies, historians have tended to work within a single set of defining markers for geographical space—be they culturally, administratively or socio-politically determined, as in studies emphasizing belief systems and socially specific perceptions, studies that define boundaries with reference to censuses, state polities and bureaucracies, or studies defining territory in the context of contested socio-political power.[36] As we seek to better understand the historical processes that crystallized into land conflicts in the Nilgiri Hills, our attention is drawn to several, differently defined, regions. They stretch from Ootacamund to Madras and London when it comes to general EIC policy; from Coimbatore to Calicut in Malabar during periods of administrative infighting and competing interests in controlling the hill regions; from Kandelmund to Nelliyalam and Kottayam as far as the influence of Malabar lordship is concerned; from Nelliyalam through Devanaickenkotta to Mysore regarding certain forms of revenue and agrarian expansion; and so on. The outer boundaries of these regions were flexible and contested. Their relevance to people's lives varied over time, just as the relevance of the hills varied in the lives of lords and subjects on the lower elevations and plains. There is therefore reason to reconsider some of the given regions in the early modern and modern history of South India, and to work with a notion of multiple regions, recognizing flexibility and the fluid character of any territorial entity as soon as we think in temporal terms.

Towards an Environmental History of Law

By studying the processes by which principles, policies, and implementation of rules for the appropriation of nature and human social environments transform human—nature relations, we can move towards an outline of what can broadly be described as an environmental history of law. A few comments along these lines may be made in conclusion of this study of claims and rights in the early colonial Nilgiri Hills. These reflections are mainly drawn from the findings of the present study, but are intended as a contribution to a wider debate on law and nature.

In studies of similar situations, a state tends to be acknowledged as one of the most powerful legal actors, and rightly so. From an institutional perspective, the right to property in land is an institution which is sanctioned by the state through its capacity to use force. This has often led researchers to base their studies on the precondition of a unified state—a state which either speaks with a single voice or aims to establish a singular policy by means of forcefully implemented legal regulation. Sudha Vasan points to the major simplifications that such structuring preconditions have produced. Her study clearly highlights the need to acknowledge the diversity not only of the process of implementation, but also of the state institutions as such.[37] Similarly, the present book demonstrates the need to avoid treating the state, or other agencies acting as a state, either as a given precondition or as a single unified actor.

The reasons for caution are manifold. Firstly, such assumptions may obscure an analysis of competing interests within the state and alliances that cut across the boundaries of state realms. This point is made not simply to draw attention to institutional competition, which has often been observed in the conflictual relationship between forest and revenue departments, as for example in Vasant Saberwal's study. More importantly, there is a need to integrate further the analysis of state and society within historical processes, in which the substance and control of both were uncertain, and to do this without founding the analytical frame on an assumption of the outcome: a strong state. This means, in addition, avoiding studying early colonial history from the vantage point of late-nineteenth-century imperial India, and hence reading the conditions of a strong colonial state into the contested and fragmented situations of territories under EIC rule.[38]

Secondly, taking for granted the state as the most powerful actor in legal battles over nature makes it more difficult to analyse situations where the state is absent, where other political entities and social formations define the sphere in which rights are determined, or where a state-like bureaucracy such as the EIC or an international organization acts as both legislative and executive authority. During periods of war and conquest, when the battle was not only for territory and wealth, but also for the right to make and impose law and to become the unquestioned legislative authority, analytical assumptions that are dependent on a state are less than useful. That is not to disregard the importance of the state, but simply to avoid giving it ultimate explanatory power. Consequently, for the purpose of better understanding the processes involved in making law, rather than implementing established law, it has been useful to ask these questions in a study of the uncertain situation of the early colonial period. Such situations arose frequently throughout the entire period of colonial rule—as studies such as those by Vasan and Bhattacharya convincingly show—but in the absence of a firmly established colonial state, the conflictual processes of legal codification under the influence of claims on and appropriation, control, and use of nature, in its material and nonmaterial aspects, will inevitably stand out.[39]

Another point that needs to be made concerns imagined nature and the means by which nature is charged with meanings of a foundational character, i.e. principles that organize the right of humans to interfere with nature, gain access to its resources and claim control over it. We may usefully observe here the contrast and interplay of the universal and the particular. In defining their relations to nature, actors—individual, community, corporate, or state—tend to identify and advocate both universal principles and particular circumstances as a basis for asserting rights. By reference to higher norms as founding principles of human—nature relations, nature may be identified with divinity, with historical and place-based legacies rooted in immemorial pasts, with universal liberties for all subjects of the British crown, or with similarly universal principles of human rights and indigenous rights. Thus, the universal places the right of the individual outside particularistic realms, yet within principles based on interest, ideology and worldview. Simultaneously, particular structuring conditions, which are a hallmark of all natural conditions in their particular locations, are continuously invoked in order to determine or contest the formation or implementation of legal codes. Such circumstances may be ecological and climatic conditions, livelihood patterns and social organization, or the specific identification of groups of people in racial terms which tie a certain people to a particular landscape. The particular thus cuts through and conditions the universal according to place and time, though organized, here too, by principles profoundly based on interest.

As a parallel logic we may consider the intimate relationship between history and law, which is manifest in the constant references made to the past for the purpose of legitimizing claims to nature in the present, as touched on in the first and discussed in the ensuing chapters of this study. A situation in which the past or history can be invoked for the sake of such claims points to the acceptance of a universal principle. At the same time, the particular meaning of the past as it is experienced in each case and the legal implications of ascertaining rights by referring to the past are a place of great diversity. However, whether the past implies place-based experience and notions of divinity and identity, documented proof of particular rights, or rights ascertained by custom and aboriginality, these are particular circumstances structuring a legal practice that accepts the past as a valid reference point for claiming rights in nature.

There is a tendency to identify the particular with the local, i.e. with tribal communities or individual interests, in contrast to the universal claims generally associated with a state. But just as particular meanings of nature are not limited to people native to a place, but are also fundamental to the working of state administrations, so universal principles are prevalent among all actors. The legal appropriation of land is one sphere in which the universal and the particular come into play in the formation of legal codes. When land law was established, it simultaneously encompassed universal principles of sovereign rights and particular conditions of localities and ecologies implied in common law and its applications in South India. The renegotiated adjustments of common law practice in the South Indian disputes prove how custom was accommodated in continuously redefined legal regulations and decisions. We may therefore observe how law is both placeless and place-bound, just as it is simultaneously timeless and time-bound.

This brings a third observation into focus, which is the notion of custom. This is a term with legal implications. Yet many studies that rely on custom as an ethnological category see it as immutable and timeless tradition. This contradictory usage of the word made it a flexible resource in the hands of colonial officers. While in legal terms custom represented negotiated law and thus had an inherent capacity to change in content and practice, in an ethnological perspective it carried fixed, even static connotations by which the concept was made a constituent part of what was perceived as an organic whole of tribal society and culture. Needless to say, in order to understand critical points of legal conflicts, custom portrayed as stable and unchanging needs to be contrasted with the notion of custom as renegotiated practice. What then stands out as particularly interesting is the simultaneous and apparently unproblematic claims to undisputed—but different—legal principles and the observation of a particular 'timeless' custom. The result of this interaction, phrased rhetorically and ideologically in the form of legal claims to nature, was a continuously changing and diverse practice.

Fourthly, we need to observe the process of making law rather than taking law as a given. Many valuable studies exploring the human—nature relationship at the time of British conquest view that relationship from the perspective of the expropriation of rights and exploitation of resources. Expropriation and exploitation did not 'just happen', they signify a situation of law at work. From a legal standpoint, the appropriation of territory implies the control of absolute rights in land and exploitation is defined by rights of usage. As discussed earlier, rather than specifically targeting legal contestations, historical studies have chosen to emphasize the role and management of natural resources and have therefore tended to prioritize usage, in terms of excessive exploitation and misuse. In either case, these studies tend to approach law once it is decided upon and set to work. But there is reason to focus on the social process of drawing up legal codes in relation to actual territorial claims. From the aggressor's point of view, the formation of codes was generally pursued for the purpose of legitimizing territorial and social conquest according to well-established principles. But when we look closely at the legal reasoning of the conqueror, the various interests inherent in territorial claims may show that codes were not adhered to for the same purposes. That is to say, conflicting land claims were made lawful by reference to different legal principles or codes. Pursuing legal studies of human—nature relations from the perspective of multiple, conflicting interests sheds light on the constant redefinitions and reinterpretations of law whereby powerful interests battled for the right to appropriate nature.

Having observed the complex and contextual character of the process of making law, we should, finally, bring into focus the people to whom the law was expected to be applied. For reasons similar to those just explained, aggressive expropriation of land may, but need not, evoke a unified response from those who lose entitlement to it. Existing indigenous social hierarchies and conflicts, together with tensions resulting from ongoing socio-economic change, may transmit into processes of colonial territorial conquest and, through such transformations, existing social oppositions may find new alliances across the colonizer-colonized divide. We may thus observe how different ideas of property can interact across rival groups in situations of changing production of value from land, such as when increasingly sedenterized agriculture competes with pastoralism or when long-term migration transforms the social composition of a population. The historical perspective is crucial.

In the endeavour to project a vision for the transformation of nature with the purpose of promoting a particular policy, law is a useful tool in the hands of a ruling authority. But the unlimited application of such a tool should not be assumed. When interests compete within the framework of a state or when legal settlements risk provoking local protest or revolt, the enforced implementation of law, in spite of protest, is only one of many alternatives. From the state's perspective, a slower but surer way of pursuing interests is also to negotiate the formation of law, in particular in situations of unstable authority—as in the Nilgiris. In the process, legal terminology and perceptions of human–nature relations, derived from varying social and legal systems, will coexist, or at least leave an imprint on the legal code. The founding of law and administration upon native custom was the determined policy of the Madras government; however, despite its ambition to uphold this strategy for instilling trust in the population and thus securing rule, it was unable to fully control the legal process. In spite of the uneven power relations, the process of negotiation—with its many different strategies of delaying investigations, avoidance, joint action, or skilful use of the legal system—embodied a sphere of legal wrestling between subject and ruling authority that could act to change the course of events. When the powers of the colonial state grew, this sphere narrowed, but it did not disappear.

Notes

1. Field notes, Tapkodumund and Nuln mund, 9 February 2005.
2. Karsten, 2002, *Between Law and Custom. High and Low Legal Cultures in the Lands of the British Diaspora—the United States, Canada, Australia, and New Zealand, 1600–1900*, 68–9. The Treaty of Waitingi (1840) Articles 1 and 2.
3. The Maori Independence Site: http://aotearoa.wellington.net.nz/
4. Karsten, 2002, *Between Law and Custom. High and Low Legal Cultures in the Lands of the British Diaspora—the United States, Canada, Australia, and New Zealand, 1600–1900*, 53-4, 103.
5. Ibid., 116–18.
6. Frykenberg, 1977, *Land Tenure and Peasant in South Asia*, 37, 48–50; Stein, 1977, '"Privileged Landholding". The Concept Stretched to Cover the Case', 75.
7. Ludden, 1985, *Peasant History in South India*, 104–7, citing TNA, TDCR, vol. 7968: 1838–9; Washbrook, 2004, 'Sovereignty, Property, Land and Labour in Colonial South India', 75–8, 80, 87–8.
8. OIOC, MRP, 1 May 1835: 1368, no. 7.
9. TNA, Translation of Badaga Petition, 1 July 1835, Madras Board of Revenue, 27 July 1835, cited in Sutton, 2001, publicly available 2006, *Other Landscapes. Hill Communities, Settlers and State on the Colonial Nilgiris,*

c. 1820–1900, 25. OIOC, MRP, 15 June 1835: 6015–16, To the Secretary to the Board of Revenue, signed I. Haig, 10 June 1835.

10. The arbitrator appointed for the Badaga claimants was Mayoor Appah Moodely and the government's arbitrator was I. Haig. Haig's landholdings in Ootacamund amounted to 21 acres as sanctioned by government and 38 acres according to a later survey conducted to find out the size of actual holdings, compared with granted lands. His very hostile attitude to the Badaga and to shifting cultivation, noted by Sutton, may also be seen in the light of vested interests in establishing European property. OIOC, MBRP, To the President and Members of the Board of Revenue, signed A. Robertson, Collector and Reg.r of Govt. Grants, 16 June 1834: 5144–8, para 2. MRP, 15 June 1835: 6015–16, To the Secretary to the Board of Revenue, signed I. Haig, 10 June 1835, and 20 July 1835: 7433–4, To the Secretary to the Board of Revenue, signed I. Haig, 4 July 1835. MBRP, 20 August 1835: 9242–3, To the Secretary to the Board of Revenue, from I. Haig Esq. at Ootacamund, 6 August 1835. Sutton, 2001, publicly available 2006, *Other Landscapes. Hill Communities, Settlers and State on the Colonial Nilgiris, c. 1820–1900*, 25–7.
11. Bagchi, 1982, *The Political Economy of Underdevelopment*, 83–4; D'Souza, 2004, 'Rigidity and the Affliction of Capitalist Property. Colonial Land Revenue and the Recasting of Nature', 238–9, 264, 270; Ibid., 2006, *Drowned and Dammed. Colonial Capitalism and Flood Control in Eastern India*.
12. Ludden, 2002, 'Spectres of Agrarian Territory in Southern India', 237, 241, 256.
13. See in particular Ramachandra Guha's elaboration of the purpose and role of the Forest Department and the Forest Acts of 1865 and 1878, which were intended to monopolize state control of forests. Guha, 1985, 'Forestry and Social Protest in British Kumaun, c. 1893–1921', 68–9; Scott, 1998, *Seeing Like a State. How Certain Schemes to Improve the Human Condition Have Failed*, Introduction.
14. Bhattacharya, 1996, 'Remaking Custom. The Discourse and Practice of Colonial Codification', 24–7, 48–9; Singh, 1998, *Natural Premises. Ecology and Peasant Life in the Western Himalaya, 1800–1950*, 92–100, 234–5. As noted earlier, Sudha Vasan argues along similar lines, though emphasizing even more the incapacity of the state to implement stringent rules. Vasan, 2006, 'Forest Settlements in the Raj. Persistent Diversity in Forest Property Regimes in Himachal Pradesh'.
15. Rangarajan, 1996, *Fencing the Forest. Conservation and Ecological Change in India's Central Provinces, 1860–1914*, 30.

16. Guha, 1989, *The Unquiet Woods. Ecological Change and Peasant Resistance in the Himalaya*, 59.
17. Ibid., 105.
18. See Chapter 3 for further discussion.
19. OIOC, MD, Fort St George Revenue Department, 21 June 1843, no. 13.
20. Karsten, 2002, *Between Law and Custom. High and Low Legal Cultures in the Lands of the British Diaspora—the United States, Canada, Australia, and New Zealand, 1600–1900*, 56–7. For a valuable comparison of the development of legal regimes in England and its colonies, emphasizing the combination of common characteristics and regional applications, see Hay and Craven, eds, 2004, *Masters, Servants, and Magistrates in Britain and the Empire, 1562–1955*, Introduction, 1–58.
21. Prakash, 1990, *Bonded Histories. Genealogies of Labor Servitude in Colonial India*; Mani, 1998, *Contentious Traditions. The Debate on Sati in Colonial India*; Singha, 1998, *A Despotism of Law. Crime and Justice in Early Colonial India*, viii, xi.
22. Ibid., 285–6, 297–9.
23. For examples of the latter, see Grigg, 1880, *The Manual of Nilagiri District*, 305, 325, 328.
24. A communication was demi-official when government officers corresponded with each other or the public without the formality of the prescribed procedure and with a view to eliciting, exchanging or communicating opinions or information before a formal decision was taken.
25. OIOC, BC, Revenue Consultation, 9 May 1837, Letter from the Sub Collector E. Smith, 27 March 1837.
26. In 2000, the new state of Uttaranchal was formed from the Garhwal and Kumaon regions of the state of Uttar Pradesh. Linkenbach, 2005, 'Nature and Politics. The Case of Uttarakhand, North India', 152–3, 165.
27. Guha, 1996 (1963), *A Rule of Property for Bengal. An Essay on the Idea of Permanent Settlement*, 13; Scott, 1998, *Seeing Like a State. How Certain Schemes to Improve the Human Condition Have Failed*, 48, 81–3.
28. I am grateful to Mahesh Rangarajan for providing the inspiration for a discussion of regional history.
29. Singh, 1998, *Natural Premises. Ecology and Peasant Life in the Western Himalaya, 1800–1950*, 92–3; Guha, 1999, *Environment and Ethnicity in India, 1200–1991*, 40–6; Sivaramakrishnan, 1999, *Modern Forests. Statemaking and Environmental Change in Colonial Eastern India*, 48–53. Research into present-day movements for political autonomy, identity formation and assertion of space in national debates and on global agendas finds it increasingly difficult to accommodate similarly polarized

conceptualizations of state *versus* indigenous people. Pernille Gooch points specifically to a new Grand Narrative in which tribals are ascribed a position in a uniform life-world, 'present as bodies but still muted and disempowered and their life-world ... again colonized'. Gooch, 2005, '"We Are Van Gujjars"', 101–3. See also Sinha Kapur, 2003, 'The Bhils in the Historic Setting of Western India', 147–53; Cederlöf and Sutton, 2005, 'The Aboriginal Toda. On Indigeneity, Exclusivism and Privileged Access to Land in the Nilgiri Hills, South India', 178–82; Van Beek, 2005, '"Sons and Daughters of India". Ladakh's Reluctant Tribes', 117–19.

30. Nair, 2006, 'Beyond Exceptionalism. South and the Modern Historical Imagination', 328–30.
31. Mandelbaum, 1989, 'The Nilgiris as a Region', 1–4, 19; Hockings, 1997, *Blue Mountains Revisited. Cultural Studies on the Nilgiri Hills*, 2.
32. Linkenbach, 2005, 'Nature and Politics. The Case of Uttarakhand, North India', 151; Mey, 2005, 'Shifting Cultivation, Images, and Development in the Chittagong Hill Tracts of Bangladesh', 255.
33. OIOC, MRC, 2 February 1830, To the President and Members of the Board of Revenue from J. Sullivan. OIOC, MRC, 1 March 1830, To the President and Members of the Board of Revenue from H.J. Chamier, Secretary to Government.
34. Ludden, 2002, 'Spectres of Agrarian Territory in Southern India', 242.
35. Baker, 1984, *An Indian Rural Economy, 1880—1955. The Tamilnad Countryside*, 3, 15, 17, 22.
36. Ludden, 2002, 'Spectres of Agrarian Territory in Southern India', 235.
37. Vasan, 2006, *Living with Diversity. Forestry Institutions in the Western Himalaya*, 3, 137–42. She points specifically to Guha, 1989, *The Unquiet Woods. Ecological Change and Peasant Resistance in the Himalaya*; Peluso, 1992, *Rich Forests, Poor People. Resource Control and Resistance in Java*; Scott, 1998, *Seeing Like a State. How Certain Schemes to Improve the Human Condition Have Failed*; Ludden, 1999, *An Agrarian History of South Asia*; Saberwal, 1999, *Pastoral Politics. Shepherds, Bureaucrats, and Conservation in the Western Himalaya*; Sivaramakrishnan, 1999, *Modern Forests. Statemaking and Environmental Change in Colonial Eastern India*.
38. Saberwal, 1999, *Pastoral Politics. Shepherds, Bureaucrats, and Conservation in the Western Himalaya*.
39. Bhattacharya, 1996, 'Remaking Custom. The Discourse and Practice of Colonial Codification'; Vasan, 2006, *Living with Diversity. Forestry Institutions in the Western Himalaya*.

Bibliography

Primary Sources

India Office Records (IOR)
- Board's Collections (BC)
- European Manuscripts
  - Thomas Munro Collection
  - Walter Elliott Collection
- Madras Board of Revenue Proceedings (MBRP)
- Madras Despatches (MD)
- Madras Revenue Consultations (MRC)
- Madras Revenue Proceedings (MRP)
- Parliamentary Papers

Tamil Nadu Archives (TNA)
- (Madras) Board of Revenue Consultations (BRC)
- (Madras) Board of Revenue Proceedings (BRP)
- Coimbatore District Records (CDR)
- Nilgiri District Records (NDR)
- Tinnevelly District Collectorate Records (TDCR)

University of Birmingham Library (UBL)
Special Collections
Church Missionary Society

The Toda's Agriculture Bank Co-operative

Gazetteers and Manuals

Francis, W., 1908, *Madras District Gazetteers, the Nilgiris*. Madras: Government Press.

Grigg, H.B., 1880, *The Manual of Nilagiri District.*

Innes, C.A., 1908, *Madras District Gazetteers. Malabar and Anjengo.*

Journals

Asiatic Journal and Monthly Register for British India and Its Dependencies

Calcutta Oriental Christian Spectator

The Hindu Magazine

Madras Mail

Madras Government Gazette

Published Reports

Report of the Conservator of Forests, Madras Presidency, Annual Reports

Nilgiri Forests, 1897

Literature

Adas, Michael, 1981, 'From Avoidance to Confrontation. Peasant Protest in Precolonial and Colonial Southeast Asia'. *Comparative Studies in Society and History* 23 (2): 217–47.

Agrawal, Arun and K. Sivaramakrishnan, Eds, 2001, *Social Nature. Resources, Representations, and Rule in India*. Oxford: Oxford University Press.

Anonymous, 1828, 'Medical and Physical Society of Calcutta'. *Asiatic Journal and Monthly Register for British India and Its Dependencies* 25: 225–6.

———, 1832, 'The Neilgherry Hills'. *Asiatic Journal and Monthly Register for British India and Its Dependencies* 8: 125–8.

Armitage, David, 2000, *The Ideological Origins of the British Empire*, Ideas in Context, 59. Cambridge, New York: Cambridge University Press.

Arnold, David, 2000, *Science, Technology, and Medicine in Colonial India*, The New Cambridge History of India, 3 (5). New York: Cambridge University Press.

———, 2005, *The Tropics and the Traveling Gaze. India, Landscape, and Science 1800–1856*, Nature, Culture, Conservation Series. New Delhi: Permanent Black.

Arunima, G., 2003, *There Comes Papa. Colonialism and the Transformation of Matriliny in Kerala, Malabar, c. 1850–1940*. New Delhi: Orient Longman.

Bagchi, Amiya Kumar, 1982, *The Political Economy of Underdevelopment*, Modern Cambridge Economics. Cambridge, New York: Cambridge University Press.

Baker, Christopher John, 1984, *An Indian Rural Economy, 1880–1955. The Tamilnad Countryside*. New Delhi, New York, Oxford: Oxford University Press.

Barber, Thomas Hervey, 1830, 'Journal of a Route to the Neelghurries from Calicut'. *Asiatic Journal (new series)* 3: 310–16.

Bayly, C.A., 2000, 'Ireland, India and the Empire: 1780–1914', in *Royal Historical Society Transactions*, 10, edited by Ian W. Archer and Jon Lawrence. Cambridge: Cambridge University Press, 377–97.

———, 2004, *The Birth of the Modern World, 1780–1914. Global Connections and Comparisons*, The Blackwell History of the World. Malden, MA: Blackwell Pub.

Bayly, Susan, 1999, *Caste, Society and Politics in India from the Eighteenth Century to the Modern Age*, The New Cambridge History of India, 4 (3). New York: Cambridge University Press.

Berge, Lars, 2000, *The Bambatha Watershed. Swedish Missionaries, African Christians and an Evolving Zulu Church in Rural Natal and Zululand 1902–1910*, Studia Missionalia Upsaliensia, 78. Uppsala: Uppsala University: distributed by Swedish Institute for Missionary Research.

Bhabha, Homi K., 1994, *The Location of Culture*. London, New York: Routledge.

Bhattacharya, Neeladri, 1996, 'Remaking Custom. The Discourse and Practice of Colonial Codification', in *Tradition, Dissent and Ideology. Essays in Honour of Romila Thapar*, edited by Romila Thapar, S. Gopal and R. Champakalakshmi. New Delhi: Oxford University Press, 20–51.

Bird-David, Nurit, 1987, 'The Kurumbas of the Nilgiris. An Ethnographic Myth?' *Modern Asian Studies* 21 (1): 173–89.

———, 1997, 'The Nilgiri Tribal Systems. A View from Below', in *Blue Mountains Revisited. Cultural Studies on the Nilgiri Hills*, edited by Paul Hockings. New Delhi, New York: Oxford University Press, 5–22.

Blackburn, Stuart H., 2004, 'Life Histories as Narrative Strategy. Prophecy, Song, and Truth-Telling in Tamil Tales and Legends', in *Telling Lives in India. Biography, Autobiography, and Life History*, edited by David Arnold and Stuart H. Blackburn. Bloomington: Indiana University Press, 203–26.

Blumenbach, Johann Friedrich, 1779, *Handbuch der Naturgeschichte*. Göttingen.

———, 1787, *Institutiones Physiologicae*. Göttingen.

———, 1820, *The Institutions of Physiology*. Translated by John Elliotson. 3rd ed. London: Burgess & Hill.

———, 1825, *A Manual of the Elements of Natural History*. Translated by Richard Thomas Gore. London: Printed for W. Simpkin & R. Marshall.

Brewer, John and Susan Staves, 1995, *Early Modern Conceptions of Property*, Consumption and Culture in the 17th and 18th Centuries. London, New York: Routledge.

Brockway, Lucile, 1979, *Science and Colonial Expansion: The Role of the British Royal Botanic Gardens*, Studies in Social Discontinuity. New York: Academic Press.

Bryant, G.J., 1985, 'Scots in India in the Eighteenth Century'. *The Scottish Historical Review* 64, 1 (177): 22–41.

Buchanan, Francis Hamilton, 1807, *A Journey from Madras through the Countries of Mysore, Canara, and Malabar*. London: T. Cadell and W. Dawis, *et al.*

Cederlöf, Gunnel, 1997, *Bonds Lost. Subordination, Conflict, and Mobilisation in Rural South India, c. 1900–1970*. New Delhi: Manohar Publications.

———, 2002, 'Narratives of Rights. Codifying People and Land in Early Nineteenth-Century Nilgiris'. *Environment and History* 8 (3): 319–62.

———, 2003, 'Social Mobilisation among People Competing at the Bottom-Level of Society. The Presence of Missions in Rural South India *c.* 1900–1950', in *Christians and Missionaries in India. Cross-Cultural Communication since 1500*, edited by Robert Frykenberg. London: Eerdmans/RoutledgeCurzon Press, 336–56.

———, 2005, 'The Agency of the Colonial Subject. Claims and Rights in Forestlands in Early Nineteenth-Century Nilgiris'. *Studies in History* 21 (2): 247–69.

———, 2005, 'The Toda Tiger. Debates on Custom, Utility and Rights in Nature, South India 1820–1843', in *Ecological Nationalisms. Nature, Livelihoods and Identities in South Asia*, edited by Gunnel Cederlöf and K. Sivaramakrishnan. New Delhi and Seattle: Permanent Black and University of Washington Press, 65–89.

———, and Deborah Sutton, 2005, 'The Aboriginal Toda. On Indigeneity, Exclusivism and Privileged Access to Land in the Nilgiri Hills, South India', in *Indigeneity in India*, edited by Bengt G. Karlsson and Tanka B. Subba. London: Kegan Paul, 160–86.

———, 2008, 'The Agency of the Colonial Subject. Claims and Rights in Forestlands in Early Nineteenth-Century Nilgiris', in *People of the Jangal. Reformulating Identities and Adaptations in Crisis*, edited by Marine Carrin and Harald Tambs-Lyche. New Delhi: Manohar Publications, 223–58.

Chakrabarty, Dipesh, 1994, 'Postcoloniality and the Artifice of History. Who Speaks for "Indian" Pasts?' in *The New Historicism Reader*, edited by H. Aram Veeser. New York: Routledge.

———, 2000, *Provincializing Europe. Postcolonial Thought and Historical Difference*, Princeton Studies in Culture/Power/History. Princeton, NJ: Princeton University Press.

Chatterjee, Partha and Anjan Ghosh, 2002, *History and the Present*. New Delhi: Permanent Black.

D'Souza, Rohan, 2004, 'Rigidity and the Affliction of Capitalist Property. Colonial Land Revenue and the Recasting of Nature'. *Studies in History* 20 (2): 237–72.

———, 2006, *Drowned and Dammed. Colonial Capitalism and Flood Control in Eastern India*. New Delhi: Oxford University Press.

Damodaran, Vinita, 2005, 'Indigenous Forests. Rights, Discourses, and Resistance in Chotanagpur, 1860–2002', in *Ecological Nationalisms. Nature, Livelihoods and Identities in South Asia*, edited by Gunnel Cederlöf and K. Sivaramakrishnan. New Delhi and Seattle: Permanent Black and University of Washington Press, 115–50.

Daniels, R.J. Ranjit, 1996, 'The Nilgiri Biosphere Reserve. Review of Conservation Status with Recommendations for a Holistic Approach to Management India', 16, Paris: UNESCO, *South-South Co-operation Programme for Environmentally Sound Socio-Economic Development in the Humid Tropics*.

Droysen, Johann Gustav, 1868, *Grundriss der Historik*. Leipzig.

Emeneau, M.B., 1944, *Kota Texts*, University of California Publications in Linguistics 2 (1–2), 3 (1–2). Berkeley: University of California Press.

———, 1971, *Toda Songs*. Oxford: Clarendon Press.

———, 1984, *Toda Grammar and Texts*. Philadelphia: American Philosophical Society.

Engels, Friedrich, 1968, *The Origin of the Family, Private Property, and the State, in the Light of the Researches of Lewis H. Morgan*. Moscow: Progress.

Eyal, Gil, 2004, 'Identity and Trauma'. *History and Memory* 16 (1): 5–36.

Finn, Margot C., 2000, *Law, Debt, and Empire in Calcutta*, British Studies. Austin: The Harry Ransom Humanities Research Centre, University of Texas at Austin.

———, 2006, 'Colonial Gifts. Family Politics and the Exchange of Goods in British India, *c.* 1780–1820'. *Modern Asian Studies* 40 (1): 203–31.

Finnström, Sverker, 2003, *Living with Bad Surroundings. War and Existential Uncertainty in Acholiland, Northern Uganda.* Vol. 35, Acta Universitatis Upsaliensis. Uppsala Studies in Cultural Anthropology. Uppsala: Department of Cultural Anthropology and Ethnology, Uppsala University.

Flanagan, Thomas, 1989, 'The Agricultural Argument and Original Appropriation. Indian Lands and Political Philosophy'. *Canadian Journal of Political Science* 22 (3): 589–602.

Foster, W., 1912, 'An English Settlement in Madagascar in 1645–6'. *The English Historical Review* 27 (106): 239–50.

Foucault, Michel, 1977, *Discipline and Punish. The Birth of the Prison.* 1st American ed. New York: Pantheon Books.

Frenz, Margret, 2003, *From Contact to Conquest. Transition to British Rule in Malabar, 1790–1805*. New Delhi: Oxford University Press.

Frost, Alan, 1981, 'New South Wales as *Terra Nullius*. The British Denial of Aboriginal Land Rights'. *Historical Studies* 19 (77): 513–23.

Frykenberg, Robert Eric, 1977, *Land Tenure and Peasant in South Asia*. New Delhi: Manohar Publications, Orient Longman.

Gadgil, Madhav and Ramachandra Guha, 1992, 'State Forestry and Social Conflict in British India', in *Peasant Resistance in India, 1858–1914*, edited by David Hardiman. New Delhi, New York: Oxford University Press.

Gleig, George Robert, 1830, *Life of Major General Sir Thomas Munro*. London.

Gold, Ann Grodzins and Bhoju Ram Gujar, 2002, *In the Time of Trees and Sorrows. Nature, Power, and Memory in Rajasthan*. Durham, NC: Duke University Press.

Gooch, Pernille, 2005, '"We Are Van Gujjars"', in *Indigeneity in India*, edited by Bengt G. Karlsson and T. B. Subba. London, New York, Bahrain: Kegan Paul, 97–115.

Gordon, Robert W., 1996, 'Paradoxical Property', in *Early Modern Conceptions of Property*, edited by John Brewer and Susan Staves. London, New York: Routledge, 95–110.

Gow, Peter, 1995, 'Land, People, and Paper in Western Amazonia', in *The Anthropology of Landscape. Perspectives on Place and Space*, edited by Eric Hirsch and Michael O'Hanlon. Oxford: Oxford University Press, 43–62.

Grove, Richard, 1993, 'Conserving Eden. The (European) East India Companies and Their Environmental Policies on St. Helena, Mauritius and in Western India, 1660 to 1854'. *Comparative Studies in Society and History* 35 (2): 318–51.

———, 1995, *Green Imperialism. Colonial Expansion, Tropical Island Edens, and the Origins of Environmentalism, 1600–1860*, Studies in Environment and History. Cambridge, New York: Cambridge University Press.

Guha, Ramachandra, 1985, 'Forestry and Social Protest in British Kumaun, *c.* 1893–1921', in *Subaltern Studies 4. Writings on South Asian History and Society*, edited by Ranajit Guha. New Delhi: Oxford University Press, 54–100.

———, 1989, *The Unquiet Woods. Ecological Change and Peasant Resistance in the Himalaya*. New Delhi: Oxford University Press.

Guha, Ranajit, 1983, *Elementary Aspects of Peasant Insurgency in Colonial India*. New Delhi: Oxford University Press.

———, 1996 (1963), *A Rule of Property for Bengal. An Essay on the Idea of Permanent Settlement*. Durham, NC: Duke University Press.

Guha, Sumit, 1999, *Environment and Ethnicity in India, 1200–1991*, Cambridge Studies in Indian History and Society, 4. New York: Cambridge University Press.

———, 2000, 'Review. *Hybrid Histories. Forests, Frontiers and Wildness in Western India* by Ajay Skaria'. *Seminar* 486.

Hall, Stuart, 1994, 'Cultural Studies. Two Paradigms', in *Culture/ Power/ History. A Reader in Contemporary Social Theory*, edited by Nicholas B. Dirks, Geoff Eley and Sherry B. Ortner. Princeton, NJ: Princeton University Press, 520–38.

Hardiman, David, 1987, *The Coming of the Devi. Adivasi Assertion in Western India*. Delhi, New York: Oxford University Press.

———, 1992, *Peasant Resistance in India, 1858–1914*, Oxford in India Readings, Themes in Indian History. New Delhi, New York: Oxford University Press.

———, 1994, 'Power in the Forest. The Dangs, 1820–1940', in *Subaltern Studies 8. Essays in Honour of Ranajit Guha*, edited by David Arnold and David Hardiman. New Delhi: Oxford University Press.

———, 1996, 'Small-Dam Systems of the Sahyadris', in *Nature, Culture, Imperialism. Essays on the Environmental History of South Asia*, edited by David Arnold and Ramachandra Guha. New Delhi: Oxford University Press, 185–209.

———, 2006, *Histories for the Subordinated*. New Delhi: Permanent Black.

Harkness, Henry, 1832, *A Description of a Singular Aboriginal Race Inhabiting the Summit of the Neilgherry Hills or the Blue Mountains of Coimbatoor, in the Southern Peninsula of India*. London: Smith Elder and Co.

Harrison, Mark, 2002, *Climates & Constitutions. Health, Race, Environment, and British Imperialism in India, 1600–1850*, Oxford India Paperbacks. New Delhi, New York: Oxford University Press.

Hay, Douglas, and Paul Craven, eds, 2004, *Masters, Servants, and Magistrates in Britain and the Empire, 1562–1955*, Chapel Hill, London: The University of North Carolina Press.

Hockings, Paul, 1978, *A Bibliography for the Nilgiri Hills of Southern India*. Rev. edn. New Haven, CO: Human Relations Area Files.

———, 1980, *Ancient Hindu Refugees. Badaga Social History 1550–1975*. The Hague, New York: Mouton.

———, 1997, *Blue Mountains Revisited. Cultural Studies on the Nilgiri Hills*. New Delhi, New York: Oxford University Press.

———, 1999, *Kindreds of the Earth. Badaga Household Structure and Demography*. Walnut Creek, CA: AltaMira Press.

Hough, James, 1829, *Letters on the Climate, Inhabitants, Productions, &C., &C., of the Neilgherries, or, Blue Mountains of Coimbatoor, South India*. London: J. Hatchard and Son.

Hutton, Patrick H., 1997, 'Mnemonic Schemes in the New History of Memory'. *History and Theory. Studies in the Philosophy of History* 36: 378–91.

Ingold, Tim, 1996, *Key Debates in Anthropology*. London, New York: Routledge.

———, 2000, *The Perception of the Environment. Essays on Livelihood, Dwelling & Skill*. London, New York: Routledge.

Jackson, Michael, 2002, *The Politics of Storytelling. Violence, Transgression, and Intersubjectivity*. Copenhagen: Museum Tusculanum Press University of Copenhagen.

———, 2004, *Existential Anthropology. Events, Exigencies, and Effects*. New York: Berghahn Books.

Jaeger, Friedrich and Jörn Rüsen, 1992, *Geschichte des Historismus. Eine Einführung*. München: C.H. Beck.

Jervis, H., 1834, *Narrative of a Journey to the Falls of the Cavery; with an Historical and Descriptive Account of the Neilgherry Hills*. London: Smith, Elder and Co., Cornhill.

Johnson, Melissa A., 2003, 'The Making of Race and Place in Nineteenth-Century British Honduras'. *Environmental History* 8 (4): 598–617.

Karsten, Peter, 2002, *Between Law and Custom. High and Low Legal Cultures in the Lands of the British Diaspora—The United States, Canada, Australia, and New Zealand, 1600–1900*. Cambridge, New York. Cambridge University Press.

Kumar, Dharma, 1982, *The Cambridge Economic History of India. Volume 2, c. 1757–c. 1970*. New Delhi: Orient Longman, Oxford University Press.

Lévi-Strauss, Claude, 1996, 'Introduction', in *A History of the Family*, edited by André Burguière, Christine Klapisch-Zuber, Martine Segalen, and Francoise Zonabend. Cambridge, MA: Belknap Press of Harvard University Press, 2 vols.

Lieberman, David, 1996, 'Property, Commerce, and the Common Law. Attitudes to Legal Change in the Eighteenth Century', in *Early Modern Conceptions of Property*, edited by John Brewer and Susan Staves. London, New York: Routledge, 144–58.

Linkenbach, Antje, 2005, 'Nature and Politics. The Case of Uttarakhand, North India', in *Ecological Nationalisms. Nature, Livelihoods, and Identities in South Asia*, edited by Gunnel Cederlöf and K. Sivaramakrishnan. New Delhi and Seattle: Permanent Black and University of Washington Press, 151–69.

Louis, Wm. Roger, 1999, 'Introduction', in *The Oxford History of the British Empire. Historiography*, 5, edited by Robin W. Winks. Oxford: Oxford University Press.

Ludden, David E., 1985, *Peasant History in South India*. Princeton, NJ: Princeton University Press.

_______, 1999, *An Agrarian History of South Asia*, The New Cambridge History of India, 4 (4). Cambridge, New York: Cambridge University Press.

_______, 2002, 'Spectres of Agrarian Territory in Southern India'. *Indian Economic and Social History Review* 39 (2 and 3): 233–57.

MacKenzie, John M., 1993, 'Essay and Reflection. On Scotland and the Empire'. *The International History Review* 15 (4): 714–39.

Mackworth, Digby, 1823, *Diary of a Tour through Southern India, Egypt and Palestine in the Years 1821 and 1822*. London: Hatchard and Son.

Mandelbaum, David G., 1941, 'Culture Change among the Nilgiri Tribes'. *American Anthropologist* 43 (1): 19–26.

_______, 1989, 'The Kotas in Their Social Setting', in *Blue Mountains. The Ethnography and Biogeography of a South Indian Region*, edited by Paul Hockings. New Delhi: Oxford University Press, 144–85.

_______, 1989, 'The Nilgiris as a Region', in *Blue Mountains. The Ethnography and Biogeography of a South Indian Region*, edited by Paul Hockings. Delhi: Oxford University Press, 1–19.

Mani, Lata, 1998, *Contentious Traditions. The Debate on Sati in Colonial India*. Berkeley: University of California Press.

Marshall, P.J., 1996, 'Parliament and Property Rights in the Late Eighteenth-Century British Empire', in *Early Modern Conceptions of Property*, edited by John Brewer and Susan Staves. London, New York: Routledge, 530–44.

Marshall, William E., 1873, *A Phrenologist Amongst the Todas or the Study of a Primitive Tribe in South India. History, Character, Customs, Religion, Infanticide, Polyandry, Language*. London: Longmans, Green and Co.

Matsuda, Matt K., 1996, *The Memory of the Modern*. New York: Oxford University Press.

McLaren, Martha, 1993, 'From Analysis to Prescription. Scottish Concepts of Asian Despotism in Early Nineteenth-Century British India'. *The International History Review* 15 (3): 469–501.

———, 2001, *British India & British Scotland, 1780–1830: Career Building, Empire Building, and a Scottish School of Thought on Indian Governance*. Series on International, Political, and Economic History. Akron, Ohio: University of Akron Press.

Menon, Ajit, 2004, 'Colonial Constructions of "Agrarian Fields" and "Forests" in the Kolli Hills'. *Indian Economic and Social History Review* 41 (3): 315–37.

Metcalf, Thomas R., 1994, *Ideologies of the Raj*, The New Cambridge History of India, 3 (4). Cambridge, New York: Cambridge University Press.

Mey, Wolfgang, 2005, 'Shifting Cultivation, Images, and Development in the Chittagong Hill Tracts of Bangladesh', in *Ecological Nationalisms. Nature, Livelihoods, and Identities in South Asia*, edited by Gunnel Cederlöf and K. Sivaramakrishnan. New Delhi and Seattle: Permanent Black and University of Washington Press, 255–73.

Morrison, Kathleen D., 2002, 'Pepper in the Hills. Upland-Lowland Exchange and the Intensification of the Spice Trade', in *Forager-Traders in South and Southeast Asia. Long-Term Histories*, edited by Kathleen D. Morrison and Laura Lee Junker. Cambridge: Cambridge University Press.

Nair, Janaki, 2006, 'Beyond Exceptionalism. South and the Modern Historical Imagination'. *Indian Economic and Social History Review* 43 (3): 323–47.

Nandy, Ashis, 1995, 'History's Forgotten Doubles'. *History and Theory. Studies in the Philosophy of History* 34: 44–66.

Narayana Rao, Velcheru, David Dean Shulman and Sanjay Subrahmanyam, 2001, *Textures of Time. Writing History in South India, 1600–1800*. New Delhi, Bangalore: Permanent Black.

Neeson, J.M., 1993, *Commoners: Common Right, Enclosure and Social Change in England, 1700–1820*. Cambridge, New York: Cambridge University Press.

Nigam, Sanjay, 1990, 'Disciplining and Policing the "Criminals by Birth". Part 1, the Making of a Colonial Stereotype—The Criminal Tribes and Castes of North India'. *The Indian Economic and Social History Review* 27 (2).

Ortner, Sherry B., 1994, 'Theory in Anthropology since the Sixties', in *Culture/Power/History. A Reader in Contemporary Social Theory*, edited by Nicholas B. Dirks, Geoff Eley and Sherry B. Ortner. Princeton, NJ: Princeton University Press, 372–411.

Ouchterlony, John, 1848, 'Geographical and Statistical Memoir of a Survey of the Neilgherry Mountains, under the Superintendence of Captain J. Ouchterlony, 1847'. *Madras Journal of Literature and Science* 9 (1849): 1–138.

Peers, Douglas M., 1995, *Between Mars and Mammon: Colonial Armies and the Garrison State in India, 1819–1835*, International Library of Historical Studies, 1. London and New York: Tauris Academic Studies and St. Martin's Press.

Pels, Peter and Oscar Salemink, 1999, *Colonial Subjects. Essays on the Practical History of Anthropology*. Ann Arbor: University of Michigan Press.

Peluso, Nancy Lee and Peter Vandergeest, 2001, 'Genealogies of the Political Forest and Customary Rights in Indonesia, Malaysia, and Thailand'. *Journal of Asian Studies* 60 (3): 761–812.

———, 1992, *Rich Forests, Poor People. Resource Control and Resistance in Java*. Berkeley: University of California Press.

Philips, C.H. and D. Philips, 1941, 'Alphabetical List of Directors of the East India Company from 1758 to 1858'. *Journal of the Royal Asiatic Society*.

Pohlandt-McCormick, Helena, 2000, '"I Saw a Nightmare …". Violence and the Construction of Memory (Soweto, June 16, 1976)'. *History and Theory* 39 (4): 23–44.

Pouchepadass, Jacques, 1995, 'British Attitudes Towards Shifting Cultivation in Colonial South India. A Case Study of South Canara District 1800–1920', in *Nature, Culture, Imperialism. Essays on the Environmental History of South Asia*, edited by David Arnold and Ramachandra Guha. New Delhi: Oxford University Press.

Prakash, Gyan, 1990, 'Writing Post-Orientalist Histories of the Third World. Perspectives from Indian Historiography'. *Comparative Studies in Society and History* 32 (2 [April]): 383–408.

———, 1990, *Bonded Histories. Genealogies of Labor Servitude in Colonial India*. Cambridge, New York: Cambridge University Press.

Pratap, Ajay, 2000, *The Hoe and the Axe. An Ethnohistory of Shifting Cultivation in Eastern India*. Edited by Ramachandra Guha and Madhav Gadgil, Studies in Social Ecology and Environmental History. New Delhi: Oxford University Press.

Pratt, Mary Louise, 1992, *Imperial Eyes. Travel Writing and Transculturation*. London, New York: Routledge.

Price, Frederick, 2000 (1908), *Ootacamund, a History*. New Delhi: Asian Educational Services.

Prichard, James Cowles, 1843, *The Natural History of Man*. London: H. Bailliere.

———, 1855, *The Natural History of Man*. 4th edn. London: H. Bailliere.

Radhakrishna, Meena, 2001, *Dishonoured by History: "Criminal Tribes" and British Colonial Policy*. Hyderabad: Orient Longman.

Raffles, Hugh, 1999, '"Local Theory". Nature and the Making of an Amazonian Place'. *Cultural Anthropology* 14 (3): 323–60.

Rajan, S. Ravi, 2006, *Modernizing Nature. Forestry and Imperial Eco-Development 1800–1950*, Oxford Historical Monographs. Oxford, New York: Clarendon Press, Oxford University Press.

Rangarajan, Mahesh, 1996, *Fencing the Forest. Conservation and Ecological Change in India's Central Provinces, 1860–1914*, Studies in Social Ecology and Environmental History. New Delhi: Oxford University Press.

———, 2001, 'From Princely Symbol to Conservation Icon. A Political History of the Lion in India', in *The Unfinished Agenda. Nation Building in South Asia*, edited by Mushirul Hasan and N. Nakazato. New Delhi: Manohar Publications, 399–441.

Reill, Peter Hanns, 2005, *Vitalizing Nature in the Enlightenment*. Berkeley: University of California Press.

Reynolds, Henry, 1987, *The Law of the Land*. Ringwood, Vic. Australia, New York: Penguin Books, Viking Penguin.

Rivers, W.H.R., 1906, *The Todas*. London, New York: Macmillan and Co. Ltd.

———, Raymond William Firth and David Murray Schneider, 1968, *Kinship and Social Organization*, Monographs on Social Anthropology, 34. London, New York: Athlone P., Humanities P.

Saberwal, Vasant K., 1999, *Pastoral Politics. Shepherds, Bureaucrats, and Conservation in the Western Himalaya*, Studies in Social Ecology and Environmental History. New Delhi, New York: Oxford University Press.

Saravanan, Velayutham, 2003, 'Colonial Commercial Forest Policy and Tribal Private Forests in Madras Presidency, 1792–1881'. *Indian Economic and Social History Review* 40 (4): 403–23.

———, 2004, 'Colonialism and Coffee Plantations. Decline of Environment and Tribals in Madras Presidency during the Nineteenth Century'. *Indian Economic and Social History Review* 41 (4): 465–88.

———, 2006, 'Economic Exploitation of Forest Resources in South India During the Early 19th Century'. XIV World Congress of Economic History, Helsinki.

Schama, Simon, 1995, *Landscape and Memory*. New York: A.A. Knopf, Random House.

Schlee, Gunther, 2002, 'Introduction. Approaches to "Identity" and "Hatred". Some Somali and Other Perspectives', in *Imagined Differences. Hatred and the Construction of Identity*, 5, edited by Günther Schlee. Hamburg. Lit., 3–32.

Scott, James C., 1998, *Seeing Like a State. How Certain Schemes to Improve the Human Condition Have Failed*, Yale Agrarian Studies. New Haven: Yale University Press.

Shah, Alpa, 2006, 'Elephants, Indigenous Communities and the Environment. The Politics of Claims in India's Jharkhand'. 19th European Conference on Modern South Asian Studies, Leiden.

Shortt, J., 1868, *An Account of the Tribes on the Neilgherries*. Madras: Higginbotham & Co.

Singh, Chetan, 1998, *Natural Premises. Ecology and Peasant Life in the Western Himalaya, 1800–1950*, Studies in Social Ecology and Environmental History. New Delhi, New York: Oxford University Press.

Singh, K.S., 1977, 'Presidential Address'. Indian History Congress, 38th session, Bhubaneswar, M. Athes Ali, Gen. Rec. IMC, AMU, Aligarh.

Singha, Radhika, 1998, *A Despotism of Law. Crime and Justice in Early Colonial India*. New Delhi, New York: Oxford University Press.

Sinha Kapur, Nandini, 2003, 'The Bhils in the Historic Setting of Western India', in *Mobile and Marginalized Peoples. Perspectives from the Past*, edited by Rudolf C. Heredia and Shereen F. Ratnagar. New Delhi: Manohar Publishers, 145–66.

Sivaramakrishnan, K., 1999, *Modern Forests. Statemaking and Environmental Change in Colonial Eastern India*. Stanford, CA: Stanford University Press.

Skaria, Ajay, 1999, *Hybrid Histories. Forests, Frontiers, and Wildness in Western India*, Studies in Social Ecology and Environmental History. New Delhi, New York: Oxford University Press.

Stein, Burton, 1977, '"Privileged Landholding". The Concept Stretched to Cover the Case', in *Land Tenure and Peasant in South Asia*, edited by Robert Eric Frykenberg. New Delhi: Manohar Publications, Orient Longman, 67–77.

———, 1989, *Thomas Munro. The Origins of the Colonial State and His Vision of Empire*. New Delhi, New York: Oxford University Press.

———, 1998, *A History of India*, Blackwell History of the World. Oxford, Malden, MA: Blackwell Publishers.

Stocking, George W., 1987, *Victorian Anthropology*. New York, London: Free Press, Collier Macmillan.

———, 1988, *Bones, Bodies, Behavior. Essays on Biological Anthropology*, History of Anthropology, 5. Madison, WI: University of Wisconsin Press.

———, 1995, *After Tylor. British Social Anthropology, 1888–1951*. Madison, WI: University of Wisconsin Press.

Stokes, Eric, 1959, *The English Utilitarians and India*. Oxford: Clarendon Press.

Sundar, Nandini, 1997, *Subalterns and Sovereigns. An Anthropological History of Bastar, 1854–1996*. Delhi, New York: Oxford University Press.

Sutton, Deborah, 2002, 'Horrid Sights and Customary Rights. The Toda Funeral on the Colonial Nilgiris'. *Indian Economic and Social History Review* 39 (1): 45–70.

Thomas, Keith, 1983, *Man and the Natural World. A History of the Modern Sensibility*. 1st American edn. New York: Pantheon Books.

Thompson, E.P., 1975, *Whigs and Hunters. The Origin of the Black Act*. London: Allen Lane.

———, 1991, *Customs in Common*. New York: New Press.

Torstendahl, Rolf, 2003, 'Fact, Truth, and Text. The Quest for a Firm Basis for Historical Knowledge around 1900'. *History and Theory. Studies in the Philosophy of History* 42 (October): 305–31.

Tosh, John, 1999, *The Pursuit of History*. 3rd ed. New York: Longman.

Van Beek, Martijn, 2005, '"Sons and Daughters of India". Ladakh's Reluctant Tribes', in *Indigeneity in India*, edited by Bengt G. Karlsson and T.B. Subba. London, New York, Bahrain: Kegan Paul, 117–41.

Vasan, Sudha, 2006, *Living with Diversity. Forestry Institutions in the Western Himalaya*. Shimla: Indian Institute of Advanced Study.

Veit-Brause, Irmline, 1996, 'Historicism Revisited'. *Storia della Storiografia* 29: 99–125.

Walker, Anthony R., 1986, *The Toda of South India. A New Look*, Studies in Sociology and Social Anthropology. New Delhi: Hindustan Pub. Corp.

———, 1989, 'Toda Society between Tradition and Modernity', in *Blue Mountains. The Ethnography and Biogeography of a South Indian Region*, edited by Paul Hockings. New Delhi, Oxford, New York: Oxford University Press, 186–205.

———, 1998, *Between Tradition and Modernity and Other Essays on the Toda of South India*. New Delhi: B.R. Pub. Corp. Distributed by D.K. Publishers Distributors.

Washbrook, David A., 1999, 'India, 1818–1860. The Two Faces of Colonialism', in *Oxford History of the British Empire. The Nineteenth Century*, edited by Andrew Porter. Oxford: Oxford University Press, 395–422.

———, 2004, 'South India 1770–1840. The Colonial Transition'. *Modern Asian Studies* 38 (3): 479–516.

——— 2004, 'Sovereignty, Property, Land and Labour in Colonial South India', in *Constituting Modernity. Private Property in the East and West*, edited by Huri İslamoğlu. London, New York: I.B. Tauris, 69–99.

Wittkau, Annette, 1994, *Historismus. Zur Geschichte des Begriffs und des Problems*. Göttingen: Vandenhoeck & Ruprecht.

Wittrock, Björn, 2000, 'Modernity. One, None, or Many? European Origins and Modernity as a Global Condition'. *Daedalus* 129 (1): 31–60.

———, 2003, 'History of Social Science. Understanding Modernity and Rethinking Social Studies of Science', in *Social Studies of Science and Technology. Locking Back Ahead*, edited by B Joerges and H. Nowotny. Dordrecht: Kluwer Academic Publishers, 79–102.

Wootton, David, 1996, *Modern Political Thought. Readings from Machiavelli to Nietzsche*. Indianapolis, IN: Hackett Pub.

Zagarell, Allen, 2002, 'Gender and Social Organization in the Reliefs of the Nilgiri Hills', in *Forager-Traders in South and Southeast Asia. Long-Term Histories*, edited by Kathleen D. Morrison and Laura Lee Junker. Cambridge: Cambridge University Press, 77–104.

Unpublished Works

Sutton, Deborah, 2001, 'Other Landscapes. Hill Communities, Settlers and State on the Colonial Nilgiris, *c.* 1820–1900'. PhD thesis, Centre for Historical Studies, School of Social Sciences, Jawaharlal Nehru University, New Delhi, publicly available 2006.

Vasan, Sudha, 2006, 'Forest Settlements in the Raj. Persistent Diversity in Forest Property Regimes in Himachal Pradesh'. Paper given at the workshop on 'Nature in the Raj. Colonial Environments and Indigenous Knowledge', Nehru Memorial Museum and Library, New Delhi.

Wilson, Jon, 2000, 'Governing Property, Making Law. Land, Local Society and Colonial Rule in Bengal, *c.* 1785–1830'. PhD thesis, Faculty of Modern History, University of Oxford.

Index

About the Author

Gunnel Cederlöf is professor of history at the Linnaeus University, Centre for Concurrences in Colonial and Postcolonial Studies and the Department of Cultural Sciences, Sweden. Her research spans modern Indian and British imperial history, and environmental and legal history. She was professor of history at Uppsala University, Sweden, and has taught at KTH Royal Institute of Technology, Sweden. Among her publications are *Founding an Empire on India's North-Eastern Frontiers, 1790–1840. Climate, Commerce, Polity* (2014), *Bonds Lost. Subordination, Conflict and Mobilisation in Rural South India c. 1900–1970* (1997), *At Nature's Edge. The Global Present and Long-Term History* (2018, with M. Rangarajan), *Subjects, Citizens and Law. Colonial and Independent India* (2017, with S. Das Gupta), and *Ecological Nationalisms. Nature, Livelihoods, and Identities in South Asia* (2006, 2012, with K. Sivaramakrishnan).